Scott Foresman

ELL Teaching Guide

Editorial Offices: Glenview, Illinois • Parsippany, New Jersey • New York, New York
Sales Offices: Needham, Massachusetts • Duluth, Georgia • Glenview, Illinois
Coppell, Texas • Sacramento, California • Mesa, Arizona

ISBN: 0-328-14602-1

4 5 6 7 8 9 10 V004 14 13 12 11 10 09 08 07

Contents

Introduction .... **iv**

Unit 1: This Land Is Your Land

Because of Winn-Dixie **1**

Lewis and Clark and Me **8**

Grandfather's Journey **15**

The Horned Toad Prince **22**

Letters Home from Yosemite **29**

Unit 2: Work & Play

What Jo Did **36**

Coyote School News **43**

Grace and the Time Machine **50**

Marven of the Great North Woods **57**

So You Want to Be President? **64**

Unit 3: Patterns in Nature

The Stranger **71**

Adelina's Whales **78**

How Night Came from the Sea **85**

Eye of the Storm **92**

The Great Kapok Tree **99**

Unit 4: Puzzles and Mysteries

The Houdini Box **106**

Encantado: Pink Dolphin of the Amazon **113**

The King in the Kitchen **120**

Seeker of Knowledge **127**

Encyclopedia Brown and the Case of the Slippery Salamander **134**

Unit 5: Adventures by Land, Air, and Water

Sailing Home: A Story of a Childhood at Sea **141**

Lost City: The Discovery of Machu Picchu **148**

Amelia and Eleanor Go for a Ride **155**

Antarctic Journal **162**

Moonwalk **169**

Unit 6: Reaching for Goals

My Brother Martin **176**

Jim Thorpe's Bright Path **183**

How Tía Lola Came to ~~Visit~~ Stay **190**

To Fly: The Story of the Wright Brothers **197**

The Man Who Went to the Far Side of the Moon **204**

ELL Reader Lessons and Study Guides **211**

Multilingual Lesson Vocabulary **272**

Scott Foresman Reading Street
Overview of Weekly Support for English Language Learners

The ELL Teaching Guide provides weekly lesson materials to support English language learners with scaffolded comprehension instruction and vocabulary development. It builds on the Student Edition and on literacy instruction in the Teacher's Edition. Support for English language learners and teachers is based on the Three Pillars, developed by Dr. Jim Cummins:
Activate Prior Knowledge/Build Background
Access Content
Extend Language

Scott Foresman Reading Street provides these resources:

- **Student Edition** that builds every student's reading and language skills
- **Decodable Readers** for practicing emergent literacy skills (grades K–3)
- **Leveled Readers** for differentiated instruction
- **Teacher's Edition** with ELL instructional strategies built into the lesson plans
- **ELL Readers** that develop English language learners' vocabulary and comprehension skills
- **ELL Posters** with high-quality illustrations and five days of activities supporting key vocabulary and concepts
- **Ten Important Sentences** to focus on comprehension while expanding English
- **ELL and Transition Handbook** that supports teachers' professional development and students' transition to advanced levels of English proficiency
- **ELL Teaching Guide** see below

ELL Teaching Guide Features

"Week at a Glance" Lesson Planners offer a quick reference to the ELL support materials for each lesson of the year.

"Picture It!" Comprehension Lessons provide teaching strategies for each comprehension skill. A reproducible "Picture It!" student practice page helps students learn the key comprehension skill through illustrations, graphic organizers, sheltered text, and ELL-friendly activities.

Vocabulary Activities and Word Cards stimulate language production and reinforce target vocabulary. Small-group and partner activities use reproducible Word Cards to practice listening, speaking, reading, and writing. Home-language activities allow students to connect their prior knowledge to key vocabulary and concepts in English.

Multilingual Summaries of each main reading selection provide a brief, accessible summary in English and translations of the summary in the next most common five languages among the U.S. school population: Spanish, Chinese, Vietnamese, Korean, and Hmong. Students and parents can use the summaries to prepare for reading, build comprehension, support retellings, and strengthen school-home connections.

ELL Reader Lessons and Study Guides support every ELL Reader with scaffolded instruction to help students understand and respond to literature. The reproducible Study Guides support students' comprehension and provide writing and take-home activities for learners at various English proficiency levels.

Multilingual Lesson Vocabulary provides translations of the target vocabulary in Spanish, Chinese, Vietnamese, Korean, and Hmong.

Because of Winn-Dixie

Student Edition pages 22–33

Week at a Glance	Customize instruction every day for your English Language Learners.				
	Day 1	**Day 2**	**Day 3**	**Day 4**	**Day 5**
Teacher's Edition	Use the ELL Notes that appear throughout each day of the lesson to support instruction and reading.				
ELL Poster 1	• Assess Prior Knowledge • Develop Concepts and Vocabulary	• Preteach Tested Vocabulary	• Television Interviews	• Review Sequence of Events	• Monitor Progress
ELL Teaching Guide	• Picture It! Lesson, pp. 1–2 • Multilingual Summaries, pp. 5–7	• ELL Reader Lesson, pp. 212–213	• Vocabulary Activities and Word Cards, pp. 3–4 • Multilingual Summaries, pp. 5–7		
ELL Readers		• Teach *Bears in Danger*	• Reread *Bears in Danger* and other texts to build fluency		
ELL and Transition Handbook	Use the following as needed to support this week's instruction and to conduct alternative assessments: • Phonics Transition Lessons • Grammar Transition Lessons • Assessment				

Picture It! Comprehension Lesson

Sequence

Use this lesson to supplement or replace the skill lesson on pages 18–19 of the Teacher's Edition.

Teach

Distribute copies of the Picture It! blackline master on page 2.

- Have students look at the pictures. Then read the captions aloud.
- Ask: *What happens first in this story?* (Ben eats cookies in the library.)
- Share the Skill Points (at right) with students.
- Have students tell what happens next and last in the story.

Practice

Read aloud the directions on page 2. Have students fill in the *First, Next, Next,* and *Last* circles in the graphic organizer. Have students keep their organizers for later reteaching.

Answers for page 2: *First:* Ben eats cookies in the library, even though it is against the rules. *Next:* Ants come to eat the crumbs. *Next:* The librarian is unhappy with Ben. *Last:* Ben cleans up the crumbs. The librarian is happy.

Skill Points

✓ Events in a story are in a special order, called **sequence.**

✓ Understanding the sequence is important to understanding the story.

✓ Sometimes events in a story are told out of sequence. Something that happens earlier may be told after something that happens later.

Name ______________________________

Look at the pictures. **Read** the story.

- What happens first? **Write** that event in the *First* circle.
- What happens next? **Write** that event in the *Next* circle.
- What happens next? **Write** that event in the second *Next* circle.
- What happens last? **Write** that event in the *Last* circle.

Ben's Cookies

One day, Ben ate cookies in the library.

Many ants came to enjoy Ben's cookies.

The librarian wasn't happy. She wanted Ben to obey the sign.

Ben cleaned up his mess. The librarian was happy.

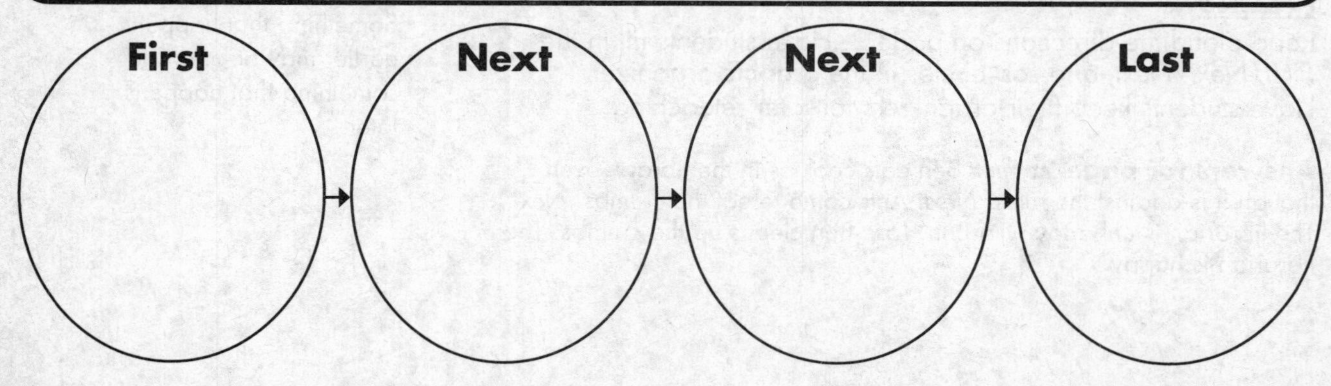

Vocabulary Activities and Word Cards

Copy the Word Cards on page 4 as needed for the following activities.
Use the blank card for an additional word that you want to teach.
Also see suggestions for teaching vocabulary in the ELL and Transition Handbook.

Find Your Partner	Part-of-Speech Word Sort	Home Language Clues
• Give one Word Card to each student, making sure that each student in the class has the same card as one other student. • Ask students to write definitions in their own words on the backs of their cards. • Ask half of the students to place their cards on their desks word side up and half of the students to place their cards definition side up. • Have each student whose card has a definition facing up stand, one at a time, and read the definition to the class. • Have all students with word-side-up cards examine their cards to see if they match the definition. If the card matches, have the student stand up. Then have the two standing students exchange cards to see whether their cards match. • Continue the game until all students whose cards show definitions have read them to the class.	• Divide the students into pairs. Give each pair of students a set of Word Cards and two sheets of paper. • Have each pair of students prepare a two-column chart with *Verbs* and *Adjectives* as the headings. • Have students sort the Word Cards, discussing where to put each word. • Then have each pair of students write sentences that use words from each column.	• Pair students who have writing proficiency in the same home language, and give each student a set of Word Cards. • Have students work together to write translations of the vocabulary words in their home language on the back of each card. (See the Multilingual Lesson Vocabulary beginning on page 272 for suggested translations.) • Have partners lay out the cards with the home language sides facing up. • Invite students to generate synonyms for each word in their home language. Then ask them to name the English vocabulary word with the same meaning. They can turn the cards over to check their answers.

grand	**memorial**
peculiar	**positive**
prideful	**recalls**
selecting	

Multilingual Summaries

English

Because of Winn-Dixie

Opal and her father have moved to Naomi, Florida. She spends many hours at the library. Opal has a big dog named Winn-Dixie. Opal teaches Winn-Dixie to watch her through the library window.

One day Miss Franny, the librarian, saw Winn-Dixie. She was frightened. She thought that Winn-Dixie was a bear. Opal told Miss Franny that Winn-Dixie was her dog. Miss Franny allowed the dog to come into the library.

Miss Franny told a story. She said that once, when she was a girl, a bear came into the library. She was frightened, but decided to fight the bear. She threw a book at it. The bear went away.

Miss Franny is sad that most of her old friends are gone. Opal is sad that she has no friends in Naomi yet. Opal says that she and Miss Franny and Winn-Dixie can be friends. Miss Franny says that would be wonderful.

Spanish

Gracias a Winn-Dixie

Opal y su papá se han mudado para Naomi, Florida. Ella pasa muchas horas en la biblioteca. Opal tiene un perro grande que se llama Winn-Dixie. Opal le enseña a Winn-Dixie a vigilarla a través de los cristales de la biblioteca.

Un día, la Srta. Franny, la bibliotecaria, vio a Winn-Dixie. Estaba muy asustada. Pensó que Winn-Dixie era un oso. Opal le dijo a la Srta. Franny que Winn-Dixie era su perro. La Srta. Franny le permitió a Winn-Dixie entrar a la biblioteca.

La Srta. Franny le contó a Opal una historia. Le dijo que una vez, cuando ella era una niña, un oso entró a la biblioteca. Ella estaba asustada, pero decidió luchar con el oso. Entonces le tiró un libro y el oso se fue.

La Srta. Franny está triste porque la mayoría de sus amigos ya no están. Opal está triste porque todavía no tiene amigos en Naomi. Opal dice que la Srta. Franny, Winn-Dixie y ella pueden ser amigos. La Srta. Franny dice que eso sería maravilloso.

Multilingual Summaries

Chinese

多虧有溫迪克斯

奧珀爾與爸爸搬家到了佛羅里達州。她經常去圖書館看書，家裏的大狗狗溫迪克斯也跟著她。奧珀爾教它在圖書館窗外站崗。

一天，圖書館管理員法蘭尼看見溫迪克斯，把它當作是熊，心裏非常害怕。奧珀爾告訴她，溫迪克斯是她的狗狗。于是法蘭尼特別允許它進入圖書館。

法蘭尼還講了一個故事，她還是小女孩時，有一隻熊闖進圖書館，法蘭尼雖然害怕，但還是决定勇敢戰鬥，朝熊扔書，把它趕跑了。

法蘭尼傷心地說，許多老朋友都已經去世了。奧珀爾在納奧米還沒有朋友，心情也很沮喪。她說她和溫迪克斯會做法蘭尼的好朋友。法蘭尼高興地說，真是太好啦！

Vietnamese

Vì Winn-Dixie

Opal và ba của cô dọn đến Naomi, Florida. Cô ở thư viện hàng giờ. Opal có một con chó to tên Winn-Dixie. Opal dạy Winn-Dixie trông cô qua cửa sổ thư viện.

Ngày nọ Cô Franny, viên quản thủ thư viện, thấy Winn-Dixie. Cô hoảng sợ. Cô tưởng Winn-Dixie là một con gấu. Opal nói cho Cô Franny biết Winn-Dixie là con chó của mình. Cô Franny cho phép con chó này vào thư viện.

Cô Franny kể lại một câu chuyện. Cô nói rằng có một lần, khi cô còn là một bé gái, một con gấu vào thư viện. Cô hoảng sợ, nhưng quyết định chống lại con gấu. Cô ném một quyển sách vào gấu. Gấu bỏ đi nơi khác.

Cô Franny buồn vì đa số các bạn cũ của cô không còn ở đó nữa. Opal buồn vì chưa có bạn ở Naomi. Opal nói rằng cô ta và Cô Franny và Winn-Dixie, có thể làm bạn với nhau. Cô Franny nói rằng điều đó là thật tuyệt.

Multilingual Summaries

Korean

윈 딕시 덕분에

오팔은 아버지와 함께 플로리다로 이사 왔다. 오팔은 도서관에서 많은 시간을 보낸다. 오팔에게는 윈-딕시라는 큰 개가 한 마리 있는데 오팔은 윈 딕시에게 도서관 창문을 통해 자신을 지켜보도록 가르친다.

어느 날 도서관 사서인 프래니 양이 윈 딕시를 보고 곰으로 착각해 겁에 질리게 된다. 오팔이 프래니 양에게 윈 딕시가 자기 개라고 얘기하자 프래니 양은 개를 도서관 안으로 들여보내 준다.

프래니 양은 자기가 어렸을 때 곰이 도서관에 들어왔던 일을 이야기해 준다. 그녀는 그때 겁이 났었지만 곰과 싸우기로 마음먹었고 책을 던져 곰을 쫓아냈다고 말해준다.

프래니 양은 옛날 친구들이 대부분 이사를 가 버려서 슬펐고 오팔은 아직 나오미에서 친구가 한 명도 없다고 슬퍼한다. 오팔은 자신과 프래니 양, 윈 딕시 이렇게 셋이 친구가 될 수 있다고 말하고 그 말을 들은 프래니 양은 아주 기뻐한다.

Hmong

Vim yog Winn-Dixie

Opal thiab nws txiv tau tsiv mus rau Florida. Nws siv sij hawm ntau nyob rau tom lub tsev khaws ntaub ntawv. Opal muaj ib tug aub loj hu ua Winn-Dixie. Opal qhia Winn-Dixie kom nyob ntawm lub qhov rais saib nws.

Muaj ib hnub Miss Franny, tus saib xyuas cov ntawv pom Winn-Dixie. Nws tau ntshai. Nws xav hais tias Winn-Dixie yog ib tug dais. Opal hais rau Miss Franny tias Winn-Dixie yog nws tus aub. Miss Franny thiaj li cia Opal coj nws tus aub los nyob rau hauv lub tsev khaws ntaub ntawv.

Miss Franny piav ib zaj dab neeg. Nws hais tias muaj ib zaug, thaum nws tseem yog ib tug me nyuam ntxhais, muaj ib tug dais los rau hauv lub tsev khaws ntaub ntawv ntawv. Nws tau ntshai, tab si hov txiav txim siab tias yuav ntaus tus dais. Nws thiaj li cuam ib phau ntawv rau ces tus dais thiaj li khiav mus lawm.

Miss Franny tu siab heev vim tias nws cov qub phooj ywg mus tag lawm. Opal los kuj tu siab vim tias nws tseem tsis tau muaj ib tug phooj ywg nyob rau Naomi. Opal hais tias nws thiab Miss Franny thiab Winn-Dixie, lawv peb tug mam li ua phoojywg. Miss Franny hais tias ua li ntawd zoo heev li.

Lewis and Clark and Me

Student Edition pages 44–59

Week at a Glance	Customize instruction every day for your English Language Learners.				
	Day 1	**Day 2**	**Day 3**	**Day 4**	**Day 5**
Teacher's Edition	Use the ELL Notes that appear throughout each day of the lesson to support instruction and reading.				
ELL Poster 2	• Assess Prior Knowledge • Develop Concepts and Vocabulary	• Preteach Tested Vocabulary	• Find Your Word Partner	• Our Journeys	• Monitor Progress
ELL Teaching Guide	• Picture It! Lesson, pp. 8–9 • Multilingual Summaries, pp. 12–14	• ELL Reader Lesson, pp. 214–215	• Vocabulary Activities and Word Cards, pp. 10–11 • Multilingual Summaries, pp. 12–14		
ELL Readers	• Reread *Bears in Danger*	• Teach *Talking to Lewis and Clark*	• Reread *Talking to Lewis and Clark* and other texts to build fluency		
ELL and Transition Handbook	Use the following as needed to support this week's instruction and to conduct alternative assessments: • Phonics Transition Lessons • Grammar Transition Lessons • Assessment				

Picture It! Comprehension Lesson

Author's Purpose

Use this lesson to supplement or replace the skill lesson on pages 40–41 of the Teacher's Edition.

Teach

Distribute copies of the Picture It! blackline master on page 9.

- Have students look at the picture and the paragraph's title.
- Read the paragraph aloud.
- Ask: *What is the author's purpose, or reason, for writing this paragraph?* (to inform the reader)
- Share the Skill Points (at right) with students.
- Have students discuss the author's purpose and how the author achieves it.

Practice

Read aloud the directions on page 9. Have students answer the questions at the bottom of the page. Have them keep their work for later reteaching.

Answers for page 9: 1. b **2.** c

Skill Points

✓ The **author's purpose** is the reason or reasons why an author writes something.

✓ Some common author's purposes are to persuade or convince the reader of something; to inform, or explain something; to entertain, or make the reader enjoy the writing; or to share ideas or feelings.

Name ______________________________

Author's Purpose

Read the paragraph. **Look** at the picture.

- **Read** each question and the four answer choices given.
- **Circle** the letter of the correct answer for each question.

Exploring the West

In the early 1800s, Meriwether Lewis and William Clark explored the West. President Thomas Jefferson sent them. They started their journey from St. Louis, Missouri, in 1804. They traveled for almost two-and-a-half years. During that time, they met Native Americans from almost fifty different tribes.

1. What is the author's purpose?

a. to persuade or try to convince the reader
b. to inform or explain something to the reader
c. to make the reader laugh
d. to frighten the reader

2. How does the author meet this purpose?

a. by telling interesting stories
b. by writing about his emotions
c. by providing facts
d. by providing opinions

Vocabulary Activities and Word Cards

Copy the Word Cards on page 11 as needed for the following activities.
Use the blank cards for additional words that you want to teach.
Also see suggestions for teaching vocabulary in the ELL and Transition Handbook.

Definition Concentration	True or False?	Write a Story
• Create one set of Word Cards and six blank cards for every pair of students. • Have pairs of students work together to write definitions for each word on the blank cards. Remind students that a definition tells what a word means. • Have students place the Word Cards and definition cards face down in rows on a table. • Instruct students to take turns turning over two cards and looking for a matched pair. A matched pair is a Word Card and its definition card. When a student finds a matched pair, the student keeps the cards. • To determine the winner, check which student has the most cards at the end of the game.	• Ask a student to select a card from a set of Word Cards. • Make up a sentence using the vocabulary word, and ask the student if the sentence is true or false. For example: Boats dock at a wharf. (true) • Ask the rest of the group whether they agree with the student's answer. • Repeat the exercise until all students have had a chance to choose a card.	• Divide the class into small story-writing groups, and give each group a set of Word Cards. • Within each group, distribute the Word Cards so that each student has at least one card. • Have students select one member of the group to record the story, another to make sure that each student contributes at least one sentence to the story, and a third to read the story to the class. • Have each group brainstorm ideas for the story. Tell the students that the story can be silly or serious but must include all of the vocabulary words. Then have each student come up with a sentence for the story using the Word Card or Cards he or she received. • Give students ten minutes to write their story. Then have one member of each group read the story to the class.

docks	**migrating**
scan	**scent**
wharf	**yearned**

Multilingual Summaries

English

Lewis and Clark and Me

Seaman is a Newfoundland dog. As Lewis and Clark prepare for their expedition, Lewis buys Seaman. Newfoundland dogs are very big. They are good swimmers. Lewis wants to take Seaman with him on the expedition.

Everyone boards the boat and the expedition begins. Seaman sees squirrels swimming across the river. Lewis tells Seaman to fetch the squirrels. Seaman catches many squirrels. He brings many squirrels to the boat. The men cook the squirrels. Everyone eats well that night.

On another day, Lewis talked with some Indians. They liked Seaman. He was so big that they thought he was a bear. They wanted to trade beaver skins for the bear-dog. Lewis said no. Seaman was too special.

Spanish

Lewis y Clark y yo

Seaman es un perro de raza terranova. Mientras Lewis y Clark se preparan para la expedición, Lewis compra a Seaman. Los perros terranova son muy grandes. Son buenos nadadores. Lewis quiere que Seaman vaya con él en la expedición.

Todos suben a bordo del bote y la expedición comienza. Seaman ve ardillas que atraviesan el río nadando. Lewis le dice a Seaman que vaya a buscar algunas ardillas. Seaman caza muchas ardillas. Lleva muchas ardillas al bote. Los hombres cocinan las ardillas. Todos comen bien esa noche.

Otro día, Lewis habló con algunos indígenas. A ellos les gustaba Seaman. Él era tan grande que los indígenas pensaban que era un oso. Ellos querían cambiar pieles de castor por el oso-perro. Lewis les dijo que no. Seaman era muy especial.

Multilingual Summaries

Chinese

劉易斯、克拉克與西蒙

西蒙是紐芬蘭犬。劉易斯與克拉克出發探險前，劉易斯買下了西蒙。紐芬蘭犬的個頭很大，非常擅長游泳，劉易斯要帶上它一起去探險。

大家登上船，探險隊出發啦。西蒙忽然發現有松鼠游過河。劉易斯命令西蒙去捕捉，一下抓獲不少獵物帶回船。廚師做成豐盛的晚餐，讓大家吃得飽飽的。

還有一天，劉易斯碰到印地安人。他們都非常喜歡西蒙，把大個頭的它當作了熊，要求用海狸皮來交換。劉易斯可不同意，因為西蒙與別的狗不一樣。

Vietnamese

Lewis cùng Clark và Tôi

Seaman là một con chó thuộc giống Newfoundland. Khi Lewis và Clark chuẩn bị cuộc thám hiểm, Lewis mua Seaman. Chó giống Newfoundland rất lớn. Chó này bơi giỏi. Lewis muốn mang Seaman theo trong kỳ thám hiểm.

Mọi người lên thuyền và cuộc thám hiểm bắt đầu. Seaman thấy những con sóc bơi băng qua sông. Lewis kêu Seaman đi bắt những con sóc này. Seaman bắt được nhiều sóc. Nó mang nhiều sóc đến thuyền. Những người trên thuyền nấu những con sóc này. Mọi người ăn uống no nê tối hôm đó.

Vào một ngày khác, Lewis nói chuyện với những Thổ Dân Da Đỏ. Họ thích Seaman. Seaman to đến nỗi họ tưởng nó là con gấu. Họ muốn đổi da hải ly để lấy con chó-gấu này. Lewis nói không. Seaman quá đặc biệt.

Multilingual Summaries

Korean

루이스와 클라크와 시맨

시맨은 뉴펀들랜드 종 개이다. 루이스는 클라크와 함께 탐험을 떠날 준비를 하면서 시맨을 산다. 뉴펀들랜드 종 개들은 몸집이 상당히 크며 수영을 잘 하기 때문에 루이스는 시맨을 탐험에 함께 데려가고 싶어한다.

모두 보트에 올라타고 탐험이 시작된다. 시맨은 다람쥐가 강을 헤엄쳐 가는 것을 본다. 루이스가 시맨에게 다람쥐를 잡아오라고 시키자 시맨은 다람쥐를 많이 잡아서 보트로 물고 온다. 그날 밤 사람들은 다람쥐를 요리해 맛있게 먹는다.

어느 날 루이스는 인디언 몇 명과 이야기를 나누게 됐는데 인디언들은 시맨을 마음에 들어한다. 그들은 시맨의 몸집이 커서 곰인 줄 알았다고 한다. 인디언들은 비버 모피와 이 곰 같은 개를 교환하자고 했지만 루이스는 싫다고 말한다. 시맨은 너무도 특별한 개이기 때문이다.

Hmong

Lewis thiab Clark thiab Kuv

Seaman yog ib tug aub Newfoundland (lub teb chaws nrhiav tau tshiab). Thaum Lewis thiab Clark tau npaj khoom rau kawg txoj hauv kev mus soj ntsuam lub teb chaws tshiab, Lewis tau yuav Seaman. Cov aub Newfoundland loj heev li. Lawv txawj ua luam dej heev li. Lewis xav coj Seaman nrog nws mus lawm txoj hau kev mus soj ntsuam lub teb chaws tshiab.

Sawvdaws tau nce lub nkoj ces txoj hauv kev soj ntsum lub teb chaws tshiab thiaj li pib. Seaman pom nas ncuav ua luam dej hla tus dej. Lewis hais kom Seaman mus caum cov nas ncuav. Seaman ntes tau ntau tus nas ncuav. Nws coj cov nas ncuas mus rau suam lub nkoj. Cov txiv neej thiaj muab cov nas ncuav ua noj. Sawv daws tau zoo noj hmo ntawd.

Muaj ib hnub, Lewis tau nrog ib cov Qhab tham. Lawm nyiam Seaman. Nws loj heev li lawv xav hais tias nws yog ib tug dais. Lawv xav muab nas dej cov paub los pauv tus aub. Lewis hais tias tsis kam. Seaman muaj nuj nqis heev li.

Grandfather's Journey Student Edition pages 70–81

Week at a Glance	Customize instruction every day for your English Language Learners.				
	Day 1	**Day 2**	**Day 3**	**Day 4**	**Day 5**
Teacher's Edition	Use the ELL Notes that appear throughout each day of the lesson to support instruction and reading.				
ELL Poster 3	• Assess Prior Knowledge • Develop Concepts and Vocabulary	• Preteach Tested Vocabulary	• Class Journey	• A Snapshot of This Country	• Monitor Progress
ELL Teaching Guide	• Picture It! Lesson, pp. 15–16 • Multilingual Summaries, pp. 19–21	• ELL Reader Lesson, pp. 216–217	• Vocabulary Activities and Word Cards, pp. 17–18 • Multilingual Summaries, pp. 19–21		
ELL Readers	• Reread *Talking to Lewis and Clark*	• Teach *Our Trip Out East*	• Reread *Our Trip Out East* and other texts to build fluency		
ELL and Transition Handbook	Use the following as needed to support this week's instruction and to conduct alternative assessments: • Phonics Transition Lessons • Grammar Transition Lessons • Assessment				

Picture It! Comprehension Lesson

Sequence

Use this lesson to supplement or replace the skill lesson on pages 66–67 of the Teacher's Edition.

Teach

Distribute copies of the Picture It! blackline master on page 16.

- Have students read the time-line captions in order. Then read the paragraph aloud. Ask: *Who came to North America first? Who came second?* (Native Americans came first; the Spanish came second.)
- Share the Skill Points (at right) with students.
- Have students find the sequence or order words.

Practice

Read aloud the directions on page 16. Have students underline the sequence words and then write the events in order on the time line. Have students keep their organizers for later reteaching.

Answers for page 16: Sequence words: *first, next, then, during, today; Thousands of years ago:* Native Americans came; *1500s*: the Spanish and French came; *1600s*: people from England and the Netherlands came; *1700s*: People from all over Europe and African people in slavery came; *Today*: People from all over the world come.

Skill Points

✓ **Sequence** means the order of the events in a story or paragraph.

✓ Dates, times, and sequence words (such as *first, next,* and *last)* can help you find the order of the events.

✓ Sometimes, two or more events happen at the same time. Sequence words such as *during* and *meanwhile* can show this.

Name ______________________________

Look at the time line. **Read** the paragraph.

- In what order did events occur? **Underline** the sequence words.
- What happened when? **Write** the events in order in the time line below showing the dates when they occurred.

Settling North America

People have been coming to North America for thousands of years. The first people to come were Native Americans. Scientists believe that they moved here from Eurasia thousands of years ago. Next came the Spanish and French, in the 1500s. Then, in the 1600s, people from England and the Netherlands came. In the 1700s, people from all over Europe began coming to North America. During this time, people from Africa were brought to North America as slaves. Today, people from all over the world continue to come.

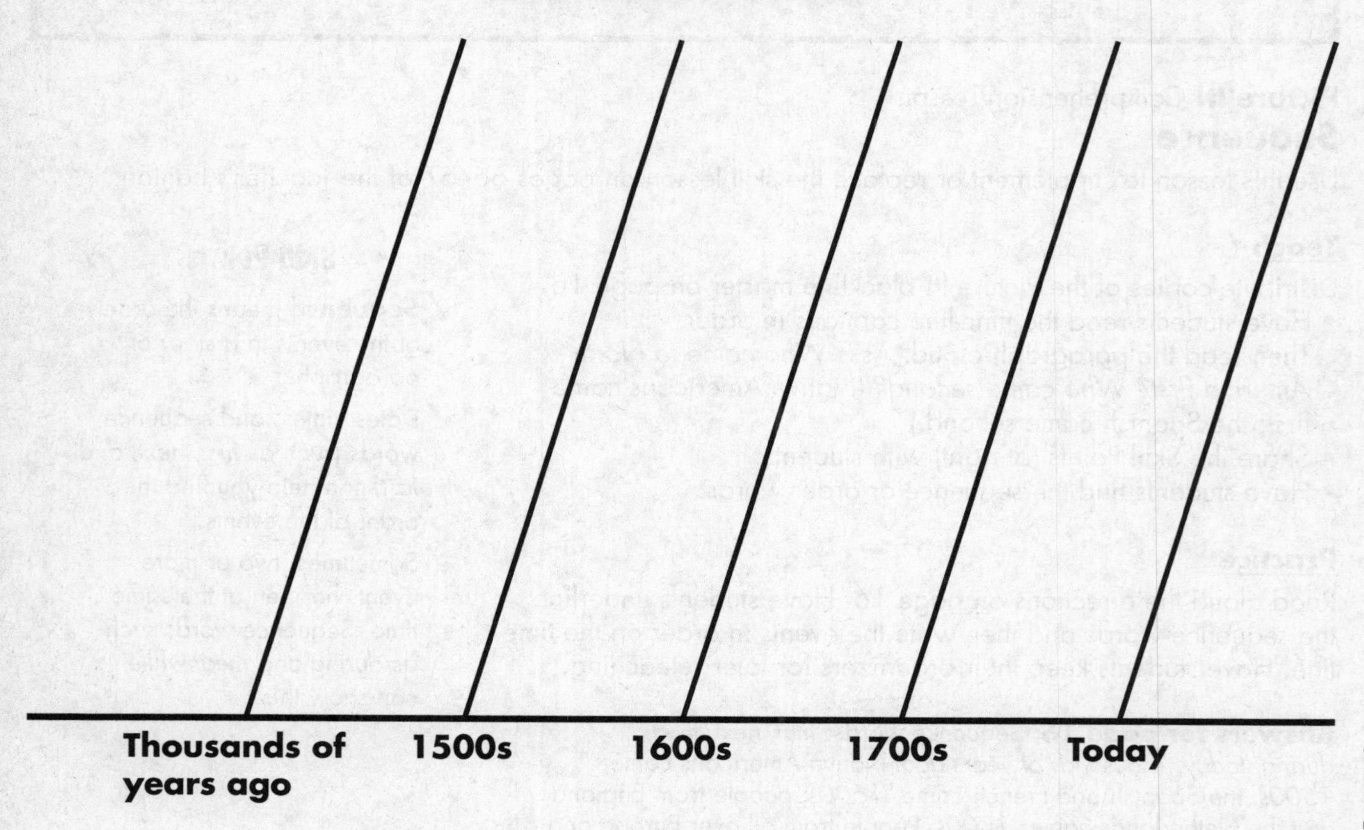

Vocabulary Activities and Word Cards

Copy the Word Cards on page 18 as needed for the following activities.
Use the blank card for an additional word that you want to teach.
Also see suggestions for teaching vocabulary in the ELL and Transition Handbook.

Cloze Sentences	Charades	Riddle Game
• Give each student a set of Word Cards and two pieces of paper. • Have students write one sentence using each vocabulary word. • On a second sheet of paper, have students rewrite each sentence, replacing the vocabulary word with a line. • Divide the class into pairs. Have each pair exchange the papers with their cloze sentences and try to fill in the missing vocabulary words. Have partners check one another's work.	• Reproduce two sets of Word Cards for the following words: *amazed, bewildered, sculptures, towering.* • Place one set of Word Cards face up so that all students can see them. • Divide students into pairs or small groups. Give each group one Word Card. • Have each group discuss how to act out its vocabulary word. • Have groups take turns acting out scenes while the others try to guess their words using the displayed set of Word Cards as clues.	• Divide the class into pairs. Give each pair a set of Word Cards. • Have students place the set of Word Cards face down in a pile. • Ask one partner to choose a card and make up a riddle about the word. Provide examples, such as: *What is something breakable that artists create?* or, *If you felt this way, you would feel very confused.* Then have students tell their riddles to their partners. • Have the partner try to guess the word. Then have students switch roles. • Continue the activity until students have created riddles for every Word Card.

amazed	**bewildered**
homeland	**longed**
sculptures	**still**
towering	

Multilingual Summaries

English

Grandfather's Journey

Grandfather came to California a long time ago. He traveled through the United States. He saw many beautiful sights. He met many new people.

Grandfather liked California best. He returned to Japan. He married. The couple moved back to San Francisco. They had a daughter. The daughter grew up. The family moved back to Japan. The daughter married. The daughter had a little boy. He loved to visit his Grandfather. Grandfather told the boy stories about California.

War came. The grandparents' house in the city was bombed. They moved to a small village. The grandfather wanted to see California again. He died before he could see California again. Now, the grandson lives in California. He returns to Japan often. When he is in California, he wants to be in Japan. When he is in Japan, he wants to be in California. Now he feels that he understands his grandfather.

Spanish

El viaje de abuelo

Abuelo llegó a California hace mucho tiempo. Viajó por Estados Unidos. Vio muchos paisajes maravillosos. Conoció a muchas personas nuevas.

Al abuelo el lugar que más le gustó fue California. Regresó a Japón. Se casó. La pareja se mudó para San Francisco. Tuvieron una hija. La hija creció. La familia regresó a Japón. La hija se casó. La hija tuvo un niño. A él le gustaba visitar a su abuelo. El abuelo le contaba historias sobre California.

Vino la guerra. La casa de los abuelos en la ciudad fue bombardeada. Ellos se mudaron para un pueblo pequeño. El abuelo quería ver otra vez California, pero murió antes de poder volver. Ahora su nieto vive en California. Él regresa con frecuencia a Japón. Cuando está en California, quiere estar en Japón. Cuando está en Japón, quiere estar en California. Ahora él siente que comprende a su abuelo.

Multilingual Summaries

Chinese

外公的漫長旅途

很久以前，外公來到美國的加州。他走遍了美國，看過許多迷人的風景，遇過很多風俗習慣不同的居民。

外公最喜歡的還是加州。回到日本結婚後，帶著太太來到舊金山。在這裏有了媽媽，等她長大後，全家才回到日本。媽媽婚後生了個男孩兒。小外孫最喜歡和外公在一起，聽外公講關于加州的故事。

戰爭突然爆發，炸毀了外公在城裏的家。他們只好搬到一個小村莊。外公很想再去加州，可是這個願望直到去世也沒有能夠實現。現在小外孫住在加州，也經常飛回日本的家。他在加州時想著日本，在日本時又念著加州，終于能夠理解外公當年的心情了。

Vietnamese

Hành Trình Của Ông Ngoại

Ông Ngoại đến California cách đây đã lâu lắm. Ông du lịch khắp Hoa Kỳ. Ông thấy nhiều cảnh vật đẹp. Ông gặp gỡ nhiều người mới.

Ông Ngoại thích California nhất. Ông trở về Nhật. Ông cưới vợ. Cặp vợ chồng dọn trở lại San Francisco. Họ có một người con gái. Cô con gái lớn lên. Gia đình dọn trở lại Nhật. Cô con gái có chồng. Cô con gái có một bé trai. Cậu bé thích đi thăm Ông Ngoại của mình. Ông kể cho cậu bé nghe những chuyện về California.

Chiến tranh đến. Ngôi nhà của ông bà ngoại ở thành phố bị bỏ bom. Họ dọn đến một ngôi làng nhỏ. Ông muốn được thấy lại California. Ông qua đời trước khi ông được thấy lại California. Bây giờ, cậu cháu ngoại sống ở California. Cậu thường trở về Nhật. Khi cậu ở California, cậu lại muốn ở Nhật. Khi cậu ở Nhật, cậu lại muốn ở California. Bây giờ cậu cảm thấy là cậu hiểu được ông Ngoại của mình.

Multilingual Summaries

Korean

할아버지의 여행

할아버지는 오래 전에 캘리포니아로 와서 미국 곳곳을 여행하며 훌륭한 경치를 많이 보고 새로운 사람들도 많이 만났다.

할아버지는 그 중에서도 캘리포니아를 제일 좋아했다. 할아버지는 일본으로 돌아가 결혼한 뒤 할머니와 함께 다시 샌프란시스코로 돌아왔다. 할아버지와 할머니에겐 딸이 한 명 있었는데 딸이 성장하자 다시 가족 모두가 일본으로 돌아갔다. 딸이 결혼해 낳은 남자아이는 할아버지 댁에 가는 것을 좋아했고 할아버지는 손자에게 캘리포니아 얘기를 해주었다.

전쟁이 일어났다. 도시에 있는 할아버지와 할머니의 집이 폭격을 맞자 할아버지 가족은 작은 마을로 이사를 갔다. 할아버지는 캘리포니아에 다시 가고 싶어했지만 그러지 못하고 돌아가셨다. 이제 할아버지의 손자가 캘리포니아에 살고 있고 손자는 일본에 자주 들른다. 캘리포니아에 있을 때는 일본에 가고 싶고, 일본에 있을 때는 캘리포니아에 가고 싶어지는 걸 보니 손자는 이제 할아버지를 이해할 수 있을 것 같다.

Hmong

Yawm Txiv Lub Neej

Yawm txiv tuaj rau California ntev heev los lawm. Nws ncig xyuas thoob lub teb chaws Miskas. Nws tau pom tej qhov chaw zoo nkauj. Nws tau ntsib ntau leej neeg tshiab.

Yawm txiv nyiam California tshaj. Nws rov los rau Yijpoo teb. Nws tau yuav poj niam. Ob niam txiv rov tsiv tuaj rau San Francisco. Nkawd muaj ib tug ntxhais. Lawv tsev neeg rov khiav mus rau Yijpoo teb. Tus ntxhais yuav txiv. Tus ntxhais muaj ib tug me nyuam tub. Nws nyiam mus saib nws yawm txiv. Yawm txiv piav dab neeg txog California rau tus me nyuam tub.

Tsov rog tshwm sim tuaj. Niam tais yawm txiv lub tsev nyob rau hauv zos loj raug hoob pob. Lawv thiaj li tsiv mus rau ib lub zos me me. Yawm txiv xav saib California ib zaug ntxiv. Tab sis mas nws tuag ua ntej nws rov pom California. Ziag no, tus tub xeeb ntxwv nyob rau California. Nws rov mus Yijpoo teb ntau zaus. Thaum nws nyob California, nws xav nyob tim Yijpoo teb. Thaum nws nyob tim Yijpoo teb, nws xav nyob California. Ziag no nws xav tias nws nkag siab nws yawm txiv.

The Horned Toad Prince

Student Edition pages 92–105

Week at a Glance	Customize instruction every day for your English Language Learners.				
	Day 1	**Day 2**	**Day 3**	**Day 4**	**Day 5**
Teacher's Edition	Use the ELL Notes that appear throughout each day of the lesson to support instruction and reading.				
ELL Poster 4	• Assess Prior Knowledge • Develop Concepts and Vocabulary	• Preteach Tested Vocabulary	• Learning About the Southwest	• Families of Animals	• Monitor Progress
ELL Teaching Guide	• Picture It! Lesson, pp. 22–23 • Multilingual Summaries, pp. 26–28	• ELL Reader Lesson, pp. 218–219	• Vocabulary Activities and Word Cards, pp. 24–25 • Multilingual Summaries, pp. 26–28		
ELL Readers	• Reread *Our Trip Out East*	• Teach *Painting the Southwest*	• Reread *Painting the Southwest* and other texts to build fluency		
ELL and Transition Handbook	Use the following as needed to support this week's instruction and to conduct alternative assessments: • Phonics Transition Lessons • Grammar Transition Lessons • Assessment				

Picture It! Comprehension Lesson

Author's Purpose

Use this lesson to supplement or replace the skill lesson on pages 88–89 of the Teacher's Edition.

Teach

Distribute copies of the Picture It! blackline master on page 23.

- Have students read the dictionary definition. Then read the paragraph aloud.
- Ask: *What is the author's purpose?* (to inform or explain something to the reader)
- Share the Skill Points (at right) with students.
- Have students discuss the ways the author shows the purpose.

Skill Points

✓ The **author's purpose** is the reason or reasons an author writes something.

✓ Some common purposes are to persuade or convince the reader of something, to inform or explain something, to entertain, or to share ideas or feelings.

Practice

Read aloud the directions on page 23. Have students circle the letter of the answer that shows the author's purpose. Then have them write a sentence or two explaining the ways the author indicates what the purpose of the paragraph is. Have students keep their work for later reteaching.

Answers for page 23: 1. b **2.** The author provides information. He or she defines what a fable is and lists examples of fables. This shows that the author's purpose is to inform or explain.

Name ______________________________

Author's Purpose

Read the definition. Then **read** the paragraph.

- What is the author's purpose? **Circle** the letter of the correct answer.
- How did the author meet his or her purpose? **Write** a short answer on the lines below.

fa·ble \fā'bəl\ *n.*: a short story that teaches a lesson, usually including animals that talk and act like people

Fables

Fables are fictional stories told to teach a lesson. Often, the stories have animals that talk and act like people. Aesop was a man from ancient Greece. He wrote many fables, which are still famous today. He wrote "The Fox and the Grapes" and "The Tortoise and the Hare." People from all over the world still tell fables to teach each other.

1. What is the author's purpose?

a. to persuade or try to convince the reader

b. to inform or explain something to the reader

c. to entertain or make the reader enjoy the paragraph

d. to write ideas and feelings

2. How does the author meet his or her purpose?

____

____

____

____

Vocabulary Activities and Word Cards

Copy the Word Cards on page 25 as needed for the following activities.
Use the blank card for an additional word that you want to teach.
Also see suggestions for teaching vocabulary in the ELL and Transition Handbook.

Tell a Story	Definition Concentration	True or False?
• Distribute one set of Word Cards to each student. • Gather the students in a circle and explain that the group will be telling a story together. • Begin the story with a sentence that uses a vocabulary word. • Have the student to your right continue the story, adding a sentence that uses any of the other vocabulary words. • Have each student continue the story, adding a sentence that uses a vocabulary word. • Let students help one another think of sentences that continue the story. • Encourage students to be creative and to try to make the story exciting or funny.	• Create one set of Word Cards and seven blank cards for every pair of students. • Have pairs of students work together to write definitions for each word on the blank cards. Remind students that a definition tells what a word means. • Have students place the Word Cards and definition cards face down in rows on a table. • Instruct students to take turns turning over two cards and looking for a matched pair. A matched pair is a Word Card and its definition card. When a student finds a matched pair, the student keeps the cards. • To determine the winner, check which student has the most cards at the end of the game.	• Make one set of Word Cards. • Ask a student to select a card. • Make up a sentence using the vocabulary word, and ask the student if the sentence is true or false. For example: *A prairie has many hills and trees.* (false) • Ask the rest of the group whether they agree with the student's answer. • Repeat the exercise until all students have had a chance to choose a card.

bargain	**favors**
lassoed	**offended**
prairie	**riverbed**
shrieked	

Multilingual Summaries

English

The Horned Toad Prince

Reba Jo played guitar. She roped things with her lasso. One day, she rode her horse to an old, dry riverbed. Suddenly, the wind blew her hat off. The hat blew into an old well.

A horned toad said he would find her hat. He asked for three things in return. He wanted some chili. He wanted to hear Reba Jo play her guitar. He wanted to take a nap in her hat. Reba Jo agreed. The toad found Reba Jo's hat. She rode away without thanking the toad.

The toad followed her home. Reba Jo gave him his wishes. The toad ate some chili and heard a song. Instead of his last wish, the toad asked for a kiss. Reba Jo agreed so the toad would leave. When she kissed him, the toad turned into a prince. Then he went away.

Spanish

El príncipe sapo

Reba Jo tocaba guitarra. Enlazaba cosas con su lazo. Un día, llegó en su caballo hasta el lecho de un río seco. De repente, el viento le voló el sombrero. El sombrero cayó dentro de un viejo pozo.

Un sapo le dijo que él podía encontrar el sombrero. Le pidió tres cosas a cambio. Quería comer un poco de chile. Quería escuchar a Reba Jo tocar la guitarra. Quería dormir una siesta en su sombrero. Reba Jo estuvo de acuerdo. El sapo le encontró el sombrero y ella se fue sin darle las gracias.

El sapo la siguió hasta la casa. Reba Jo le cumplió los tres deseos que había prometido. Le dio un poco de chile, le cantó una canción. En lugar de pedir su último deseo, el sapo le pidió un beso. Reba Jo estuvo de acuerdo porque así el sapo se podía ir. Cuando lo besó, el sapo se convirtió en un príncipe. Después, se fue.

Multilingual Summaries

Chinese

蟾蜍王子

麗巴不僅能彈吉它，還會使用套索。有一天，她騎馬去乾涸的老河床。突然帽子讓一陣風吹走，掉進井裏面。

蟾蜍保證為她找回帽子，但先要答應三件事。它想要一些辣椒，聽麗巴彈吉它，還想在帽子裏打個盹。麗巴全都同意了。可找回帽子後，麗巴沒說謝謝就騎馬走了。

蟾蜍一直跟到家裏，麗巴只好滿足它的願望。讓它吃了辣椒，為它彈了歌曲。蟾蜍說不想打盹，最好能吻一下。為了讓它趕快走，麗巴勉強同意了。輕輕一吻，蟾蜍竟然變成了英俊的王子！可是王子轉身離開了麗巴的家。

Vietnamese

Hoàng Tử Cóc Sừng

Reba Jo chơi đàn ghi-ta. Cô buộc đồ vật bằng sợi dây thòng lọng của mình. Ngày nọ, cô cỡi ngựa đến một lòng sông xưa cũ đã khô. Thình lình, gió thổi bay nón của cô. Nón bay xuống một cái giếng cũ.

Một con cóc sừng nói là nó sẽ tìm được cái nón của cô. Để bù lại cóc yêu cầu ba điều. Cóc muốn được một ít súp đậu. Cóc muốn được nghe Reba Jo chơi đàn ghi-ta. Cóc muốn ngủ trưa trong cái nón của cô. Reba Jo đồng ý. Cóc tìm ra chiếc nón của Reba Jo. Cô cỡi ngựa đi mà không cám ơn chàng cóc.

Chàng cóc theo cô về tận nhà. Reba Jo cho cóc được những điều ước. Cóc ăn một ít súp đậu và nghe một bài hát. Thay vào điều ước cuối cùng của mình, cóc xin được một nụ hôn. Reba Jo đồng ý làm để cho cóc đi chỗ khác. Khi cô hôn cóc, cóc trở thành một chàng hoàng tử. Rồi chàng bỏ đi.

Multilingual Summaries

Korean

뿔 달린 두꺼비 왕자

레바 조는 기타를 연주한다. 그녀는 올가미로 물건을 낚아채기도 한다. 어느 날 그녀는 말을 타고 오래되어 말라버린 강바닥에 갔다가 갑자기 바람이 불어 그녀의 모자가 날아가서 오래된 우물 속에 빠져버린다.

그러자 뿔 달린 두꺼비 한 마리가 나타나 모자를 찾아주겠다고 말한다. 두꺼비는 그 대신 그녀에게 세 가지를 요구하는데 그것은 칠리 고추 몇 개, 레바 조의 기타 연주 듣기, 그리고 그녀의 모자 안에서 낮잠을 자는 것이었다. 레바 조가 그러겠다고 하자 두꺼비는 모자를 찾아 주지만 레바 조는 두꺼비에게 고맙다는 말도 없이 말을 타고 떠나 버린다.

두꺼비가 그녀의 집까지 따라오자 레바 조는 두꺼비의 소원을 들어준다. 두꺼비는 칠리 고추 몇 개를 먹고 음악을 듣고는 마지막 소원 대신 키스를 해달라고 한다. 레바 조는 두꺼비를 내보내기 위해 그러겠다고 하고 두꺼비에게 키스하자 두꺼비는 왕자로 변한다. 하지만 왕자는 떠나가버린다.

Hmong

Tub Qav Kaws Vaj Ntxwv Tuaj Kub

Reba Jo ntaus kij taj. Nws muab nws txoj hlua pov khi ntau yam. Muaj ib hnub, nws tau caij nees mus txog ib tug dej qub thiab qhuav lawm. Tos nco xwb, cua cia li tshuab nws lub kaus mom ya lawm. Lub kaus mom raug tshuab mus poob rau ib lub qhov dej.

Ib tug qav kaws tuaj kub hais tias nws mam li nrhiav lub kaus mom. Nws tau nug peb yam khoom rov qab. Nws xav tau ib cov kua txob ntxuag taum thiab nqaij nyuj (chili) los noj. Nws xav hnov Reba Jo ntaus kij taj. Thiab, nws xav pw ib tsig hauv lub kaus mom. Reba Jo pom zoo li. Tus qav nrhiav tau Reba Jo lub kaus mom. Reba Jo caij nees mus tsis nco ua tus qav kaws tsaug.

Tus qav kaws raws nws los tsev. Reba Jo thiaj li muaj tej yam uas tus qav kaws xav tau. Tus qav noj kua txob ntxuag taum thiab mloog ib zaj nkauj. Tabsis tus qav kaws tsis yuav yam kawg nws thov lawm, tus qav kaws txawm thov nwj ib pas xwb. Reba Jo pom zoo li, kom tus qav kaws thiaj li khiav mus. Thaum nws nwj tus qav kaws, tus qav kaws cia li txias los ua ib tug tub vaj ntxwv. Ces nws thiaj li khiav mus lawm.

Letters Home from Yosemite Student Edition pages 116–127

Week at a Glance	Customize instruction every day for your English Language Learners.				
	Day 1	**Day 2**	**Day 3**	**Day 4**	**Day 5**
Teacher's Edition	Use the ELL Notes that appear throughout each day of the lesson to support instruction and reading.				
ELL Poster 5	• Assess Prior Knowledge • Develop Concepts and Vocabulary	• Preteach Tested Vocabulary	• Going on a Hike	• Class Consensus	• Monitor Progress
ELL Teaching Guide	• Picture It! Lesson, pp. 29–30 • Multilingual Summaries, pp. 33–35	• ELL Reader Lesson, pp. 220–221	• Vocabulary Activities and Word Cards, pp. 31–32 • Multilingual Summaries, pp. 33–35		
ELL Readers	• Reread *Painting the Southwest*	• Teach *For Purple Mountain Majesties*	• Reread *For Purple Mountain Majesties* and other texts to build fluency		
ELL and Transition Handbook	Use the following as needed to support this week's instruction and to conduct alternative assessments: • Phonics Transition Lessons • Grammar Transition Lessons • Assessment				

Picture It! Comprehension Lesson

Main Idea and Details

Use this lesson to supplement or replace the skill lesson on pages 112–113 of the Teacher's Edition.

Teach

Distribute copies of the Picture It! blackline master on page 30.

- Have students read the map. Then read the paragraph aloud.
- Ask: *What is this paragraph about?* (national parks)
- Share the Skill Points (at right) with students.
- Have students find the sentence that tells the main idea. Then have them find the sentences that give details.

Practice

Read aloud the directions on page 30. Have students write the main idea and details in the graphic organizer. Have students keep their organizers for later reteaching.

Answers for page 30: *Main Idea:* Some national parks are historic places. *Details:* At the Abraham Lincoln Birthplace, visitors see the boyhood home of the 16th President. At the Edgar Allan Poe Site, visitors see where a famous writer lived. Visitors to the African American Civil War Memorial learn about African Americans' contributions during the Civil War.

Skill Points

✓ The most important idea in a paragraph is the **main idea.**

✓ To find the main idea, ask: *What is this paragraph mostly about?* See if there is a sentence that gives the main idea.

✓ Other sentences in the paragraph tell more about the main idea. They give **details** about the main idea.

Name ______________________________

Look at the map. **Read** the paragraph.

- Which sentence tells the main idea? **Write** it in the *Main Idea* box.
- Which sentences give details? **Write** those sentences in the *Detail* boxes.

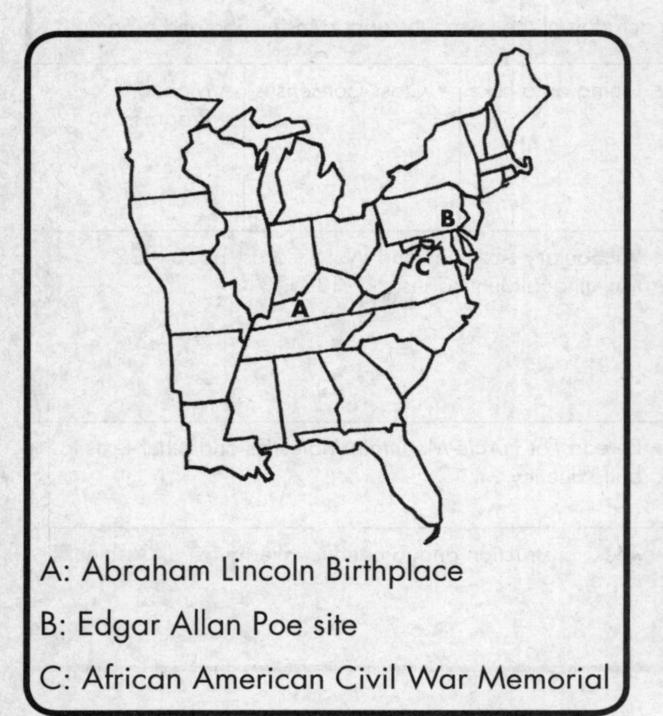

National Parks in the United States

Some national parks in the United States are historic places. These parks teach visitors about America's past. At the Abraham Lincoln Birthplace National Historic Site, visitors can see the boyhood home of the 16th President. At the Edgar Allan Poe National Historic Site, visitors can see where a famous writer lived. Visitors to the African American Civil War Memorial can learn about African Americans' contributions during the Civil War.

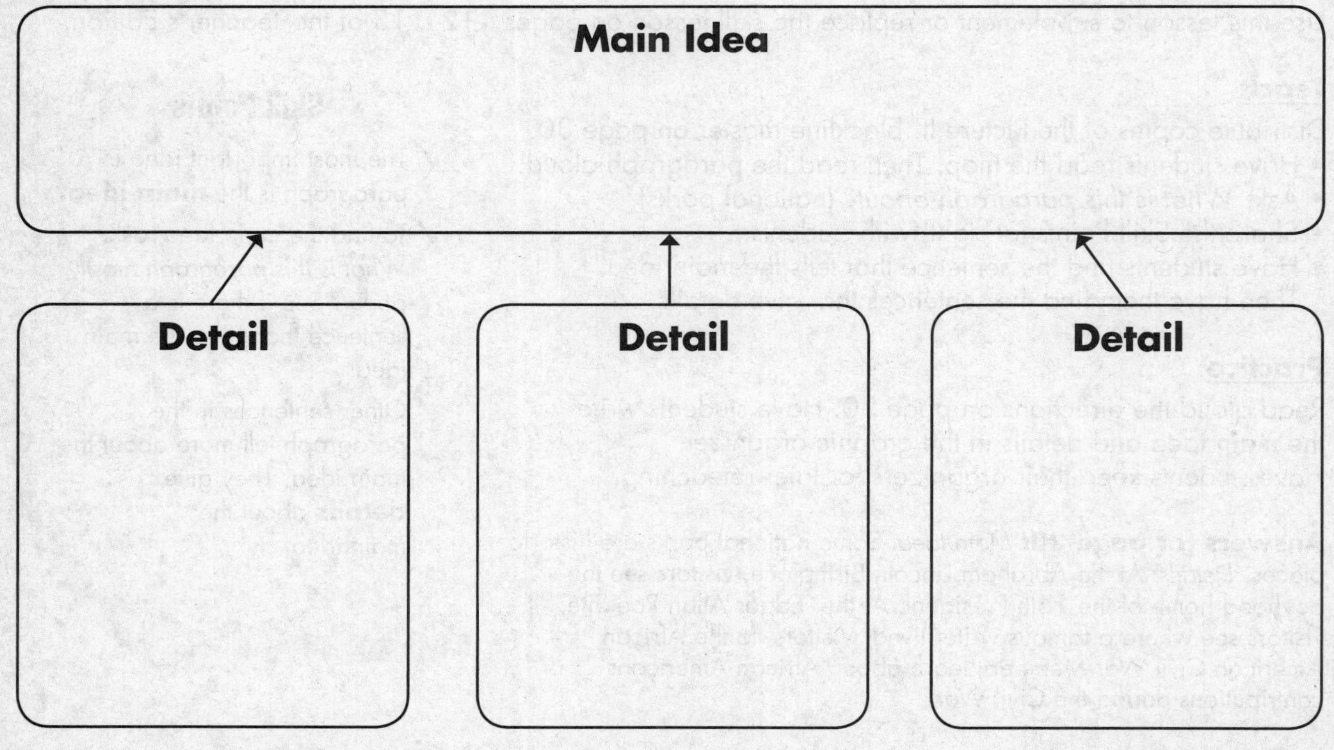

Vocabulary Activities and Word Cards

Copy the Word Cards on page 32 as needed for the following activities.
Use the blank card for an additional word that you want to teach.
Also see suggestions for teaching vocabulary in the ELL and Transition Handbook.

Home Language Clues	Context Game	Write a Story
• Pair students who have writing proficiency in the same home language, and give each student a set of Word Cards. • Have students work together to write translations of the vocabulary words in their home language on the back of each card. (See the Multilingual Lesson Vocabulary beginning on page 272 for suggested translations.) • Have partners lay out the cards with the home language sides facing up. • Invite students to generate synonyms for each word in their home language. Then ask them to name the English vocabulary word with the same meaning. They can flip the cards over to check their answers.	• Give a set of Word Cards to each student. • Have each student write a context sentence for each word on the back of each card. Remind students that context sentences are sentences that show the meaning of the word. Instruct students not to include the vocabulary word in the context sentence but to leave a blank where the word belongs. • Have students form pairs and exchange their cards with the context sides up. • Have students take turns looking at their partner's context sentence and guessing the vocabulary word. Have them discard each card into a correct or incorrect pile, depending on their guess. • To determine the winner, check which student has the most cards in the correct pile at the end of the game.	• Divide the class into small story-writing groups, and give each group a set of Word Cards. • Within each group, distribute the Word Cards so that each student has at least one card. • Have students select one member of the group to record the story, another to make sure that each student contributes at least one sentence to the story, and a third to read the story to the class. • Have each group brainstorm ideas for the story. Tell the students that the story can be silly or serious but must include all of the vocabulary words. Then have each student come up with a sentence for the story using the Word Card or Cards he or she received. • Give students ten minutes to write their story. Then have one member of each group read the story to the class.

glacier

impressive

naturalist

preserve

slopes

species

wilderness

Multilingual Summaries

English

Letters Home from Yosemite

Yosemite became a national park in 1890. It is in the Sierra Nevada Mountains. The park is named for a Native American name for grizzly bear. More than 3.5 million people visit Yosemite every year.

Bridal Veil Falls is one of the highest waterfalls in America. More than half of the highest waterfalls in America are in Yosemite. Giant old sequoia trees grow in Yosemite. Wild animals such as black bears and bighorn sheep live in the park.

Glacier Point is a little more than one-half mile above the floor of Yosemite Valley. El Capitan is the biggest block of granite in the country. Yosemite Falls is three waterfalls in one. A glacier is on Mt. Lyell, the park's highest peak. Tioga Pass runs through the park. It is the highest highway in the Sierra Nevada Mountains.

Spanish

Cartas desde Yosemite

Yosemite se convirtió en un parque nacional en 1890. Está situado en las montañas de la Sierra Nevada. El parque recibió este nombre por el nombre que le daban al oso pardo los indígenas norteamericanos. Más de 3.5 millones de personas visitan Yosemite cada año.

La catarata de Bridal Veil es una de las cataratas más altas en América del Norte. Más de la mitad de las cataratas más altas de América del Norte están en Yosemite. Enormes y viejos árboles de secuoya crecen en Yosemite. Animales salvajes como osos negros y carneros de cuernos grandes viven en el parque.

Glacier Point está a un poco más de la mitad de una milla encima del valle Yosemite. El Capitán es el bloque más grande de granito del país. Las cataratas de Yosemite son tres cataratas en una. Un glaciar está en el monte Lyell, la cima más alta del parque. El paso de Tioga corre a través del parque. Es la carretera más alta en las montañas de la Sierra Nevada.

Multilingual Summaries

Chinese

優勝美地公園

優勝美地於1890年成為國家公園，它位於內華達山區，在印地安語中是“大灰熊”的意思。每年有超過350萬人來這裏觀光。

新娘面紗瀑布是美國最高的瀑布之一，全國最高的瀑布有一半以上在優勝美地。這裏還有古老的美洲巨杉，生活著黑熊、大角羊等野生動物。

冰川點距離優勝美地谷底800多米。酋長石是美國最大的花崗岩巨石。優勝美地瀑布分三段俯衝直下。公園最高的萊爾峰上也有冰川。迪歐戈公路穿過公園，是內華達山區海拔最高的公路。

Vietnamese

Thư Gởi Về Nhà từ Yosemite

Yosemite trở thành khu vườn quốc gia vào năm 1890. Nó nằm trong Dãy Núi Sierra Nevada. Khu vườn được đặt tên theo chữ gấu lớn màu nâu (grizzly bear) của tiếng Thổ Dân Mỹ. Có hơn 3.5 triệu người đến tham quan Yosemite mỗi năm.

Thác nước Bridal Veil (Mạng Che Mặt Cô Dâu) là một trong những thác nước cao nhất ở Hoa Kỳ. Yosemite có trên phân nửa số thác nước cao nhất ở Hoa Kỳ. Những cây tùng đồ sộ lâu đời mọc lên ở Yosemite. Thú rừng như gấu đen và cừu to sừng sinh sống trong khu vườn này.

Điểm Glacier ở bên trên nền thung lũng Yosemite hơn nửa dặm. El Capitan là một trong những tảng hoa cương lớn nhất của cả nước. Thác nước Yosemite là ba thác nước nhập một. Một dãy băng trên ngọn Mt. Lyell, đỉnh cao nhất của khu vườn. Đường đèo Tioga Pass đi xuyên qua khu vườn. Đó là xa lộ cao nhất trong Dãy Núi Sierra Nevada.

Multilingual Summaries

Korean

요세미티에서 온 편지

시에라 네바다 산맥 속에 있는 요세미티는 1890년에 국립공원으로 지정되었다. 요세미티란 이름은 아메리카 원주민어의 회색 곰이라는 말에서 따왔으며 매년 350만 명 이상이 이 공원을 찾는다.

브라이들 베일(면사포) 폭포는 미국에서 가장 높은 폭포 중 하나로 이런 폭포의 반 이상이 요세미티 안에 자리잡고 있다. 거대하고 오래된 세쿼이아 나무들이 요세미티에서 자라고 있으며 흑곰이나 큰뿔양 같은 야생동물도 이곳에 살고 있다.

글래시어 포인트는 요세미티 계곡 바닥에서 위쪽으로 반 마일보다 약간 더 높은 곳에 있다. 엘 캐피턴은 미국에서 가장 큰 화강암 바위이다. 요세미티 폭포는 폭포 세 개가 하나로 합쳐진 것이다. 공원에서 가장 높은 봉우리인 라이엘 산에는 빙하가 하나 있다. 티오가 패스는 공원을 관통해 이어져있는데 이것은 시에라 네바다 산맥에서 가장 높은 고속도로이다.

Hmong

Sau Tsab Ntawv Mus Tsev los ntawm Yosemite

Xyoo 1890, Yosemite raug tsa ua ib lub thaj chaw national park. Nws nyob rau hauv roob toj siab Sierra Nevada. Thaj chaw park ntawd raug tis npe los ntawm ib lo lus Qhab Miskas rau ib tug dais. Niaj xyoo, ntau tshaj li 3.5 lab neeg tuaj xyuas Yosemite.

Bridal Veil Falls yog ib tug dej tsaws tsag ntawm cov loj tshaj hauv teb chaws Miskas. Cov dej tsaws tsag loj tshaj plaws feem coob nyob Miskas teb nyob rau hauv Yosemite. Tsob ntoo sequoia loj tuaj hauv Yosemite. Tsiaj txhu qus xws li cov dais dub thiab cov yaj tuaj kub loj nyob rau hauv thaj chaw park no.

Lub Roob Glacier Point siab siab tshaj ib nrab las (mile) los ntawm Tiaj Yosemite. El Capitan yog lub roob ua pob zeb granite loj tshaj plaws hauv teb chaws Miskas. Yosemite Falls yog peb dej tsaws tsag los ua ib lub. Muaj ib thooj dej khov nyob rau saum lub roob Mt. Lyell, thaj chaw park ntawd lub ncov roob siab tshaj. Txoj kev Tioga Pass nyob rau hauv thaj chaw park ntawd thiab yog txoj kev siab tshaj nyob rau hauv cov roob Sierra Nevada.

What Jo Did Student Edition pages 146–155

Week at a Glance	Customize instruction every day for your English Language Learners.				
	Day 1	**Day 2**	**Day 3**	**Day 4**	**Day 5**
Teacher's Edition	Use the ELL Notes that appear throughout each day of the lesson to support instruction and reading.				
ELL Poster 6	• Assess Prior Knowledge • Develop Concepts and Vocabulary	• Preteach Tested Vocabulary	• Appreciating Talents	• Narrating the Game	• Monitor Progress
ELL Teaching Guide	• Picture It! Lesson, pp. 36–37 • Multilingual Summaries, pp. 40–42	• ELL Reader Lesson, pp. 222–223	• Vocabulary Activities and Word Cards, pp. 38–39 • Multilingual Summaries, pp. 40–42		
ELL Readers	• Reread *For Purple Mountain Majesties*	• Teach *Girls Playing Basketball*	• Reread *Girls Playing Basketball* and other texts to build fluency		
ELL and Transition Handbook	Use the following as needed to support this week's instruction and to conduct alternative assessments: • Phonics Transition Lessons • Grammar Transition Lessons • Assessment				

Picture It! Comprehension Lesson

Cause and Effect

Use this lesson to supplement or replace the skill lesson on pages 142–143 of the Teacher's Edition.

Teach

Distribute copies of the Picture It! blackline master on page 37.

- Have students read the labels on the basketball player. Then read the paragraph aloud.
- Ask: *What causes basketball players' legs to be strong?*
- Share the Skill Points (at right) with students.
- Have students find the clue words. Then have them find the causes and effects.

Skill Points

✓ An **effect** is something that happens. A **cause** is what makes it happen.

✓ Clue words such as *because, so,* and *cause* sometimes show a cause-and-effect relationship.

Practice

Read aloud the directions on page 37. Have students underline the clue words. Then ask them to fill in the causes and effects in their graphic organizers. Have students keep their organizers for later reteaching.

Answers for page 37: *Clue words:* so, because, because, causes. *Causes:* running up and down the court, jumping up high; *Effect:* Basketball players have strong legs. *Causes:* passing and shooting the ball, holding hands up; *Effect:* Basketball players have strong arms.

Name ______________________________

Look at the picture. **Read** the paragraph.

- What causes a basketball player's legs to be strong? **Underline** the clue words. Then **write** the two causes and the effect in the first set of boxes below.
- What causes a basketball player's arms to be strong? **Underline** the clue words. Then **write** the two causes and the effect in the second set of boxes below.

Strong Basketball Players

Basketball players are strong. They run up and down the court, so their legs become very powerful. They develop big leg muscles, because they jump up high to shoot baskets. Basketball players' arms are strong because they pass and shoot the ball many times during a game. Holding their arms up in front of opponents to block shots also causes their arms to become strong.

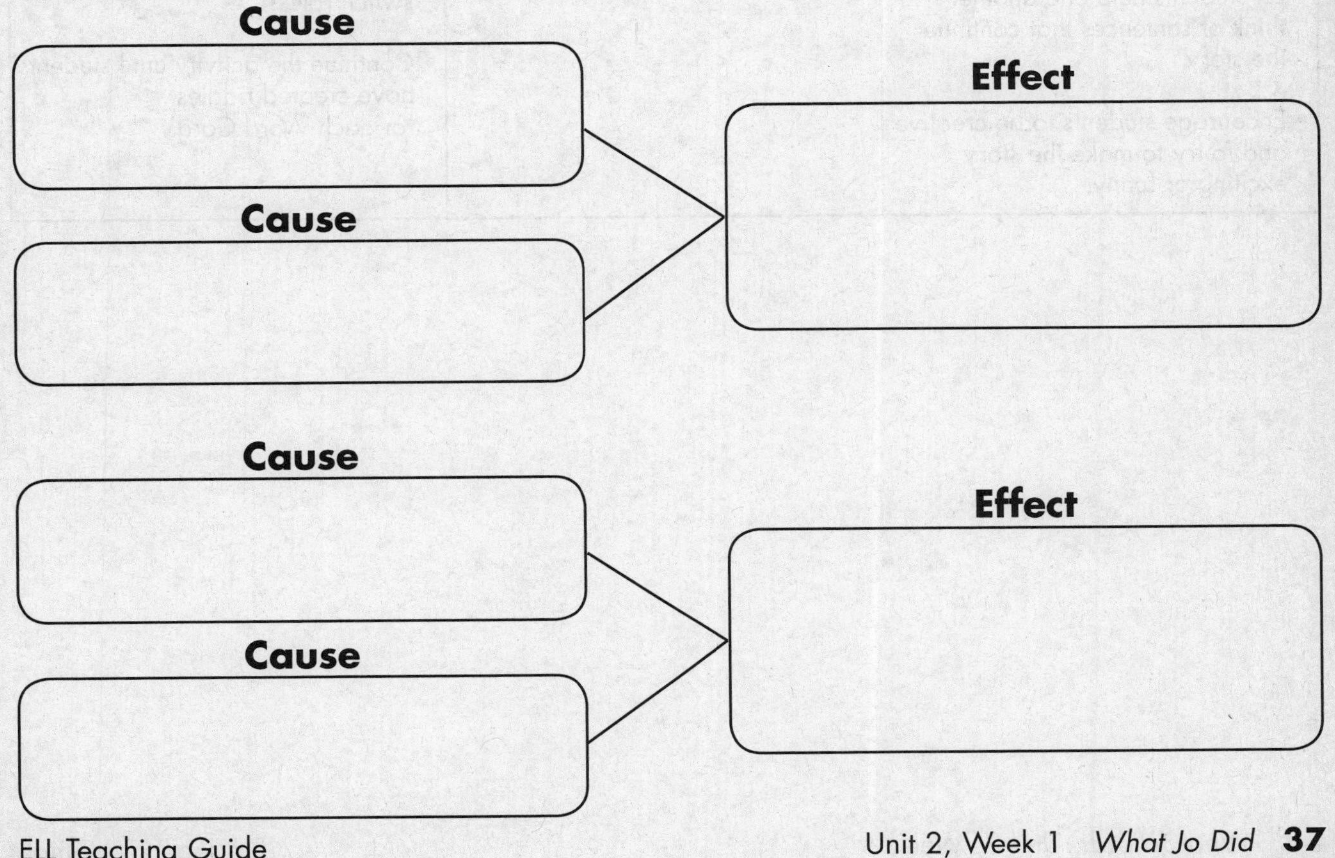

Vocabulary Activities and Word Cards

Copy the Word Cards on page 39 as needed for the following activities.
Use the blank card for an additional word that you want to teach.
Also see suggestions for teaching vocabulary in the ELL and Transition Handbook.

Tell a Story	Charades	Riddle Game
• Distribute one set of Word Cards to each student. • Gather the students in a circle and explain that the group will be telling a story together. • Begin the story with a sentence that uses a vocabulary word. • Have the student to your right continue the story, adding a sentence that uses any of the other vocabulary words. • Have each student continue the story, adding a sentence that uses a vocabulary word. • Let students help one another think of sentences that continue the story. • Encourage students to be creative and to try to make the story exciting or funny.	• Divide the class into small groups, and give each group one Word Card. • Have each group discuss how to silently act out the meaning of its vocabulary word. • Allow time for the groups to practice their charades before performing them for the class. • When they are ready, have groups take turns acting out their charades while their classmates try to guess the word.	• Divide the class into pairs. Give each pair a set of Word Cards. • Have students place the set of Word Cards face down in a pile. • Ask one partner to choose a card and make up a riddle about the word. Provide examples, such as: *If the ball hits this part of the hoop, it may or may not go in;* or, *Some people wear this piece of clothing instead of a T-shirt when they play sports.* Then have students tell their riddles to their partners. • Have the partner try to guess the word. Then have students switch roles. • Continue the activity until students have created riddles for each Word Card.

fouled

hoop

jersey

marveled

rim

speechless

swatted

Multilingual Summaries

English

What Jo Did

Joanna plays basketball at home. Her basket is sixteen feet high. Her parents do not know that regulation baskets are only ten feet high. Joanna learns to jump very high.

One day, Joanna's mother sends her to the store. On her way home, she sees boys playing basketball. They ask her to play with them. She is wearing a hat that covers her hair. They think that she is a boy. She tells them that her name is Jo.

Everyone sees that Jo is good at basketball. They ask her to dunk the ball. She does! Her hat falls off and they see that she is a girl. They are surprised. They ask her to play with them again.

Spanish

Lo que hizo Jo

Joanna juega baloncesto en casa. Su canasta está a dieciséis pies de altura. Sus padres no saben que las regulaciones para las canastas son sólo de diez pies hasta el aro. Joanna aprende a saltar muy alto.

Un día, la mamá de Joanna la manda a la tienda. En el camino de regreso, ella ve a unos niños jugando baloncesto. Ellos la invitan a jugar. Joanna tiene puesto un sombrero que le cubre su cabello. Los niños piensan que es un niño. Ella les dice que se llama Jo.

Todos ven que Jo es buena jugadora de baloncesto. Ellos la invitan a clavar la pelota. ¡Ella lo hace! Su sombrero se cae y ellos ven que es una niña. Están sorprendidos, pero la invitan a volver a jugar con ellos.

Multilingual Summaries

Chinese

喬的故事

喬安娜常在家裏打籃球。父母親不知道標準是10英尺，將她的籃筐提高到16英尺，因此喬安娜學會跳得很高。

有一次媽媽叫喬安娜去買東西，她回來時看見男孩們在打籃球。喬安娜戴著帽子，遮住了頭髮，大家以為她是男孩，叫她一塊打籃球。她說自己名字叫喬。

每人都說喬是好球員。請她做扣籃，她輕鬆地完成！可是帽子掉了，大家發現喬原來是女孩，不過還是請她一起玩。

Vietnamese

Điều Jo Đã Làm

Joanna chơi bóng rổ ở nhà. Khung rổ của cô cao đến mười sáu bộ. Ba mẹ của cô không biết là theo quy định thì những khung rổ chỉ được cao mười bộ. Joanna học nhảy lên rất cao.

Ngày kia, mẹ của Joanna nhờ cô đi đến một cửa tiệm. Trên đường về nhà, cô thấy các cậu con trai đang chơi bóng rổ. Họ rủ cô chơi với họ. Cô đang đội một cái nón che hết tóc của mình. Họ tưởng cô là một cậu con trai. Cô nói cho họ biết tên mình là Jo.

Mọi người thấy là Jo chơi bóng rổ giỏi. Họ kêu cô đánh bóng vào rổ. Cô làm được! Nón rơi xuống và họ nhận ra cô là một cô gái. Họ ngạc nhiên. Họ rủ cô chơi với họ nữa.

Multilingual Summaries

Korean

조가 한 일

조안나는 집에서 농구를 한다. 그녀의 농구 바스켓은 높이가 16피트인데 부모님은 바스켓의 규정 높이가 10피트 밖에 안 된다는 것을 모른다. 조안나는 높이 점프하는 법을 배운다.

어느 날 조안나는 어머니의 심부름으로 가게에 갔다가 집에 돌아오는 길에 남자아이들이 농구 하는 것을 본다. 아이들은 조안나에게 경기를 함께 하자고 제안한다. 조안나가 머리를 덮는 모자를 쓰고 있기 때문에 아이들이 조안나를 남자아이로 생각한 것이다. 조안나는 아이들에게 자기 이름을 조라고 말한다.

모두들 조가 농구에 뛰어나다는 것을 알게 되고 아이들은 조안나에게 덩크슛을 해보라고 권한다. 그리고 조안나는 덩크슛을 해낸다. 그런데 조안나의 모자가 땅에 떨어지면서 아이들은 조안나가 여자아이라는 것을 알게 되고 모두 놀라워한다. 아이들은 조안나에게 경기를 또 하자고 한다.

Hmong

Tej Yam Jo Tau Ua

Joanna pov npas basketball nram tsev. Nws lub tawb pov npas siab li kaum rau feet. Nws niam thiab nws txiv lawv tsis paub hais tias raws li txoj cai lub tawb pov npas tsuas siab li kaum feet xwb. Joanna kawm dhia tau siab heev li.

Muaj ib hnub, Joanna niam kom nws mus tom kiab khw. Thaum nws los txog ib tog kev, nws pom ib co me nyuam tub pov npas basketball ua si. Lawv caw nws nrog lawv ua si. Joanna ntoo ib lub kaus mom ua vov nws cov plaub hau. Lawv xav hais tias nws yog ib tug me nyuam tub. Nws qhia rau lawv tias nws lub npe hu ua Jo.

Sawv daws pom tias nws pov npas tau zoo heev. Lawm kom nws dhia ya pov lub npas rau hauv lub tawb pov npas. Nws txawm ua li ntawd. Nws lub kaus mom poob hle los ces lawv pom tias nws yog ib tug me nyuam ntxhais. Lawv ceeb tag. Lawv nug nws rov nrog lawv ua si dua.

Coyote School News Student Edition pages 166–183

Week at a Glance	Customize instruction every day for your English Language Learners.				
	Day 1	**Day 2**	**Day 3**	**Day 4**	**Day 5**
Teacher's Edition	Use the ELL Notes that appear throughout each day of the lesson to support instruction and reading.				
ELL Poster 7	• Assess Prior Knowledge • Develop Concepts and Vocabulary	• Preteach Tested Vocabulary	• Working Together	• Achieving Your Goals	• Monitor Progress
ELL Teaching Guide	• Picture It! Lesson, pp. 43–44 • Multilingual Summaries, pp. 47–49	• ELL Reader Lesson, pp. 224–225	• Vocabulary Activities and Word Cards, pp. 45–46 • Multilingual Summaries, pp. 47–49		
ELL Readers	• Reread *Girls Playing Basketball*	• Teach *First, It Was a* Rancho	• Reread *First, It Was a* Rancho and other texts to build fluency		
ELL and Transition Handbook	Use the following as needed to support this week's instruction and to conduct alternative assessments: • Phonics Transition Lessons • Grammar Transition Lessons • Assessment				

Picture It! Comprehension Lesson

Draw Conclusions

Use this lesson to supplement or replace the skill lesson on pages 162–163 of the Teacher's Edition.

Teach

Distribute copies of the Picture It! blackline master on page 44.

- Have students describe what they see in the illustrations. Then read the paragraph aloud.
- Ask: *What are some of the things a ranch hand does?* (puts up fences, repairs machines, repairs barns, takes care of horses, goes into town to buy supplies)
- Share the Skill Points (at right) with students.
- Have students identify a conclusion they can draw from the paragraph about life as a ranch hand.

Practice

Read aloud the directions on page 44. Have students complete the graphic organizer. Have them save their organizers for later reteaching.

Skill Points

✓ When you read, you form an opinion based on what you already know or on the facts and details in the text. This opinion is called a **conclusion**.

✓ You can check your conclusions or an author's conclusions by asking: *Does this conclusion make sense? Are the facts and details correct?*

Answers for page 44: *Conclusion:* Possible response: Being a ranch hand is hard work. *Supporting Facts:* Ranch hands put up fences, repair machines, repair barns, take care of horses, go into town to buy supplies, get up at 5 A.M., and work until late at night.

Name ______________________________

Draw Conclusions

Look at the picture. **Read** the paragraph below.

- What conclusion about being a ranch hand can you draw from the paragraph? **Write** it in the box below.
- What facts or details support this conclusion? **Write** them in the boxes below.

Life as a Ranch Hand

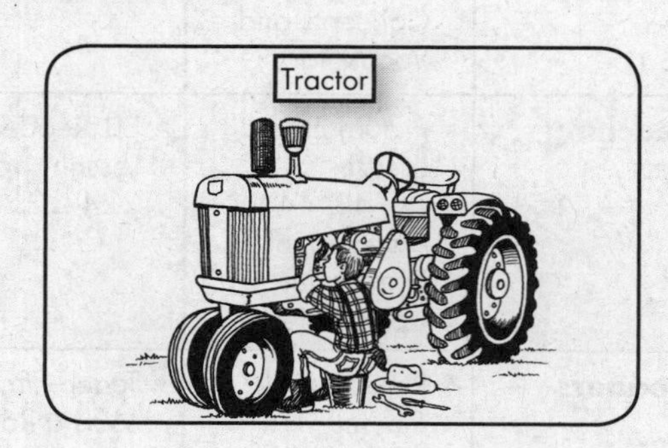

Jimmy Wilcox works on a ranch in Texas. He is called a ranch hand. Jimmy digs holes to put up fences. He repairs tractors and other machines. He repairs barns and takes care of the horses. Sometimes, the owner of the ranch asks Jimmy to pick up some supplies. Jimmy takes his truck and goes into town to buy them. There is so much work for Jimmy to do that he usually gets up at five o'clock in the morning and works until late at night.

Conclusion

Supporting Facts

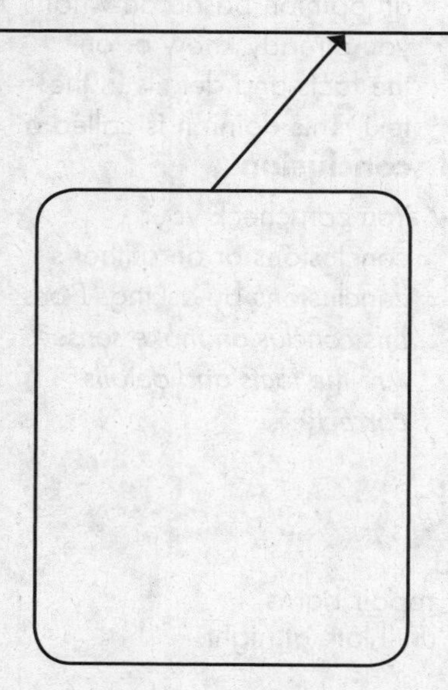

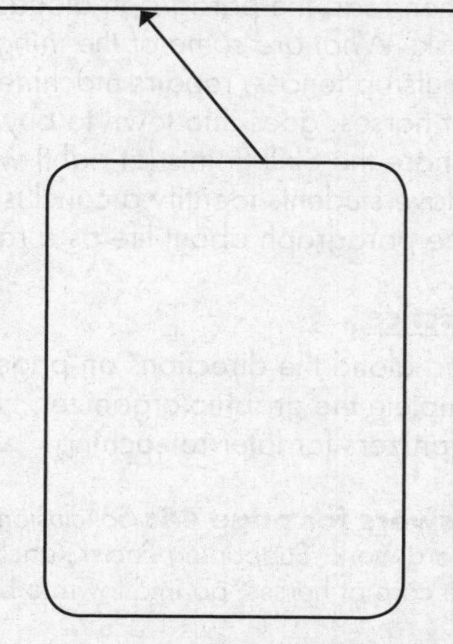

Vocabulary Activities and Word Cards

Copy the Word Cards on page 46 as needed for the following activities.
Use the blank cards for additional words that you want to teach.
Also see suggestions for teaching vocabulary in the ELL and Transition Handbook.

Poster Clues	Cloze Sentences	Home Language Clues
• Distribute sets of Word Cards to students. Then, from your own set of Word Cards, have one student pick a card without letting the others see it. • The student stands at the ELL Poster, points to the relevant area on it, and uses the information on the Poster to give hints about the vocabulary word. • Other students should try to guess which vocabulary word the student has. The first person to guess correctly may choose the next Word Card and make up clues about it. • Continue until all of the vocabulary words have been used.	• Give each student a set of Word Cards and two pieces of paper. • Have students write one sentence using each vocabulary word. • On a second sheet of paper, have students rewrite each sentence, replacing the vocabulary word with a blank line. • Divide the class into pairs. Have each pair of students exchange the papers with their cloze sentences and try to fill in the missing vocabulary words. Have partners check one another's work.	• Pair students who have writing proficiency in the same home language, and give each student a set of Word Cards. • Have students work together to write translations of the vocabulary words in their home language on the back of each card. (See the Multilingual Lesson Vocabulary beginning on page 272 for suggested translations.) • Have partners lay out the cards with the home language sides facing up. • Invite students to generate synonyms for each word in their home language. Then ask them to name the English vocabulary word with the same meaning. They can flip the cards over to check their answers.

bawling

coyote

dudes

roundup

spurs

Multilingual Summaries

English

Coyote School News

Monchi lives on a ranch in Arizona. He goes to Coyote School. The teacher, Miss Byers, helps the students to start a newspaper called *Coyote News*. All the students write stories for it. Miss Byers offers a prize for perfect attendance—a silver dollar.

Monchi and his family pick chiles after school. Monchi is hurt when a bag of chiles falls on him. He breaks his wrist.

Monchi's family has a big Christmas Eve party. They make a piñata and eat and dance. This year Monchi's present is a silver belt buckle with a hole for a silver dollar.

Monchi and his older brother help with roundup on the ranch. They stay home from school. Monchi is sad he will not get a perfect attendance award.

At the end of the school year, Monchi wins a silver dollar for helping with the newspaper. He puts the dollar in his buckle.

Spanish

Noticias de la escuela Coyote

Monchi vive en un rancho de Arizona. Él va a la escuela Coyote. La maestra, la señorita Byers, ayuda a los estudiantes a hacer un periódico que se llama *Noticias Coyote*. Todos los estudiantes escriben historias para el periódico. La señorita Byers promete dar un dólar de plata como premio por la asistencia perfecta.

Monchi y su familia recolectan chiles después de la escuela. Monchi se hace daño con una bolsa de chiles que se le cae encima. Se rompe la muñeca.

La familia de Monchi hace una gran fiesta de Nochebuena. Hacen una piñata y comen y bailan. Este año el regalo de Monchi es una hebilla de cinturón con un hueco para un dólar de plata.

Monchi y su hermano ayudan en el rodeo del rancho. Ellos no van a la escuela. Monchi está triste porque no tendrá el premio de asistencia perfecta.

Al final del año escolar, Monchi gana un dólar de plata por su ayuda en el periódico. Él coloca el dólar en su hebilla.

Multilingual Summaries

Chinese

凱奧特學校新聞報

蒙奇住在亞利桑那州的農場，他的學校名叫凱奧特。同學們跟著白老師辦報紙，起名叫凱奧特新聞報，每個人都給報紙投稿。白老師說哪位同學不缺課，就給予獎勵一銀元。

放學後，蒙奇幫家裏摘辣椒。一不小心，大包辣椒掉下來，扭傷了他的手腕。

聖誕前夕，蒙奇家舉行盛大的宴會。他們製做彼那塔陶罐、吃許多東西和一起跳舞。今年蒙奇收到的禮物是銀帶扣，上面有個小洞要放一個銀元。

可是蒙奇與哥哥要幫農場趕牛群，不能按時去學校。拿不到老師的獎勵，蒙奇心裏很傷心。

學期結束時，由於蒙奇辦報紙出色，還是獲得銀元獎，他高興地把它放在帶扣上。

Vietnamese

Tin Của Trường Coyote

Monchi sống trong một trang trại ở Arizona. Cậu đi học ở Trường Coyote. Cô giáo, Cô Byers, giúp học sinh khởi sự làm một tờ báo gọi là Tin Của Coyote. Tất cả học sinh đều phải viết bài cho báo. Cô Byers đưa ra một giải thưởng cho ai đi học đều đặn—một đồng đô-la bằng bạc.

Monchi và gia đình cậu hái ớt sau giờ học. Monchi bị thương khi một túi ớt ngả lên mình. Cậu bị gẫy cổ tay.

Gia đình của Monchi có một bữa tiệc lớn trước ngày lễ Giáng Sinh. Họ làm một con thú nhồi kẹo và ăn uống và nhảy múa. Năm nay món quà cho Monchi là một cái khóa thắt lưng bằng bạc với một cái lỗ trống để nhét đồng đô-la bạc.

Monchi và người anh giúp lùa súc vật ở trang trại. Họ phải nghỉ học. Monchi buồn vì cậu sẽ không được phần thưởng đi học đều.

Vào cuối niên học, Monchi đạt được đồng đô-la bạc vì đã giúp đỡ tờ báo. Cậu để đồng đô-la vào cái khóa thắt lưng của mình.

Multilingual Summaries

Korean

코요테 학교 뉴스

애리조나의 대농장에서 살고 있는 몬치는 코요테 학교에 다닌다. 바이어스 선생님은 학생들이 코요테 뉴스라는 신문을 만들 수 있도록 도왔고 학생들은 모두 신문에 실을 이야기를 쓴다. 바이어스 선생님은 1년 개근한 학생에게 상으로 은화 1달러를 주겠다고 제안한다.

몬치는 방과 후 가족과 칠레 고추를 따다가 고추가 든 가방이 떨어지는 바람에 손목이 부러진다.

몬치의 가족은 크리스마스 이브 파티를 성대하게 열어 피나타를 만들어 먹고 춤을 춘다. 올해 몬치가 받은 선물은 은화 달러를 달 수 있는 구멍이 나있는 은 벨트 버클이다.

몬치와 형은 농장의 가축을 모는 일을 돕느라 학교에 가지 못한다. 몬치는 개근상을 받지 못한다고 슬퍼한다.

학기말이 되었을 때 몬치는 신문 발행을 도운 공로로 은화 달러를 받고 그 은화를 벨트 버클에 끼워 넣는다.

Hmong

Tsev Kawm Ntawv Coyote Xov Xwm

Monchi nyob rau ib lub tsev yaj sab yug tsiaj nyob rau Arizona. Nws mus lub tsev kawm ntawv Coyote. Tus xib fwb, Miss Byers, pab nws cov tub ntxhais kawm ntawv tsim ib daim xov xwm hu ua Xov Xwm Coyote. Tag nrho cov tub ntxhais kawm ntawv sau dab neeg rau hauv. Miss Byers muaj khoom plig rau tus ua tuaj kawm ntawv txhua hnub - ib lub nyiaj duas-las.

Monchi thiab nws tsev neeg khaws kua txob tom qab tsev kawm ntawv lawb. Monchi tau raug mob thaum ib hnab kua txob poob ntaus nws. Nws qis tes thiaj li dam.

Monchi tsev neeg muaj ib lub koom txoos hmo ua ntej Christmas. Lawv ua Pinata thiab noj mov thiab seev ceev. Xyoo no, Monchi's qhov khoom plig yog ib txoj siv muaj lub pov siv nyiaj nrog ib lub qhov rau lub nyiaj duas-las.

Monchi thiab nws tus tij laug pab sau cov tsiaj mus khaws cia nyob rau tom tsev. Nkawv nyob tsev tsis mus kawm ntawv. Monchi tu siab tias nws yuav tsis tau qhov khoom plig ua tuaj txhua hnub tom tsev kawm ntawv.

Thaum xyoo yuav kawg, Monchi yeej ib lub nyiaj duas-las vim nws pab lawv ua daim xov xwm. Nws muab lub nyiaj duas-las rau nws lub pob siv.

Grace and the Time Machine

Student Edition pages 192–207

Week at a Glance	Customize instruction every day for your English Language Learners.				
	Day 1	**Day 2**	**Day 3**	**Day 4**	**Day 5**
Teacher's Edition	Use the ELL Notes that appear throughout each day of the lesson to support instruction and reading.				
ELL Poster 8	• Assess Prior Knowledge • Develop Concepts and Vocabulary	• Preteach Tested Vocabulary	• Repeating Lists	• Life Without the Railroads	• Monitor Progress
ELL Teaching Guide	• Picture It! Lesson, pp. 50–51 • Multilingual Summaries, pp. 54–56	• ELL Reader Lesson, pp. 226–227	• Vocabulary Activities and Word Cards, pp. 52–53 • Multilingual Summaries, pp. 54–56		
ELL Readers	• Reread *First, It Was a* Rancho	• Teach *Hello, Good-bye, and Other Customs*	• Reread *Hello, Good-bye, and Other Customs* and other texts to build fluency		
ELL and Transition Handbook	Use the following as needed to support this week's instruction and to conduct alternative assessments: • Phonics Transition Lessons • Grammar Transition Lessons • Assessment				

Picture It! Comprehension Lesson

Draw Conclusions

Use this lesson to supplement or replace the skill lesson on pages 188–189 of the Teacher's Edition.

Teach

Distribute copies of the Picture It! blackline master on page 51.

- Have students look at the pictures. Then read the scenes aloud.
- Ask: *How do Denya and Jamal visit the past?* (by watching videos of themselves when they were younger)
- Share the Skill Points (at right) with students.
- Have students find the details that support their conclusion.

Practice

Read aloud the directions on page 51. Have students complete the graphic organizer. Have them keep their organizers for later reteaching.

Answers for page 51: *Conclusion:* They visit the past by watching videos of themselves and remembering their past. *Facts and Details:* There are a TV, VCR, and videotapes. They are watching videotapes of events from their past.

Skill Points

✓ **Drawing conclusions** while you read or after you read is forming an opinion based on what you already know or on the facts and details in a text.

✓ Details show whether the conclusion you or the author reaches is correct.

Name ______________________________ **Draw Conclusions**

Look at the pictures. **Read** the scenes.

- How do Denya and Jamal visit the past? Draw a conclusion. **Write** it in the *Conclusion* box below.
- What facts and details help you make that conclusion? **Write** the details in the *Facts* and *Details* boxes below.

The Time Machine

Denya: Jamal! Come here! Do you want to travel back in time with me?

Jamal: OK.

Denya: Let's go to your first birthday party.

Jamal: Great! I love birthdays!

Jamal: Is that me? I look so little! What am I wearing?

Denya: Those were your special birthday clothes. Do you want to travel back to last summer?

Jamal: Look! There you are riding your new bike!

Mom: Jamal, Denya, time for dinner!

Denya and Jamal: OK! We're coming!

Conclusion

Facts

Details

Vocabulary Activities and Word Cards

Copy the Word Cards on pages 52–53 as needed for the following activities.
Use the blank card for an additional word that you want to teach.
Also see suggestions for teaching vocabulary in the ELL and Transition Handbook.

Part-of-Speech Word Sort	Context Game	Write a Story
• Divide the class into pairs. Give each pair of students a set of Word Cards and two sheets of paper. • Have each pair of students prepare a three-column chart labeled *Nouns, Verbs,* and *Adjectives.* • Have students sort the Word Cards, discussing where to put each word. • Then have each pair of students write sentences that use words from each column.	• Give a set of Word Cards to each student. • Have each student write a context sentence for each word on the back of each card. Remind students that context sentences are sentences that show the meaning of the word. Instruct students not to include the vocabulary word in the context sentence but to leave a blank where the word belongs. • Have students form pairs and exchange their cards with the context sides up. • Have students take turns looking at their partner's context sentence and guessing the vocabulary word. Have them discard each card into a correct or incorrect pile, depending on their guess. • To determine the winner, check which student has the most cards in the correct pile at the end of the game.	• Divide the class into small story-writing groups, and give each group a set of Word Cards. • Within each group, distribute the Word Cards so that each student has at least one card. • Have students select one member of the group to record the story, another to make sure that each student contributes at least one sentence to the story, and a third to read the story to the class. • Have each group brainstorm ideas for the story. Tell them that the story can be silly or serious but must include all of the vocabulary words. Then have each student come up with a sentence for the story using the Word Card or Cards he or she received. • Give students ten minutes to write their story. Then have one member of each group read the story to the class.

aboard

atlas

awkward	**capable**
chant	**mechanical**
miracle	**reseats**
vehicle	

Multilingual Summaries

English

Grace and the Time Machine

Grace's mother, Ava, is at work. Grace stays home with her grandmother, Nana. Grace's friends Aimee, Kester, Raj, and Maria come over to play. They decide to invent a time machine.

Grace is the first to drive the time machine. The children go to the future. Robots greet them. There are no humans. Raj drives the time machine to the past. The children see dinosaurs. Then they go to Gambia. Nana comes outside. She says that the dinosaurs woke her.

Nana drives the time machine to her childhood in Trinidad. Then their neighbor, Mrs. Myerson, comes outside. Usually, Mrs. Myerson never leaves her house. She decides to try the time machine. She travels to her childhood in 1925 Germany. She remembers how happy she was. Ava comes home. Everyone is in the backyard with the time machine. Grace tells her mother what happened. Ava says that the time machine is a wonderful invention.

Spanish

Grace y la máquina del tiempo

Ava, la mamá de Grace, está en el trabajo. Grace se queda en casa con Nana, su abuela. Los amigos de Grace, Aimee, Kester, Raj y María, llegan a su casa a jugar. Deciden inventar una máquina del tiempo.

Grace es la primera en conducir la máquina del tiempo. Los niños van al futuro. Allí son recibidos por robots. No hay seres humanos. Raj conduce la máquina del tiempo al pasado. Los niños ven dinosaurios. Luego van a Gambia. Nana sale de la casa. Dice que los dinosaurios la despertaron.

Nana conduce la máquina del tiempo a su infancia en Trinidad. Luego su vecina, la señora Myerson, sale de la casa. Usualmente, la señora Myerson nunca sale de su casa. Ella decide probar la máquina del tiempo. Viaja a su infancia en 1925, en Alemania. Ella recuerda lo feliz que era. Ava regresa a casa. Todos están en el patio con la máquina del tiempo. Grace le dice a su mamá lo que pasó. Ava dice que la máquina del tiempo es un invento maravilloso.

Multilingual Summaries

Chinese

格雷斯的時間船

媽媽要工作，格雷斯與奶奶待在家。小朋友艾米、凱斯特、瑞奇和瑪麗亞過來玩。大家決定發明時間船。

第一次由格雷斯來駕駛，他們飛到未來，許多機器人來歡迎，但是沒有人類。瑞奇駕船回到過去，他們看見了恐龍，然後又去了岡比亞。奶奶跑出來說，大恐龍吵醒了她。

奶奶駕船回到童年的特立尼達。鄰居梅爾森太太從不離開自己的家，這回也出來要看看時間船。她想乘著時間船回到1925年童年時的德國，那個時候她非常快樂。媽媽回來時，大家都聚在後院看時間船。格雷斯把今天的經歷告訴媽媽，媽媽說時間船是一項很了不起的發明。

Vietnamese

Grace và Chiếc Máy Thời Gian

Mẹ của Grace, Ava, đang ở sở làm. Grace ở nhà với bà của cô, Nana. Các bạn của Grace là Aimee, Kester, Raj, và Maria đến chơi. Họ quyết định chế tạo ra chiếc máy thời gian.

Grace là người đầu tiên lái chiếc máy thời gian. Đám bạn trẻ đi đến tương lai. Các người máy chào đón họ. Không có con người. Raj lái chiếc máy thời gian về quá khứ. Đám bạn trẻ thấy những con khủng long. Rồi họ đi đến Gambia. Nana đi ra ngoài. Bà nói là những con khủng long đã đánh thức bà.

Nana lái chiếc máy thời gian trở về thời thơ ấu của bà ở Trinidad. Rồi người láng giềng của họ, Bà Myerson, đi ra ngoài. Thông thường, Bà Myerson không bao giờ rời khỏi nhà. Bà ấy quyết định thử chiếc máy thời gian. Bà du hành về thời niên thiếu ở Đức Quốc vào năm 1925. Bà nhớ lại mình đã vui sướng biết bao. Ava về đến nhà. Mọi người đang ở sau vườn với chiếc máy thời gian. Grace kể mẹ nghe điều gì đã xảy ra. Ava nói rằng chiếc máy thời gian là một phát minh tuyệt vời.

Multilingual Summaries

Korean

그레이스와 타임머신

그레이스의 어머니인 아바는 직장에서 근무 중이고 그레이스는 나나 할머니와 함께 집에 있다. 그레이스의 친구인 에이미와 케스터, 라즈, 그리고 마리아가 집에 놀러 오고 아이들은 타임머신을 만들기로 한다.

그레이스가 제일 먼저 타임머신을 작동시켜 아이들은 미래로 가게 된다. 로봇들이 아이들에게 인사를 하는데 사람들은 보이지 않는다. 라즈가 타임머신을 작동해 과거로 간다. 아이들은 공룡을 보고 나서 감비아로 간다. 그 때 나나 할머니가 집 밖으로 나오며 공룡 때문에 잠이 깼다고 말한다.

나나 할머니는 트리니다드에서 보낸 자신의 어린 시절로 타임머신을 작동시킨다. 그러자 이웃집 마이어슨 부인이 집 밖으로 나온다. 보통 마이어슨 부인은 절대 집을 떠나지 않지만 타임머신을 한 번 타 보기로 한다. 그녀는 1925년 독일에서의 어린 시절로 여행하며 자신이 얼마나 행복했었는지를 회상한다. 그 후 그레이스의 엄마가 집에 돌아온다. 사람들은 모두 타임머신을 타고 뒤뜰에 있었다. 그레이스는 엄마에게 무슨 일이 있었는지를 이야기하고 엄마는 타임머신이 훌륭한 발명품이라고 말해 준다.

Hmong

Grace thiab lub Tshuab Tig Sij Hawm

Grace niam, Ava, nyob tom hauj lwm. Grace nyob tsev nrog nws pog, Nana. Grace cov phoojywg Aimee, Kester, Raj, thiab Maria tuaj nrog nws ua si. Lawv xav tsim ib lub tshuab tig sij hawm.

Grace yog thawj tug tsav lub tshuab. Cov me nyuam mus rau lub sij hawm yav pem suab. Robots txais tos lawv. Tsis muaj ib tug tib neeg li. Raj tsav lub tshuab tig sij hawm rov rau lub sij hawm yav tag dhau los. Cov me nyuam pom cov tsiaj dinosaurs. Ces lawv mus rau Gambia. Nana tawm nraum zoov los saib lawv. Nws hais tias cov dinosaur tsa nws sawv.

Nana tsav lub tshuab tig sij hawm mus rau lub caij thaum nws tseem yog me nyuam yaus nyob rau Trinidad. Ces tus neeg nyob ntawm lawv ib sab, Mrs. Myerson, tawm tuaj nraum zoov. Ntau zaug, Mrs. Myerson yeej tsis tawm nws lub tsev li. Nws xav siv lub tshuab tig sij hawm. Nws caij mus rau lub sij hawm thaum nws tseem yog me nyuam yaus nyob rau xyoo 1925 Yiv-las-mees (Germany). Nws nco txog thaum nws zoo siab. Ava los tsev. Sawv daws nyob nraum qab tsib taug nrog lub tshuab tig sij hawm. Grace qhia nws niam txhua yam tau tshwm sim los. Ava hais tias lub tshuab tig sij hawm yog ib qho khoom tsim tau zoo heev li.

Marven of the Great North Woods

Student Edition pages 216–232

Week at a Glance	Customize instruction every day for your English Language Learners.				
	Day 1	**Day 2**	**Day 3**	**Day 4**	**Day 5**
Teacher's Edition	Use the ELL Notes that appear throughout each day of the lesson to support instruction and reading.				
ELL Poster 9	• Assess Prior Knowledge • Develop Concepts and Vocabulary	• Preteach Tested Vocabulary	• Once Upon a Time	• Job Well Done	• Monitor Progress
ELL Teaching Guide	• Picture It! Lesson, pp. 57–58 • Multilingual Summaries, pp. 61–63	• ELL Reader Lesson, pp. 228–229	• Vocabulary Activities and Word Cards, pp. 59–60 • Multilingual Summaries, pp. 61–63		
ELL Readers	• Reread *Hello, Good-bye, and Other Customs*	• Teach *A Mill Girl's Day*	• Reread *A Mill Girl's Day* and other texts to build fluency		
ELL and Transition Handbook	Use the following as needed to support this week's instruction and to conduct alternative assessments: • Phonics Transition Lessons • Grammar Transition Lessons • Assessment				

Picture It! Comprehension Lesson

Fact and Opinion

Use this lesson to supplement or replace the skill lesson on pages 212–213 of the Teacher's Edition.

Teach

Distribute copies of the Picture It! blackline master on page 58.

- Have students read the labels on the illustration. Then read the paragraph aloud.
- Ask: *What words are clues that the author is expressing an opinion?* (I don't think, best, should)
- Share the Skill Points (at right) with students.
- Have students identify all of the statements of fact in the paragraph. Then have them find all of the statements of opinion.

Practice

Read aloud the directions on page 58. Have students complete the questions at the bottom of the page. Have them keep their work for later reteaching.

Answers for page 58: 1. fact; check dictionary **2.** fact; check encyclopedia or Internet **3.** opinion **4.** fact; check encyclopedia or Internet **5.** opinion

Skill Points

✓ A sentence that is a **fact** can be shown to be true or false. To check a fact, you can look in a book, check the Internet, or use your own knowledge and experience.

✓ A sentence that is an **opinion** cannot be shown to be true or false. It is a belief. Some clue words that show an opinion are *best, should, beautiful, in my opinion,* and *I believe.*

Name ______________________________

Fact and Opinion

Look at the picture. **Read** the paragraph.

- **Read** each sentence at the bottom of the page. **Put a check** to show whether it is a fact or an opinion.
- If the sentence is a fact, **write** how you could find out whether it is correct.

Lumberjacks

Lumberjacks are people who cut down trees. Once, they used saws and axes to cut down trees. The work was very hard. The job was so hard that I don't think anyone could have liked doing it. Today, lumberjacks use machines to cut down trees. Now, being a lumberjack is one of the best jobs in the world! In my opinion, anyone who enjoys hard work and being outdoors should try to find a job as a lumberjack.

1. Lumberjacks are people who cut down trees. Fact _____ Opinion _____

____

2. Once, they used saws and axes to cut down trees. Fact _____ Opinion _____

____

3. The work was very hard. Fact _____ Opinion _____

____

4. Today, lumberjacks use machines to cut down trees. Fact _____ Opinion _____

____

5. Now, being a lumberjack is one of the best jobs in the world! Fact _____ Opinion _____

____

Vocabulary Activities and Word Cards

Copy the Word Cards on page 60 as needed for the following activities.
Use the blank cards for additional words that you want to teach.
Also see suggestions for teaching vocabulary in the ELL and Transition Handbook.

Riddle Game	Definition Concentration	Find Your Partner
• Divide the class into pairs. Give each pair a set of Word Cards. • Have students place the set of Word Cards face down in a pile. • Ask one partner to choose a card and make up a riddle about the word. Provide examples, such as: *If you saw something that made you sad, you might feel this emotion;* or, *If something became very large, you might use this word to describe it.* Then have students tell their riddles to their partners. • Have the partner try to guess the word. Then have students switch roles. • Continue the activity until students have created riddles for every Word Card.	• Create one set of Word Cards and five blank cards for every pair of students. • Have pairs of students work together to write definitions for each word on the blank cards. Remind students that a definition tells what a word means. • Have students place the Word Cards and definition cards face down in rows on a table. • Instruct students to take turns turning over two cards and looking for a matched pair. A matched pair is a Word Card and its definition card. When a student finds a matched pair, the student keeps the cards. • To determine the winner, check which student has the most cards at the end of the game.	• Give one Word Card to each student, making sure that each student in the class has the same card as one other student. • Ask students to write a definition in their own words on the back of their Word Card. • Ask half the class to place their cards on their desks word side up and half the class to place their cards definition side up. • Have each student whose card has a definition facing up stand, one at a time, and read the definition to the class. • Have all students with word- side-up cards examine their cards to see if they match the definition. If a card matches, have that student stand up. Then have the two standing students exchange cards to see whether their cards match. • Continue the game until all students whose cards show definitions have read them to the class.

cord

dismay

grizzly

immense

payroll

Multilingual Summaries

English

Marven of the Great North Woods

When Marven is ten years old, many people are dying of influenza. His parents send him away so that he will be safe. He is sent to a logging camp. His job is to work as the camp's bookkeeper. Marven must also wake up the lumberjacks who sleep late. Marven works hard. He learns to wake the lumberjacks early in the morning. He creates a system to pay the lumberjacks. Soon, he does his job so well that he can finish work early.

One day Marven puts on his skis and goes into the woods. He hears noises, and sees something moving. He thinks that it is a grizzly bear. Marven is frightened. But it is not a bear. It is one of the lumberjacks! Marven goes back to camp with the lumberjack.

Spanish

Marven de los grandes bosques del Norte

Cuando Marven tiene diez años, mucha gente está muriendo de influenza. Sus padres lo mandan lejos para protegerlo. Marven es enviado a un campamento de tala de árboles. Su trabajo consiste en llevar la contabilidad del campamento. Marven también tiene que despertar a los leñadores que se quedan dormidos. Marven trabaja duro. Aprende a despertar a los leñadores muy temprano. Él crea un sistema de paga para los leñadores. Muy pronto, él hace el trabajo tan bien que puede terminar de trabajar temprano.

Un día, Marven se pone sus esquís y se va al bosque. Escucha ruidos y ve algo que se mueve. Piensa que es un oso pardo. Marven está asustado. Pero no es un oso. ¡Es uno de los leñadores! Marven regresa al campamento con el leñador.

Multilingual Summaries

Chinese

住在北方大森林的馬文

馬文10歲時，流感爆發死了許多人。父母親把馬文送到遠方，那裏比較安全。馬文到伐木場當了一名書記員。伐木工人要是睡過頭，就由馬文叫醒他。馬文工作很努力，清晨早起叫工人，還想出計算工資的好辦法。沒過多久，他的工作就做得又快又好。

有一次，馬文獨自劃著雪橇去森林，突然聽到些聲音，看見有什麼東西走過來。開始他還以為是大灰熊，心裏非常害怕。仔細一看原來是伐木工人，於是他們就一起回伐木場。

Vietnamese

Marven của Rừng Bắc Hùng Vĩ

Khi Marven mười tuổi, nhiều người bị chết vì bệnh cúm. Ba mẹ của cậu cho cậu đi nơi khác để cậu được an toàn. Cậu được gởi đến một trại đốn gỗ. Công việc của cậu là kế toán giữ sổ sách của trại. Marven cũng phải đánh thức những thợ đốn gỗ nào ngủ trễ. Marven cần cù làm việc. Cậu học được là phải đánh thức các thợ đốn gỗ lúc sáng sớm. Cậu lập ra một hệ thống để trả lương cho các thợ đốn gỗ. Không bao lâu, cậu làm việc giỏi đến mức cậu có thể làm xong công việc sớm.

Ngày kia Marven mang giày trượt tuyết vào và đi vào rừng. Cậu nghe có tiếng động, và thấy một vật gì di động. Cậu nghĩ đó là một con gấu nâu hung tợn. Marven hoảng sợ. Nhưng không phải con gấu. Đấy là một người trong số thợ đốn gỗ! Marven trở lại trại với người thợ đốn gỗ này.

Multilingual Summaries

Korean

북쪽 큰 숲의 마벤

마벤이 열 살이던 때 많은 사람들이 독감으로 죽어가고 있었다. 마벤의 부모님은 마벤의 안전을 위해 멀리 떠나 보낸다. 그는 벌채 막사로 보내지고 막사에서 경리와 늦잠 자는 벌목꾼들을 깨우는 일을 하게 된다. 마벤은 열심히 일을 하여 벌목꾼들을 아침 일찍 깨울 수 있는 방법을 익히고 벌목꾼들에게 돈을 지불하는 방식도 고안해낸다. 곧 그는 일을 아주 잘 해내 빨리 끝낼 수 있게 된다.

어느 날 마벤은 스키를 신고 숲 속으로 들어간다. 그는 이상한 소리를 듣고 무엇인가가 움직이는 것을 본다. 그는 그것이 회색곰이라고 생각하고 겁에 질린다. 하지만 그것은 곰이 아니라 벌목꾼들 중 한 명이었다. 마벤은 벌목꾼과 막사로 돌아간다.

Hmong

Marven Nyob Hav Ntoo Nuj Ntxees

Thaum Marven muaj kaum xyoo, ntau leej neeg tau tuag los ntawm tus mob ua npaws. Nws niam thiab nws txiv xa nws ncaim mus kom nws thiaj li tsis kis mob. Nws raug xa mus rau ib qhov chaws rau cov neeg txiav ntoo. Nws txoj hauj lwm yog saib xyuas qhov chaws txiav ntoo ntaub ntawv them nyiaj. Marven yuav tsum tsa cov neeg txiav ntoo ua pw lig. Marven rau rau siab ua nws txoj hauj lwm. Nws xyaum tsa cov neeg txiav ntoo thaum sawv ntxov. Nws tsim tau ib txoj kev los them nyiaj rau cov neeg txiav ntoo. Tsis ntev, nws ua tau nws txoj hauj lwm zoo heev ces nws thiaj ua hauj lwm tas txhua hnub ntxov heev li.

Muaj ib hnub Marven rau nws txhais khau daus (ski) thiaj mus rau tom hav ntoo. Nws hnov suab thiab pom dab tsi txav txav. Nws xav hais tias yog ib tug dais dub. Marven tau ntshai. Tab si tsis yog ib tug dais. Yog ib tug neeg txiav ntoo! Marven nrog tus neeg txiav ntoo rov los tom qhov chaws txiav ntoo.

So You Want to Be President? Student Edition pages 244–255

Week at a Glance	Customize instruction every day for your English Language Learners.				
	Day 1	**Day 2**	**Day 3**	**Day 4**	**Day 5**
Teacher's Edition	Use the ELL Notes that appear throughout each day of the lesson to support instruction and reading.				
ELL Poster 10	• Assess Prior Knowledge • Develop Concepts and Vocabulary	• Preteach Tested Vocabulary	• Review Main Idea and Supporting Details	• Letters to the President	• Monitor Progress
ELL Teaching Guide	• Picture It! Lesson, pp. 64–65 • Multilingual Summaries, pp. 68–70	• ELL Reader Lesson, pp. 230–231	• Vocabulary Activities and Word Cards, pp. 66–67 • Multilingual Summaries, pp. 68–70		
ELL Readers	• Reread *A Mill Girl's Day*	• Teach *The Fourth Grade Election*	• Reread *The Fourth Grade Election* and other texts to build fluency		
ELL and Transition Handbook	Use the following as needed to support this week's instruction and to conduct alternative assessments: • Phonics Transition Lessons • Grammar Transition Lessons • Assessment				

Picture It! Comprehension Lesson

Main Idea and Details

Use this lesson to supplement or replace the skill lesson on pages 240–241 of the Teacher's Edition.

Teach

Distribute copies of the Picture It! blackline master on page 65.

- Have students read the captions under the pictures. Then read the paragraph aloud.
- Ask: *What is the main idea of the paragraph?*
- Share the Skill Points (at right) with students.
- Have students find the supporting details for the main idea.

Practice

Read aloud the directions on page 65. Ask students to fill in the graphic organizer. Have them keep their organizers for later reteaching.

Answers for page 65: *Topic:* homes of Presidents; *Main Idea:* Most Presidents have their own houses, even though they live and work in the White House. *Supporting Details:* President Theodore Roosevelt had a house in New York State. President George H.W. Bush has a home on the coast of Maine. President Thomas Jefferson had a house in Virginia.

Skill Points

✓ The **topic** is what a paragraph is all about.

✓ The **main idea** is the most important thing an author has to say about the topic.

✓ **Supporting details** are pieces of information that tell more about the main idea.

Name ______________________

Main Idea and Details

Look at the picture. **Read** the paragraph.

- What is the topic of this paragraph? **Write** it on the line below.
- What is the main idea of this paragraph? **Write** it in the box below.
- What are the supporting details? **List** them in the boxes.

Presidents' Homes

All Presidents of the United States live and work in the White House. But most of them have had other homes too. President Theodore Roosevelt had a house in New York State. He went there to relax. President George H.W. Bush has a home on the coast of Maine. President Thomas Jefferson had a home in Virginia. He called it Monticello.

Topic: ______________________

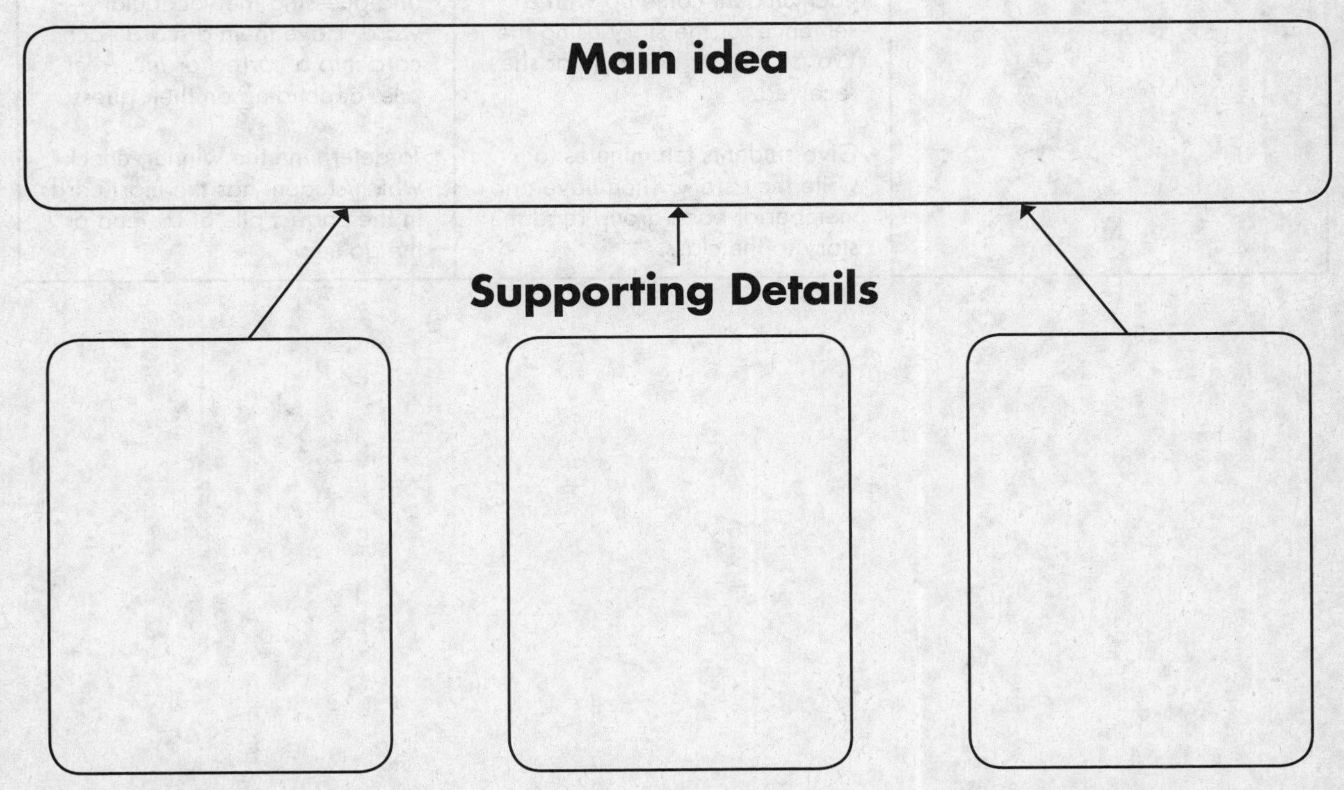

Vocabulary Activities and Word Cards

Copy the Word Cards on page 67 as needed for the following activities.
Use the blank card for an additional word that you want to teach.
Also see suggestions for teaching vocabulary in the ELL and Transition Handbook.

Secret Word Game	Write a Story	Context Game
• Divide the class into pairs. Give each pair a set of Word Cards. • Have each pair spread a set of Word Cards face up where both students can see them. • Have one student choose a word and give verbal and visual clues for it. Ask students to pause after each clue so that their partners can try to guess the word. • Have students take turns giving clues and guessing words.	• Divide the class into small story-writing groups, and give each group a set of Word Cards. • Within each group, distribute the Word Cards so that each student has at least one card. • Have students select one member of the group to record the story, another to make sure that each student contributes at least one sentence to the story, and a third to read the story to the class. • Have each group brainstorm ideas for the story. Tell them that the story can be silly or serious but must include all of the vocabulary words. Then have each student come up with a sentence for the story using the Word Card or Cards he or she received. • Give students ten minutes to write their story. Then have one member of each group read the story to the class.	• Give a set of Word Cards to each student. • Have each student write a context sentence for each word on the back of each card. Remind students that context sentences are sentences that show the meaning of the word. Instruct students not to include the vocabulary word in the context sentence but to leave a blank where the word belongs. • Have students form pairs and exchange their cards with the context sides up. • Have students take turns looking at their partner's context sentence and guessing the vocabulary word. Have them discard each card into a *correct* or *incorrect* pile, depending on their guess. • To determine the winner, check which student has the most cards in the *correct* pile at the end of the game.

Constitution	**howling**
humble	**politics**
responsibility	**solemnly**
vain	

Multilingual Summaries

English

So You Want to Be President?

The President of the United States can have fun. The White House has a swimming pool, a movie theater, and a bowling alley. Presidents can eat anything that they want to.

However, the President must dress up every day. The President must always be polite. The President has homework every day.

Presidents have been tall, short, thin, and fat. Some were outgoing. Some were shy. To be President, you must be at least 35 years old.

Some Presidents have had a father or cousin who also served as President. Presidents have had all kinds of pets.

Nine Presidents never went to college. Other Presidents have worked as engineers, farmers, lawyers, surveyors, shopkeepers, soldiers, or sailors before they were elected.

Being President is a big responsibility. The President must serve the country and the people.

Spanish

Entonces, ¿quieres ser presidente?

El presidente de Estados Unidos puede divertirse. La Casa Blanca tiene una piscina, un cine y una pista para jugar a los bolos. Los presidentes pueden comer lo que quieran.

Sin embargo, el presidente se tiene que vestir con ropa elegante todos los días. También, tiene que comportarse siempre con cortesía. El presidente tiene trabajo todos los días.

Los presidentes han sido altos, bajos, delgados y gordos. Algunos eran extrovertidos. Algunos eran tímidos. Para ser presidente tienes que tener por lo menos 35 años.

Algunos presidentes han tenido un padre o un primo que también fue presidente. Los presidentes han tenido todo tipo de mascotas.

Nueve presidentes nunca fueron a la universidad. Otros presidentes han trabajado como ingenieros, granjeros, abogados, topógrafos, comerciantes, soldados o marinos antes de haber sido elegidos.

Ser presidente es una gran responsabilidad. El presidente tiene que servir al país y a la gente.

Multilingual Summaries

Chinese

你想成為總統嗎？

做美國總統有許多樂趣。白宮裏有游泳池、電影院和保齡球道。總統想吃什麼，就能馬上吃到。

但是，總統必須天天穿得整整齊齊，要很有禮貌，每天還要做很多工作。

總統有高的矮的，有胖的瘦的；有些性格外向，而有些卻很內向。不過，所有總統都必須年滿35歲。

有些總統的父親或堂兄也當過總統。總統的寵物也各不相同。有位總統讓兒子在白宮的電梯裏養了匹小馬。

有九位總統從來沒上過大學。其他總統原先是工程師、農民、律師、測量師、商人、士兵或海員。

總統要擔負很大的責任，必須為國家與人民服務。

Vietnamese

Vậy Bạn Muốn Làm Tổng Thống Chăng?

Làm Tổng Thống của Hoa Kỳ có thể vui. Tòa Bạch Ốc có hồ bơi, rạp chiếu phim, và nhà chơi bóng gỗ lăn. Tổng Thống có thể được ăn bất cứ món gì họ muốn.

Tuy nhiên, Tổng Thống phải ăn mặc đẹp mỗi ngày. Tổng Thống lúc nào cũng phải lịch sự. Tổng Thống có bài tập làm ở nhà mỗi ngày.

Các Tổng Thống cao, thấp, gầy, và béo. Vài vị bặt thiệp. Vài vị rụt rè. Để làm Tổng Thống, bạn phải ít nhất là 35 tuổi.

Vài vị Tổng Thống đã có cha hoặc anh em họ cũng từng là Tổng Thống. Các vị Tổng Thống có đủ loại thú nuôi trong nhà. Có con trai của một vị Tổng Thống đã đem một con lừa vào trong thang máy của Tòa Bạch Ốc!

Có chín vị Tổng Thống không bao giờ học đại học. Các Tổng Thống khác đã từng làm kỹ sư, nhà nông, luật sư, thanh tra trắc đạc, chủ tiệm, binh sĩ, hoặc thủy thủ trước khi đắc cử.

Làm Tổng Thống là một trách nhiệm to lớn. Tổng Thống phải phục vụ tổ quốc và dân chúng.

Multilingual Summaries

Korean

대통령이 되고 싶다고?

미국 대통령이 되면 즐거운 일이 가득하다. 백악관에는 수영장과 영화관 그리고 볼링장도 있다. 대통령은 먹고 싶은 것은 무엇이든 먹을 수 있다.

하지만 대통령은 매일 정장을 갖춰 입어야 하고 항상 정중해야 하며 매일 숙제가 있다.

대통령들은 키가 크기도, 작기도, 마르기도, 뚱뚱하기도 하다. 어떤 대통령들은 외향적이었고 어떤 대통령들은 부끄럼을 타기도 했다. 대통령이 되려면 최소한 35살은 되어야 한다.

어떤 대통령들은 아버지나 사촌이 대통령직을 수행하기도 했다. 대통령들은 온갖 종류의 애완동물을 키우는데 어느 대통령의 아들은 백악관 엘리베이터 안에 조랑말을 데려다 놓기도 했다.

대통령들 중 열에 아홉은 전혀 대학을 다닌 적이 없다. 다른 대통령들은 대통령으로 뽑히기 전에 기술자나 농부, 변호사, 측량 기사, 소매 상인, 군인, 선원이었다.

대통령이 되는 일에는 큰 책임감이 따르며 대통령은 국가와 국민들을 위해 봉사해야 한다.

Hmong

Koj Xav Ua Thawj Tswj hwm lub Teb chaws Mis kas, Lov?

Tus thawj tswj hwm nyob rau mis kas muaj kev lom zem. Lub tsev dawb muaj ib lub pas dej, ib lub tsev saib yeeb yaj kiab, thiab ib qhov chaw kiv npas tshum cov koob ntoo (bowling). Tus thawj tswj hwm xav noj dab tsi los tau.

Tab sis, tus thawj tswj hwm yuav tsum hnav khaub ncaws zoo txhua hnub. Tus thawj tswj hwm yuav tsum paub cai txhua lub sij hawm. Tus thawj tswj hwm muaj hauj lwm ua txhua hnub.

Cov thawj tswj hwm dhau los, muaj cov siab, qis taub, yuag, thiab rog. Ib co kuj nquag thiab nyiam ua ntau yam. Ib co kuj txaj muag. Los ua tus thawj tswj hwm, koj yuav tsuam muaj hnub nyoog li 35 xyoos.

Ib cov thawj tswj hwm kuj muaj txiv los sis kwv tij tau ua tus thawj tswj hwm dhau los lawm. Cov Thawj tswj hwm nyiam yug ntau yam tsiaj. Ib tug thawj tswj hwm tus tub muab ib tug me nyuam nees rau hauv lub tsev dawb lub cav nqa tib neeg (elevator).

Cuaj tus thawj tswj hwm yeej tsis tau mus kawm ntawv qib siab ib zaug li! Lwm tus thawj tswj hwm twb ua hauj lwm ua cov kws txuj, cov qoob loo ua teb, cov kws li choj, cov kws soj ntsuam thaj av, cov neeg muag khoom tom taj laj, cov tub rog, los sis cov kws tsav nkoj dej ua ntej lawv raug tsa ua tus thawj tswj hwm.

Ua tus thawj tswj hwm yog ib txoj hauj lwm loj heev li. Tus thawj tswj hwm yuav tsum ua hauj lwm rau nws lub teb chaws thiab pej xeem sawv daws.

The Stranger Student Edition pages 272–285

Week at a Glance	Customize instruction every day for your English Language Learners.				
	Day 1	**Day 2**	**Day 3**	**Day 4**	**Day 5**
Teacher's Edition	Use the ELL Notes that appear throughout each day of the lesson to support instruction and reading.				
ELL Poster 11	• Assess Prior Knowledge • Develop Concepts and Vocabulary	• Preteach Tested Vocabulary	• Before and After	• Multiple Meaning Words	• Monitor Progress
ELL Teaching Guide	• Picture It! Lesson, pp. 71–72 • Multilingual Summaries, pp. 75–77	• ELL Reader Lesson, pp. 232–233	• Vocabulary Activities and Word Cards, pp. 73–74 • Multilingual Summaries, pp. 75–77		
ELL Readers	• Reread *The Fourth Grade Election*	• Teach *Leaves*	• Reread *Leaves* and other texts to build fluency		
ELL and Transition Handbook	Use the following as needed to support this week's instruction and to conduct alternative assessments: • Phonics Transition Lessons • Grammar Transition Lessons • Assessment				

Picture It! Comprehension Lesson

Cause and Effect

Use this lesson to supplement or replace the skill lesson on pages 268–269 of the Teacher's Edition.

Teach

Distribute copies of the Picture It! blackline master on page 72.

- Have students look at the illustration. Then read the paragraph aloud.
- Ask: *What causes leaves to be green in the summer?* (The leaves are using the Sun to make food.)
- Share the Skill Points (at right) with students.
- Have students find and underline the cause-and-effect clue words in the paragraph. Then have them find the causes of the different events.

Skill Points

✓ An **effect** is something that happens. A **cause** is why it happens.

✓ Sometimes clues words such as *because, so,* and *causes* show causes and effects. Sometimes you must find causes and effects without clue words.

Practice

Read aloud the directions on page 72. Have students underline the clue words. Then have them fill in the causes in the graphic organizer. Have students keep their organizers for later reteaching.

Answers for page 72: *Clue words:* because, so. *Box 1:* They are making food from the Sun. *Box 2:* They stop making food. *Box 3:* They become dry.

Name ______________________________

Cause and Effect

Look at the pictures below. **Read** the paragraph.

- **Underline** the cause-and-effect clue words in the paragraph.
- In the boxes below, **write** the causes of the effects shown.

Leaves Change Color

In the summer, when trees are growing, their leaves are green. They are green because they use the light from the Sun to make food. In the autumn, the leaves feel the cold air and stop making food. This makes them lose their green color, so they look red, yellow, brown, and orange. The leaves become dry, so they fall off the branches.

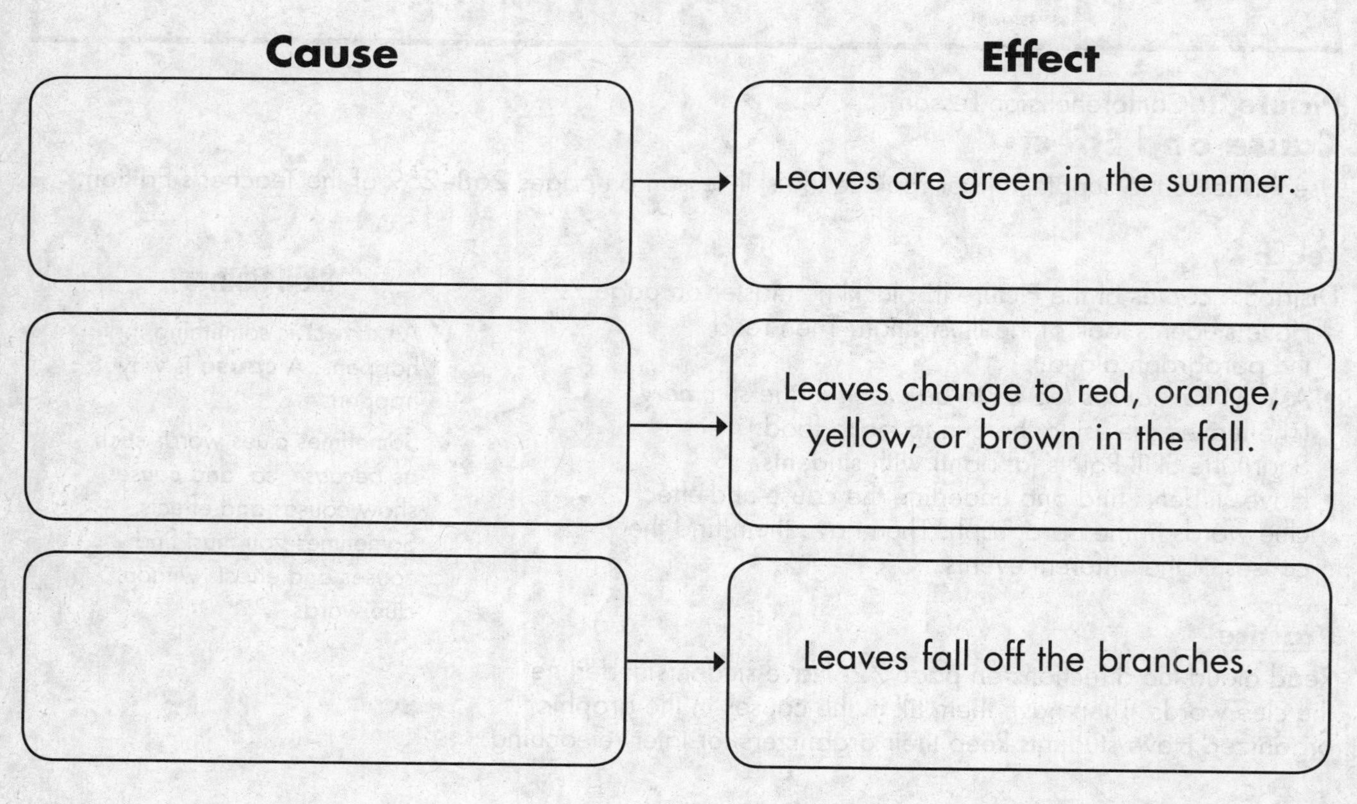

Vocabulary Activities and Word Cards

Copy the Word Cards on page 74 as needed for the following activities.
Use the blank card for an additional word that you want to teach.
Also see suggestions for teaching vocabulary in the ELL and Transition Handbook.

Riddle Game	Charades	Write a Story
• Divide the class into pairs. Give each pair a set of Word Cards. • Have students place the set of Word Cards face down in a pile. • Ask one partner to choose a card and make up a riddle about the word. Provide examples, such as: *This appears when it gets very cold;* or, *This is what you feel when you feel very, very scared.* Then have students tell their riddles to their partners. • Have the partner try to guess the word. Then have students switch roles. • Continue the activity until students have created riddles for every Word Card.	• Divide the class into small groups, and give each group one Word Card. • Have each group discuss how to silently act out the meaning of its vocabulary word. • Allow time for the groups to practice their charades before performing them for the class. • When they are ready, have groups take turns acting out their charades while their classmates try to guess the words.	• Divide the class into small story-writing groups, and give each group a set of Word Cards. • Within each group, distribute the cards so that each student has at least one. • Have students select one member of the group to record the story, another to make sure that each student contributes at least one sentence to the story, and a third to read the story to the class. • Have each group brainstorm ideas for the story. Tell the students that the story can be silly or serious but must include all of the vocabulary words. Then have each student come up with a sentence for the story using the Word Card or Cards he or she received. • Give students ten minutes to write their story. Then have one member of each group read the story to the class.

draft

etched

fascinated

frost

parlor

terror

timid

Multilingual Summaries

English

The Stranger

One day Farmer Bailey hit a man with his truck. He took the man home with him and called a doctor. The doctor said the man had lost his memory. The Baileys let the stranger stay with them.

The man helped Mr. Bailey on the farm. The man worked hard and never got tired. He seemed very happy with the Baileys.

Summer was ending, but the weather stayed warm. The leaves did not change colors, as they should have. When the stranger saw this, he knew something was wrong. He left. Then the leaves suddenly changed colors and the air turned cold. Autumn had come.

Now every year, the same thing happens. The weather stays warm for a week longer than anywhere else. Then the Baileys find a message written in the frost on a window.

Spanish

El extranjero

Un día el granjero Bailey atropelló a un hombre con su camión. Por eso lo llevó a su casa y llamó al doctor. El doctor le dijo que el hombre había perdido la memoria. Los Bailey permitieron que el hombre se quedara a vivir con ellos.

El hombre ayudaba al Sr. Bailey en la granja. Trabajaba duro y nunca se cansaba. Parecía muy feliz con los Bailey.

El verano se estaba terminando, pero todavía hacía calor. Las hojas no cambiaban de color como se suponía que lo hicieran. Cuando el extranjero vio esto, supo que algo estaba mal. Entonces se fue. Después, las hojas cambiaron repentinamente de color y el aire se tornó frío. El otoño había llegado.

Ahora, cada año, siempre pasa lo mismo. El clima se mantiene caluroso una semana más que en ningún otro lugar. Entonces, los Bailey encuentran un mensaje escrito en la escarcha de la ventana.

Multilingual Summaries

Chinese

陌生人

有一天，農場主人貝雷開卡車的時候不小心撞倒了一個人，他把那個人帶回家還請了醫生看他。醫生說那個人已經失去記憶，什麼都想不起來了。貝雷一家人好心收留了他。

那個人在農場裡幫貝雷先生做事，他工作很認真，好像一點也不會累。他看來很喜歡跟貝雷一家人住在一起。

夏天要結束了，可是天氣還是很溫暖，葉子也沒變色，以前在這個時候葉子都會變色。陌生人看見這些奇怪的現象後，他知道有些事情不對勁了，所以他離開了貝雷家。陌生人走了之後，葉子突然變色了，空氣也變得冷颼颼。秋天已經來了。

從此以後，每年都會發生同樣的事情，這裡的溫暖氣候會比其他地方多一個星期。後來貝雷一家人發現在窗子的結霜上寫著一個信息。

Vietnamese

Người Khách Lạ

Một ngày nọ Ông Nông Phu Bailey chạy xe tải đụng phải một người đàn ông. Ông đưa người đàn ông này về nhà mình và gọi bác sĩ. Bác sĩ nói là ông này đã bị mất trí nhớ. Gia đình Ông Bailey để người khách lạ này ở lại với họ.

Người khách lạ phụ giúp Ông Bailey làm việc ở trang trại. Ông ấy làm việc chuyên cần và không bao giờ thấy mệt. Ông ấy dường như rất vui vẻ với gia đình Ông Bailey.

Sắp hết mùa hè, nhưng thời tiết vẫn còn ấm. Lá cây không thay đổi màu sắc như mọi năm. Khi người khách lạ thấy vậy, ông ấy biết có điều gì đó không đúng. Ông ấy bỏ đi. Lúc ấy lá cây bỗng nhiên đổi màu và không khí trở nên lạnh hơn. Mùa thu đến.

Bây giờ cứ mỗi năm điều này lại xảy ra. Thời tiết vẫn ấm áp một tuần lâu hơn bất cứ nơi nào khác. Rồi đến khi gia đình ông Bailey tìm thấy lời nhắn viết trên lớp sương tuyết trên cửa sổ.

Multilingual Summaries

Korean

이방인

어느 날 베일리라는 농부가 트럭으로 사람을 치고는 그 사람을 집으로 데리고 간다. 집에 온 의사는 그 사람이 기억을 상실했다고 진단하고 베일리 가족은 그 이방인을 집에 머물게 한다.

그 사람은 베일리의 농사일을 도우며 열심히 일하고 피곤한 기색이 비치는 일이 결코 없다. 베일리 가족들과 함께 있는 그가 매우 행복해 보인다.

여름이 끝나고 있지만 날씨는 계속 따뜻하다. 단풍이 들 때가 되었는데도 잎사귀의 색깔은 변하지 않는다. 이방인은 이것을 보자 뭔가가 잘못 되었다고 생각하고 떠난다. 그러자 잎사귀의 색깔이 갑자기 바뀌고 공기가 차가워지면서 가을이 온다.

이제 매 년 똑같은 일이 일어난다. 일주일 이상 다른 지역보다 따듯한 날이 계속되면 베일리 가족은 창문 서리 위에 쓰여진 메시지를 발견한다.

Hmong

Tus Neeg Txawv

Muaj ib hnub Farmer Bailey ua nws lub tsheb raug ib tug txiv neej. Nws coj tus txiv neej nrog nws thiab mush u ib tug kws tshuaj. Tus kws tshuaj tau hais tias tus txiv neej xiam nws txoj kev ceem ceeb. Tsev neeg Baileys cia tus neeg txawv nrog lawv coj.

Tus neej tau pab Yawg Bailey ua teb. Tus txiv neej rau siab ua hauj lwm thiab yeej tsis nkees li. Nws zoo siab zoo nrog tsev neeg Baileys.

Lub caij so twb yuav xaus, tiam sis huab cua tseem so. Cov nplooj tsis pauv xim, raws li lawv ua pauv tas los. Thaum tus neeg txawv tau pom qhov no, nws paub hais tias tau muaj tej yam tsis yog lawm. Nws tau ncaim mus lawm. Ces cov nplooj ntoo txawm tau pauv xim thiab cov huab cua tau pib no. Lub caij nplooj ntoo tau los lawm.

Nim no txhua xyoo, qhov no pheej muaj. Cov huab cua pheej so ib lub lim tiam ntau ntxiv lwm tej chaw. Ces tsev neeg Baileys nrhiav tau ib zaj lus sau rau ntawm lub qhov rais.

Adelina's Whales

Student Edition pages 296–307

Week at a Glance	Customize instruction every day for your English Language Learners.				
	Day 1	**Day 2**	**Day 3**	**Day 4**	**Day 5**
Teacher's Edition	Use the ELL Notes that appear throughout each day of the lesson to support instruction and reading.				
ELL Poster 12	• Assess Prior Knowledge • Develop Concepts and Vocabulary	• Preteach Tested Vocabulary	• Animal Skits	• Categories of Animals	• Monitor Progress
ELL Teaching Guide	• Picture It! Lesson, pp. 78–79 • Multilingual Summaries, pp. 82–84	• ELL Reader Lesson, pp. 234–235	• Vocabulary Activities and Word Cards, pp. 80–81 • Multilingual Summaries, pp. 82–84		
ELL Readers	• Reread *Leaves*	• Teach *Friendly Giants*	• Reread *Friendly Giants* and other texts to build fluency		
ELL and Transition Handbook	Use the following as needed to support this week's instruction and to conduct alternative assessments: • Phonics Transition Lessons • Grammar Transition Lessons • Assessment				

Picture It! Comprehension Lesson

Fact and Opinion

Use this lesson to supplement or replace the skill lesson on pages 292–293 of the Teacher's Edition.

Teach

Distribute copies of the Picture It! blackline master on page 79.

- Have students describe what they see in the picture. Then read the paragraph aloud.
- Ask: *What clue words tell you an opinion is being stated?* (in my opinion, unfortunately, most, should)
- Share the Skill Points (at right) with students.
- Have students identify facts and opinions in the paragraph.

Practice

Read aloud the directions on page 79. Have students identify each statement as fact or opinion. Have them keep their work for later reteaching.

Answers for page 79: 1. O **2.** O **3.** F **4.** F **5.** O

Skill Points

✓ A **fact** can be correct or incorrect. You can check it by doing research.

✓ An **opinion** should be supported. A valid opinion is well supported. A faulty opinion is not.

✓ Some sentences have both facts and opinions in them.

Name ______________________________

Look at the pictures. **Read** the paragraph.

- **Read** the sentences below the paragraph. Which ones are facts? **Write** an *F* next to sentences that tell facts.
- Which sentences are opinions? **Write** an *O* next to sentences that tell opinions.

Two Kinds of Whales

To prevent whales from becoming extinct, the countries of the world signed an agreement. They agreed not to allow whales to be killed. In my opinion, this agreement was very good. It protected the most beautiful sea animal in the world. Unfortunately, some countries still kill whales. Iceland and Japan say that they allow whale hunting for scientific reasons. Norway allows whale hunting because it says the whales eat too many fish. These are terrible reasons for hunting whales. All whale hunting should be stopped.

1. Whales are the most beautiful sea animals in the world. ______

2. Whales should be protected. ______

3. Iceland, Japan, and Norway allow whale hunting. ______

4. The countries of the world signed an agreement making it illegal to kill whales. ______

5. Killing whales is wrong. ______

Vocabulary Activities and Word Cards

Copy the Word Cards on page 81 as needed for the following activities.
Use the blank cards for additional words that you want to teach.
Also see suggestions for teaching vocabulary in the ELL and Transition Handbook.

Secret Word Game	Skits	Poster Clues
• Divide the students into pairs, and give each pair a set of Word Cards. • Have each pair spread a set of Word Cards face up where both students can see them. • Have one student choose a word and give verbal and visual clues for it. Ask students to pause after each clue so that their partners can try to guess the word. • Have students take turns giving clues and guessing words.	• Have students form small groups, and give each group a set of Word Cards. • Ask each group to write a short skit that uses all the vocabulary words. Encourage students to be creative, making their skits interesting, exciting, funny, or silly. Allow them to improvise props and costumes from items in the classroom. • Invite each group to perform its skit for the class.	• Distribute sets of Word Cards to students. Then, from your own set of Word Cards, have one student pick a card without letting the others see it. • The student stands at the ELL Poster, points to the relevant area on it, and uses the information on the Poster to give hints about the vocabulary word. • Other students should try to guess which vocabulary word the student has. The first person to guess correctly may choose the next Word Card and make up clues about it. • Continue until all of the vocabulary words have been used.

biologist	**bluff**
lagoon	**massive**
rumbling	**tropical**

Multilingual Summaries

English

Adelina's Whales

Adelina lives on the shore of Laguna San Ignacio in Baja California, Mexico. Gray whales come to the lagoon in January to have their babies. They stay for three months. The whales are friendly there. They let people touch them.

Adelina's grandfather was the first person to tell about a visit from a whale. One day he was fishing with his partner. A whale came alongside their boat, and they were afraid. But the whale was friendly.

Adelina loves the time of year when the whales visit La Laguna. She likes to learn about the whales and watch them. Some day she may have a job working with or studying whales.

Spanish

Las ballenas de Adelina

Adelina vive a orillas de la Laguna de San Ignacio, en Baja California, México. Las ballenas grises llegan en enero para tener a sus bebés en la laguna y se quedan allí durante tres meses. Las ballenas son amistosas. Dejan que la gente las toque.

El abuelo de Adelina fue la primera persona que habló de la visita de una ballena. Un día, estaba pescando con un amigo. Una ballena se acercó al bote y ellos sintieron miedo. Pero la ballena se mostró amistosa.

Adelina adora la epoca del año en que las ballenas visitan La Laguna. Le gusta aprender de las ballenas y observarlas. Algún día, tal vez ella trabajará con las ballenas o estudiará algo relacionado con ellas.

Multilingual Summaries

Chinese

阿德莉娜的鯨魚

阿德莉娜住在墨西哥下加州省的拉古拿聖伊格納西奧湖旁邊。每年一月，灰鯨都會來這個礁湖生小鯨魚，並待上三個月。那地方的鯨魚非常友善，會讓人摸牠們的身體。

阿德莉娜的祖父是第一個把看見鯨魚的事講出來的人。有一天，正當祖父和他的夥伴一起捕魚的時候，有一隻鯨魚突然游到他們的小船旁邊，他們害怕極了，不過幸好那鯨魚表現得很友善。

一年裡面阿德莉娜最喜歡的時候，就是鯨魚來拉拉古拿的季節。她喜歡研究鯨魚，也喜歡盯著他們看。她以後很可能跟鯨魚一起工作，或者是變成專門研究鯨魚的專家。

Vietnamese

Những Con Cá Voi của Adelina

Adelina sống ở bờ biển Laguna San Ignacio ở Baja California, Mexico. Vào tháng Giêng, các cá voi sám đến vùng hồ nước biển này để đẻ con. Chúng ở đó ba tháng. Các con cá voi rất thân thiện. Chúng cho người ta sờ vào mình.

Ông nội của Adelina là người đầu tiên kể chuyện cá voi đến thăm. Một ngày kia ông đang đi đánh cá với người bạn của mình. Một con cá voi bơi dọc theo chiếc thuyền của họ, và họ lo sợ. Nhưng chú cá voi rất thân thiện.

Adelina thích khoản thời gian có các cá voi đến thăm vùng La Laguna. Cô bé thích học hỏi về cá voi và quan sát chúng. Một ngày nào đó cô bé có thể sẽ có công việc làm với cá voi hoặc nghiên cứu chúng.

Multilingual Summaries

Korean

아델리나의 고래

아델리나는 멕시코의 바자 켈리포니아에 있는 라구나 산 이그나시오 해변에 산다. 1월에 회색 고래가 새끼를 갖기 위해 환초로 둘러싸인 얕은 바다로 와서 3개월 동안 머문다. 회색 고래들은 우호적이어서 사람들이 만져도 가만히 있는다.

아델리나의 할아버지는 고래의 방문에 대해 얘기해 준 첫 번째 사람이다. 어느 날 할아버지가 동료와 낚시를 즐기고 있는데 고래 한 마리가 배 근처로 다가온다. 그들은 무서웠지만 고래는 친근하게 군다.

아델리나는 고래들이 라 라구나에 오는 시기를 좋아하며 고래에 대해 배우고 고래를 관찰하는 것을 좋아한다. 나중에 그녀는 고래와 일하는 직업을 갖거나 고래를 연구할 지도 모른다.

Hmong

Adelina tus Ntses Loj

Adelina nyob ze tus ciam dej Laguna San Ignacio hauv Baja California, Mexico. Cov ntses loj los hauv lub me nyuam pas dej los yug cov lawv me nyuam. Lawv nyob hauv lub pas dej peb lub lim tiam. Cov ntses loj yeej tsis qus. Lawv cia tib neeg los kov lawv.

Adelina yawm txiv yog thawj tus neeg ua tau qhia txog ib lub sij hawm thaum ib tug ntses loj los xyuas nws. Muaj ib hnub thaum nws mus nus ntses nrog nws ib tug phooj ywg. Ib tug ntses loj tau los ntawm lub nkoj ib sab, thiab nkawv ntshai heev. Tiam sis tus ntses loj no tsis qus.

Adelina nyiam heev thaum muaj ib lub sij hawm thaum cov ntses loj los xyuas La Laguna. Nws nyiam kawm txog cov ntses loj thiab saib lawv. Ib hnub tej zaum nws yuav tau ib txoj hauj lwm nrog cov ntses loj thiab kawm cov ntses loj.

How Night Came from the Sea

Student Edition pages 318–331

Week at a Glance	Customize instruction every day for your English Language Learners.				
	Day 1	**Day 2**	**Day 3**	**Day 4**	**Day 5**
Teacher's Edition	Use the ELL Notes that appear throughout each day of the lesson to support instruction and reading.				
ELL Poster 13	• Assess Prior Knowledge • Develop Concepts and Vocabulary	• Preteach Tested Vocabulary	• Charades	• Stories from Around the World	• Monitor Progress
ELL Teaching Guide	• Picture It! Lesson, pp. 85–86 • Multilingual Summaries, pp. 89–91	• ELL Reader Lesson, pp. 236–237	• Vocabulary Activities and Word Cards, pp. 87–88 • Multilingual Summaries, pp. 89–91		
ELL Readers	• Reread *Friendly Giants*	• Teach *Meet the Moon!*	• Reread *Meet the Moon!* and other texts to build fluency		
ELL and Transition Handbook	Use the following as needed to support this week's instruction and to conduct alternative assessments: • Phonics Transition Lessons • Grammar Transition Lessons • Assessment				

Picture It! Comprehension Lesson

Generalize

Use this lesson to supplement or replace the skill lesson on pages 314–315 of the Teacher's Edition.

Teach

Distribute copies of the Picture It! blackline master on page 86.

- Have students describe what they see in each frame of the comic strip. Then read the paragraph aloud.
- Ask: *What generalization can you make about which season most children like better?* (They like the summer better.)
- Share the Skill Points (at right) with students.
- Have students find the clue words. Then have them find the generalizations that match the clue words.

Practice

Read aloud the directions on page 86. Have students complete the graphic organizer. Have them keep their organizers for later reteaching.

Answers for page 86: *Clue Words:* generally, most; *Generalizations:* Children generally like the summer, because the weather is warm and the days are longer. Most children don't like the short days of the winter.

Skill Points

✓ A **generalization** is a sentence or rule that explains many examples.

✓ Clue words such as *all, most, always, usually,* and *generally* show that an author is making a generalization.

✓ Generalizations should be supported by facts or details.

Name ______________________________

Look at the pictures. **Read** the paragraph.

- What generalization clue words can you find? **Write** them in the chart below.
- What generalizations do the clue words show? **Write** them in the boxes next to their clue words.

Short and Long Days

Children generally like the summer, because the weather is warm and the days are longer. In many places in the United States, daylight lasts until after eight o'clock at night. In countries farther north, it stays light until eleven o'clock at night! In the winter, the days are much shorter. Most children don't like the short days of the winter. They don't like having to go to school in the dark.

Clue Word	Generalization

Vocabulary Activities and Word Cards

Copy the Word Cards on page 88 as needed for the following activities.
Use the blank cards for additional words that you want to teach.
Also see suggestions for teaching vocabulary in the ELL and Transition Handbook.

Home Language Clues	Synonym Search	Part-of-Speech Word Sort
• Pair students who have writing proficiency in the same home language, and give each student a set of Word Cards. • Have students work together to write translations of the vocabulary words in their home language on the back of each card. (See the Multilingual Lesson Vocabulary beginning on page 272 for suggested translations.) • Have partners lay out the cards with the home language sides facing up. • Invite students to generate synonyms for each word in their home language. Then ask them to name the English vocabulary word with the same meaning. They can flip the cards over to check their answers.	• Reproduce one set of Word Cards for each student. • Have each student place the cards face up on a desk or on a table. • Remind students what a synonym is. Then say synonyms or near synonyms for the words. Examples: *sparkling, singing group, person without bravery, shined, voyage, wavering.* • After each word, ask students to hold up the card for the vocabulary word that is closest in meaning.	• Divide the students into pairs. Give each pair of students a set of Word Cards and two sheets of paper. • Have each pair of students prepare a three-column chart with *Nouns, Verbs,* and *Adjectives* as the headings. • Have students sort the Word Cards, discussing where to put each word. • Then have each pair of students write sentences that use words from each column.

brilliant	chorus
coward	gleamed
journey	shimmering

Multilingual Summaries

English

How Night Came from the Sea

At the beginning of time, the only darkness was under the sea, in the kingdom ruled by Iemanjá (yay-mahn-JAH). Iemanjá's daughter married a man from the land. She loved the land. But the light was too bright for her. She wanted darkness to rest her eyes.

Her husband sent three men to Iemanjá to ask for some night. Iemanjá gave them a bag of night. She warned that only her daughter could open it. But when the men returned to land, one of them opened the bag. The night creatures escaped, and the moon and stars jumped out. Luckily Iemanjá's daughter was there. She calmed the creatures. Then she went to sleep. When she woke up, she gave three gifts: the morning star, the rooster to announce the morning, and the birds singing beautiful morning songs.

Spanish

Cómo la noche fue creada del mar

Al principio, la única oscuridad estaba debajo del mar, en el reino gobernado por Yemayá. La hija de Yemayá se casó con un hombre de la tierra. Amaba la tierra, pero la luz era demasiado brillante para ella. Quería también oscuridad para descansar sus ojos.

Su esposo mandó tres hombres a ver a Yemayá y a pedirle un poco de noche. Yemayá les dio un saco lleno de noche y les dijo que sólo su hija podía abrirlo. Sin embargo, cuando llegaron a la tierra, uno de los hombres abrió el saco. Las criaturas de la noche se escaparon y la luna y las estrellas saltaron fuera del saco. Afortunadamente, la hija de Yemayá estaba allí. Calmó a las criaturas y después se fue a dormir. Cuando se levantó, regaló tres cosas: la estrella de la mañana, el gallo para anunciar el amanecer y los pájaros cantando bellas canciones matutinas.

Multilingual Summaries

Chinese

夜晚的由來

在時間巨輪剛剛開始運轉的時候，這世界上唯一的黑暗就在海底下，那是一個由海洋女神所統治的王國。海洋女神的女兒嫁給一個陸地上的男人，她愛陸地上的一切，可是唯一不適應的地方是那裡的光線太亮了，她實在受不了，真希望有點黑暗讓眼睛好好休息一下。

她的丈夫派了三個人去海洋女神那兒要點黑暗，海洋女神給了他們一袋黑暗，不過卻警告他們，只有她女兒才能打開袋子。這三個男人回到陸地之後，其中有一個人實在忍不住好奇心，偷偷打開了袋子。一瞬間，有好多夜晚的動物從袋子裡逃了出來，月亮和星星也蹦蹦跳跳地跑了出來。還好有海洋女神的女兒在，她讓動物們安靜下來，然後她自己也趁著這難得的黑夜上床睡個好覺。隔天早上醒來，她給了大家三份禮物：晨星、宣佈早晨來臨的公雞，還有在早上唱出美妙樂曲的鳥兒。

Vietnamese

Vì Sao Đêm Tối Đến Từ Biển

Từ thuở xa xưa, bóng tối duy nhất là ở dưới biển, trong vương quốc do nữ vương Iemanjá (đọc là dê-man-giá) cai trị. Con gái của Iemanjá có chồng là người trên đất liền. Cô yêu đất liền. Nhưng ánh sáng quá chói chang cho cô. Cô muốn có được bóng tối để đôi mắt của cô được nghỉ.

Chồng của cô sai ba người đi đến Iemanjá xin một ít đêm tối. Iemanjá cho họ một túi đêm tối. Bà ấy dặn là chỉ có con gái của bà mới có thể mở túi này. Nhưng khi ba người trở về đất liền, một người trong bọn mở túi đó. Những con vật của đêm tối thoát ra, rồi trăng và sao nhảy ra. May là con gái của Iemanjá có mặt ở đó. Cô trấn an những con vật. Rồi cô đi ngủ. Khi cô thức dậy, cô tặng ba món quà: sao mai, gà trống để báo bình minh, và các con chim líu lo hót những bài ca bình minh tươi đẹp.

Multilingual Summaries

Korean

밤이 바다에서 온 방법

태초에 야만야가 통치하는 왕국의 바다 아래에는 오직 어둠만이 있었다. 야만야의 딸은 육지에서 온 남자와 결혼한다. 그녀는 육지를 좋아한다. 하지만 빛이 너무 밝아서 눈을 쉬게 해주는 어둠을 원했다.

그녀의 남편은 세 명의 남자를 야만야에게 보내 어두운 밤을 달라고 요청한다. 야만야는 그들에게 어두운 밤 한 자루를 주었는데 오직 자신의 딸만 자루를 열어볼 수 있다고 주의를 준다. 하지만 육지로 돌아올 때 그들 중 한 명이 자루를 열고 만다. 그러자 밤이 도망가고 달과 별이 자루에서 뛰어나온다. 다행히 야만야의 딸이 그곳에 있다. 그녀는 그 생물들을 진정시키고 나서 잠을 청한다. 그녀가 깨어났을 때 그녀는 자루에 담긴 생물 대신 세 가지 선물을 주는데 그것은 샛별, 아침을 알리는 수탉 그리고 아름다운 아침 노래를 부르는 새들이다.

Hmong

Ua Li Cas Yav Tsaus Ntuj Los Hauv Dej Hiav Txwv Los

Txij thaum ntuj tsim teb raug los, qhov uas tsuas tsaus ntuj yog hauv dej hiav txwv, hauv ib lub nceeg vaj uas raug kav los ntawm ib tug hu ua Iemanjá (yay-mahn-JAH). Iemanjá tus ntxhais tau yuav ib tug txiv neej nyob hauv qhuab nruab. Nws nyiam nyob saum qhuab nruab. Tiam sis lub hnub ci ci heev rau nws. Nws xav kom muaj yav tsaus ntuj kom nws qi tau muag.

Nws tus txiv txib peb tug txiv neej mus thov kom Iemanjá muab yav tsaus ntuj. Iemanjá tau muab ib lub hnab ntim yav tsaus ntuj rau hauv. Nws ceeb toom tias tsaus yog nws tus ntxhais thiaj li qhib tau lub hnab. Cov tsiaj txu tau dim, thiab lub hli thiab cov hnub qub tau khiav tawm hauv lub hnab. Muaj hmoo kawg Iemanjá tus ntxhais tau nyob ntawd thaum lub hnab tau qhib. Nws ua kom cov tsiaj txu nyob twj ywm. Ces nws mus pw tsaug zog. Thaum nws tau sawv, nws pub peb qho khoom plig: cov hnub qub thaum yav sawv ntxov, tus qaij kom nws qua yav sawv ntxov, thiab cov noog uas hu nkauj yav sawv ntxov.

Eye of the Storm

Student Edition pages 342–353

Week at a Glance	Customize instruction every day for your English Language Learners.				
	Day 1	**Day 2**	**Day 3**	**Day 4**	**Day 5**
Teacher's Edition	Use the ELL Notes that appear throughout each day of the lesson to support instruction and reading.				
ELL Poster 14	• Assess Prior Knowledge • Develop Concepts and Vocabulary	• Preteach Tested Vocabulary	• Weather Verbs	• Weatherman Skills	• Monitor Progress
ELL Teaching Guide	• Picture It! Lesson, pp. 92–93 • Multilingual Summaries, pp. 96–98	• ELL Reader Lesson, pp. 238–239	• Vocabulary Activities and Word Cards, pp. 94–95 • Multilingual Summaries, pp. 96–98		
ELL Readers	• Reread *Meet the Moon!*	• Teach *Watch Out for Hurricanes!*	• Reread *Watch Out for Hurricanes!* and other texts to build fluency		
ELL and Transition Handbook	Use the following as needed to support this week's instruction and to conduct alternative assessments: • Phonics Transition Lessons • Grammar Transition Lessons • Assessment				

Picture It! Comprehension Lesson

Graphic Sources

Use this lesson to supplement or replace the skill lesson on pages 338–339 of the Teacher's Edition.

Teach

Distribute copies of the Picture It! blackline master on page 93.

- Have students read the chart. Then read the paragraph aloud.
- Ask: *What does the chart show?* (how much snow fell during the largest blizzards of the past one hundred years)
- Share the Skill Points (at right) with students.
- Have students compare information in the chart with information in the paragraph.

Practice

Read aloud the directions on page 93. Have students answer the questions. Have them keep their work for later reteaching.

Answers for page 93: 1. 1993 **2.** 60 **3.** 37 inches

Skill Points

✓ A **graphic source** shows or explains information in the text. Charts, maps, pictures, time lines, and diagrams are all examples of graphic sources.

✓ As you read, use graphic sources to help you understand information. Compare information in the text with information in the graphic source.

Name ___________________________

Look at the chart. **Read** the paragraph.

- **Use** the chart and the paragraph to **answer** the questions below.

Big Blizzards of the Past

Blizzards are huge, powerful snowstorms. They usually cover a large area of land with many inches of snow. The largest blizzard was in 1993. Five feet of snow fell across some parts of the country, from Alabama to New York. When this much snow falls, many schools and businesses are closed.

Largest Blizzards in Past One Hundred Years

Place and Year	Snow (inches)
Kansas to Wisconsin (1940)	26
Kansas to Illinois (1967)	24
Pennsylvania to Wisconsin (1978)	36
Alabama to New York (1993)	60
New England and upper Midwest (2005)	37

1. Which year had the largest blizzard of the last one hundred years?

____

2. How many inches of snow fell during that blizzard?

____

3. How much snow fell in the blizzard of 2005?

____

Vocabulary Activities and Word Cards

Copy the Word Cards on page 95 as needed for the following activities.
Use the blank cards for additional words that you want to teach.
Also see suggestions for teaching vocabulary in the ELL and Transition Handbook.

Cloze Sentences	Definition Concentration	True or False?
• Give each student a set of Word Cards and two pieces of paper. • Have students write one sentence using each vocabulary word. • On a second sheet of paper, have students rewrite each sentence, replacing the vocabulary word with a line. • Divide the students into pairs. Have each pair exchange the papers with their cloze sentences and try to fill in the missing vocabulary words. Have partners check one another's work.	• Create one set of Word Cards and six blank cards for every pair of students. • Have pairs of students work together to write definitions for each word on the blank cards. Remind students that a definition tells what a word means. • Have students place the Word Cards and definition cards face down in rows on a table. • Instruct students to take turns turning over two cards and looking for a matched pair. A matched pair is a Word Card and its definition card. When a student finds a matched pair, the student keeps the cards. • To determine the winner, check which student has the most cards at the end of the game.	• Make one set of Word Cards. • Ask one student to select a card. • Make up a sentence using the vocabulary word, and ask the student if the sentence is true or false. For example: *Forecasts tell what happened in the past.* (false) • Ask the rest of the group whether they agree with the student's answer. • Repeat the exercise until all students have had a chance to choose a card.

destruction	**expected**
forecasts	**inland**
shatter	**surge**

Multilingual Summaries

English

Eye of the Storm

Warren Faidley is a storm chaser. He travels around the United States to photograph tornadoes, thunderstorms, and hurricanes. Warren pays close attention to weather forecasts. When the forecast says a hurricane is coming, Warren flies to the place where it will be. He went to Florida in 1992 to see Hurricane Andrew.

Warren and two other storm chasers stayed in a parking garage. They listened to weather reports. The storm came at 2:30 in the morning. The wind was loud and strong. Around 5:15, the storm reached its peak and the parking garage started to shake. They heard car alarms and windows breaking.

Around 6:00, it began to get light outside. Warren carefully went out. Broken boats were on the beach and in the streets. Trees were bent by the wind. Buildings were damaged. Warren took lots of pictures.

Spanish

El ojo de la tormenta

Warren Faidley es un cazador de tormentas. Viaja por todo el territorio de Estados Unidos para sacar fotografías de tornados, tormentas y huracanes. Warren siempre está muy atento a lo que dicen los pronósticos del tiempo. Cuando un pronóstico dice que se acerca un huracán, Warren vuela al sitio donde la tormenta llegará. Él fue a la Florida en 1992 para ver el huracán Andrew.

Warren y otros dos cazadores de tormentas estaban en un estacionamiento. Escuchaban los reportes del tiempo. La tormenta llegó a las 2:30 de la madrugada. El viento era fuerte y hacía mucho ruido. Alrededor de las 5:15, la tormenta alcanzó su máximo y el estacionamiento comenzó a temblar. Escucharon el sonido de muchas alarmas de autos y de vidrios de las ventanas rompiéndose.

Alrededor de las 6:00, comenzó a amanecer. Con mucho cuidado, Warren salió del lugar donde se encontraba. Había botes destrozados tanto en la playa como en las calles. Los árboles se habían doblado por la fuerza del viento. Muchos edificios estaban destruidos. Warren tomó muchísimas fotos.

Multilingual Summaries

Chinese

風暴的眼睛

華倫・費德萊是一名風暴追逐者，他跑遍整個美國，為的是要拍下龍捲風、大雷雨和颶風的照片。華倫非常注意天氣預報，只要預報說有颶風要來，華倫一定馬上搭飛機飛到將會出現颶風的地方。1992 年的時候他曾經到佛羅里達州親身經歷安德魯颶風的威力。

華倫和其他兩名風暴追逐者待在車庫裡，他們留心聽著天氣預報，預報說風暴會在凌晨兩點三十分的時候來。外面的風好強，風呼呼吹的聲音好大。大概在五點十五分的時候，風暴開始發揮它最強的威力，連車庫都開始震動，還可以聽到汽車警報和窗子破裂的聲音。

大約六點時，外面風雨開始變小，天也漸漸亮了。華倫小心翼翼地走出去一探究竟。被風吹壞的小船散佈在海灘和街道上，樹被吹歪，大樓也被風吹起來的東西砸得亂七八糟。華倫等的就是這個，他興奮地拍了好多照片。

Vietnamese

Mắt Bão

Warren Faidley là một người săn đuổi bão. Ông ấy du lịch vòng quanh Hoa Kỳ để chụp ảnh những cơn lốc xoáy, mưa bão sấm sét, và bão lớn. Warren rất chú ý đến các dự báo thời tiết. Khi dự báo nói rằng có cơn bão lớn sắp đến. Warren bay đến nơi sẽ có bão. Ông đã đi đến Florida vào năm 1992 để xem cơn Bão Andrew.

Warren và hai người săn đuổi bão khác ở trong một khu nhà đậu xe. Họ nghe báo cáo thời tiết. Cơn bão đến vào lúc 2:30 giờ sáng. Gió ầm ĩ và mạnh. Vào khoảng 5:15 giờ, cơn bão lên đến mức mạnh nhất và khu nhà đậu xe bắt đầu rung chuyển. Họ nghe những máy báo động chống trộm trong các chiếc xe kêu vang và cửa sổ xe rạn vỡ.

Vào khoảng 6:00 giờ, bên ngoài trời bắt đầu sáng lại. Warren thận trọng bước ra ngoài. Tàu thuyền gẫy vỡ nằm trên bãi biển và trên đường. Cây cối bị gió uốn cong. Nhà cửa bị hư hại. Warren chụp được nhiều ảnh.

Multilingual Summaries

Korean

폭풍의 눈

워렌 페이들리는 폭풍을 추적하는 사람으로 미국 전역을 여행하며 토네이도, 뇌우, 허리케인 등을 사진에 담는다. 워렌은 일기예보에 특히 귀를 기울이는데 허리케인이 예보되면 비행기를 타고 예보된 장소로 날아간다. 그는 1992년 허리케인 앤드류를 보기 위해 플로리다로 갔다.

워렌과 두 명의 다른 폭풍 추적자들이 차고에서 일기예보를 듣고 있었다. 폭풍은 새벽 2시 30분에 닥쳤다. 바람은 요란했다. 5시15분쯤 폭풍은 최고조에 달했고 차고가 흔들거리기 시작했다. 그들은 차의 경보음과 창문이 깨지는 소리를 들었다.

6시경에는 밖이 환해지기 시작했다. 워렌은 조심스럽게 밖으로 나갔다. 부서진 배들이 해변과 길가에 즐비했고 나무들은 바람에 휘어졌으며 건물들도 손상을 입었다. 워렌은 많은 사진을 찍었다.

Hmong

Hauv Nruab Nrab Ntawm Kob Nag Loj

Warren Faidley yog ib tug uas caum nag xob nag cua. Nws mus ncig lub United States mus thaij duab txog tej cua kauj zig, tej nag xob nag cua, thiab tej cua daj cua dub. Warrens saib ntsoov tej huab cua. Thaum lawv qhuaj hais tias yuav muaj ib kob cua daj cua dub, Warren ya dav hlau mus rau qhov chaw ntawd. Nws tau mus hauv Florida thaum lub 1992 mus saib Kob Cua Daj Cua Dub Andrew.

Warren thiab ob tug uas caum nag xob nag cua tau nyob hauv ib qhov chaw nres tshej. Lawv mloog xov xwm huab cua. Tau muaj kob nag xob thaum 2:30 yas sawv ntxov. Cov cua nrov thiab muaj zog heev. Thaum li 5:15, kob nag xob tau muaj zog heev thiab qhov chaw nres tshej tau pib co. Lawv hnov tej tshej pib quaj thiab tej tshej tej qhov rais pib txawg.

Thaum li 6:00, nws pib kab nraum zoov. Warren maj mam mus nraum zoov. Tej nkoj tau piam tau nyob ntawm ntug dej hiav txwv thiab ntawv tej kev. Cov cua tau ua tej ntoo lov. Tej tsev tau piam. Warren tau thaij ntau daim duab.

The Great Kapok Tree Student Edition pages 364–377

Week at a Glance	Customize instruction every day for your English Language Learners.				
	Day 1	**Day 2**	**Day 3**	**Day 4**	**Day 5**
Teacher's Edition	Use the ELL Notes that appear throughout each day of the lesson to support instruction and reading.				
ELL Poster 15	• Assess Prior Knowledge • Develop Concepts and Vocabulary	• Preteach Tested Vocabulary	• Suffixes and Related Words	• Look Outside	• Monitor Progress
ELL Teaching Guide	• Picture It! Lesson, pp. 99–100 • Multilingual Summaries, pp. 103–105	• ELL Reader Lesson, pp. 240–241	• Vocabulary Activities and Word Cards, pp. 101–102 • Multilingual Summaries, pp. 103–105		
ELL Readers	• Reread *Watch Out for Hurricanes*	• Teach *No Swimming Today!*	• Reread *No Swimming Today!* and other texts to build fluency		
ELL and Transition Handbook	Use the following as needed to support this week's instruction and to conduct alternative assessments: • Phonics Transition Lessons • Grammar Transition Lessons • Assessment				

Picture It! Comprehension Lesson

Generalize

Use this lesson to supplement or replace the skill lesson on pages 360–361 of the Teacher's Edition.

Teach

Distribute copies of the Picture It! blackline master on page 100.

- Have students look at the picture and name the different items they recognize. Then read the paragraph aloud.
- Ask: *What did Jason think about the animals in the rain forest?* (He thought that they seemed friendly.)
- Share the Skill Points (at right) with students.
- Have students find the generalization and support in the story.

Practice

Read aloud the directions on page 100. Have students complete the graphic organizer. Have them keep their organizers for later reteaching.

Answers for page 100: *Generalization:* Animals in the rain forest are friendly. *Support:* The frog was friendly. The birds were friendly. The fish were friendly.

Skill Points

✓ A **generalization** is a sentence or rule that explains many examples.

✓ A good generalization is supported by many examples.

Name ___________________________________

Look at the picture. **Read** the story.

- What generalization does Jason make about the animals he meets in the rain forest? **Write** the sentence in the large center oval below.
- What makes Jason reach this generalization? **Write** the sentences in the smaller ovals.

Friendly Animals in the Rain Forest

Jason saw many animals in the rain forest. First, he saw a frog. "Hello, little boy," said the frog. "I am happy that you have come to the rain forest." Next, Jason saw some birds. "Hello, young man," they said. "Welcome to our home!" Jason kept walking. He came to a river. "Hey, there," said the fish. "Glad you're here!" Jason was very happy. Everyone seemed friendly in this new place.

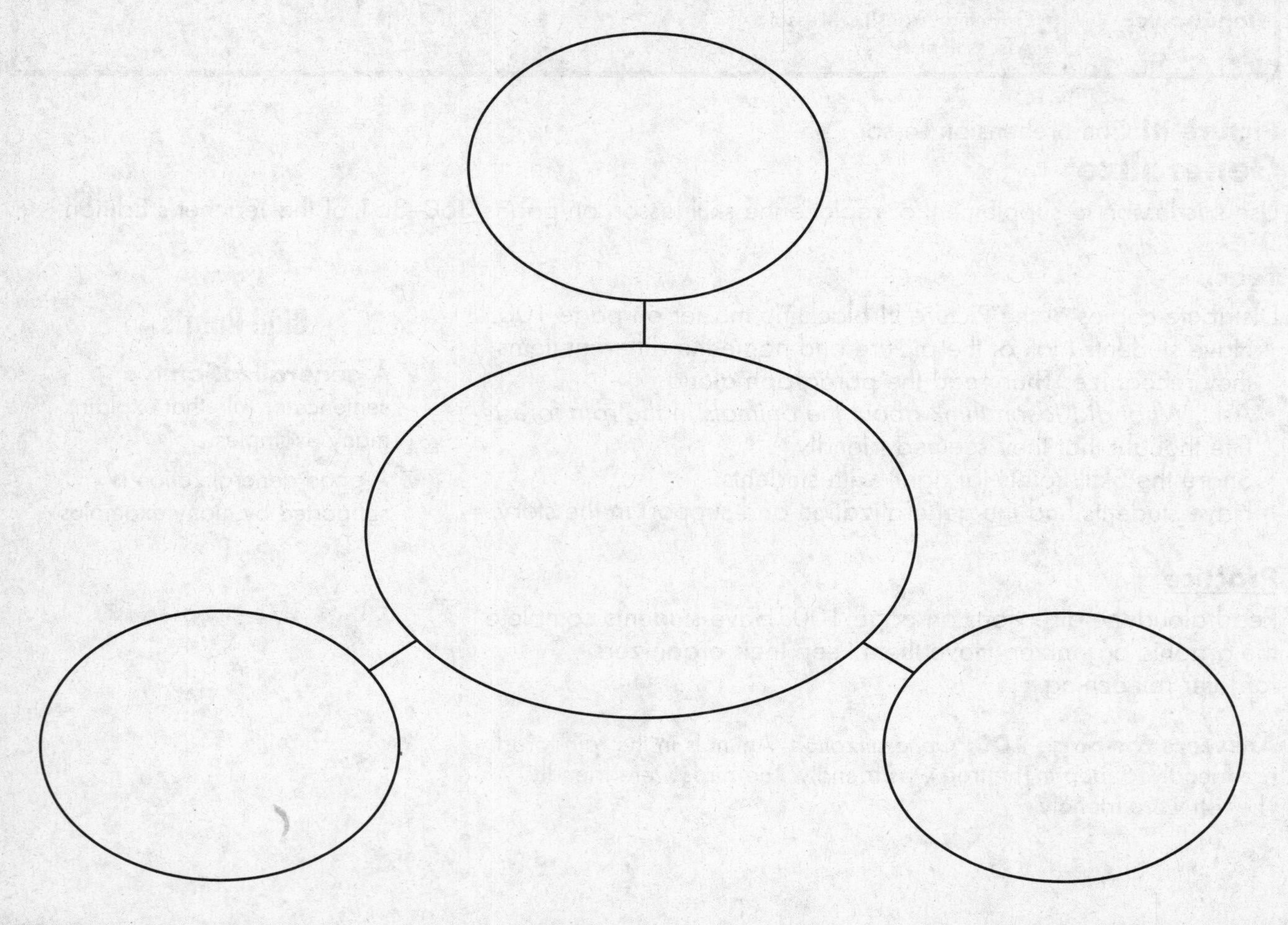

Vocabulary Activities and Word Cards

Copy the Word Cards on page 102 as needed for the following activities.
Use the blank cards for additional words that you want to teach.
Also see suggestions for teaching vocabulary in the ELL and Transition Handbook.

Riddle Game	Tell a Story	Find Your Partner
• Divide the students into pairs, and give each pair a set of Word Cards. • Have students place the set of Word Cards face down in a pile. • Ask one partner to choose a card and make up a riddle about the word. Provide examples, such as: *This describes some flowers;* or, *When bees do this, they make honey.* Then have students tell their riddles to their partners. • Have the partner try to guess the word. Then have students switch roles. • Continue the activity until students have created riddles for every Word Card.	• Distribute one set of Word Cards to each student. • Gather the students in a circle and explain that the group will be telling a story together. • Begin the story with a sentence that uses one of the vocabulary words. • Have the student to your right continue the story, adding a sentence that uses any of the other vocabulary words. • Have each student continue the story, adding a sentence that uses a vocabulary word. • Let students help one another think of sentences that continue the story. • Encourage students to be creative and to try to make the story exciting or funny.	• Give one Word Card to each student, making sure that each student in the class has the same card as one other student. • Ask students to write definitions in their own words on the backs of their Word Cards. • Ask half of the students to place their cards on their desks word side up and half of the students to place their cards definition side up. • Have each student whose card has a definition facing up stand, one at a time, and read the definition to the class. • Have all students with word-side up cards examine their cards to see if they match the definition. If a card matches, have that student stand up. Then have the two standing students exchange cards to see whether their cards match. • Continue the game until all students whose cards show definitions have read them to the class.

canopy	**dangle**
dappled	**fragrant**
pollen	**pollinate**
slithered	**wondrous**

Multilingual Summaries

English

The Great Kapok Tree

Two men walked into the Amazon rain forest. One pointed to a big Kapok tree and went away. The other began to chop down the tree. The man grew tired. He fell asleep under the tree.

While he slept, animals came to him. They told him they needed the tree for their homes. They told him the tree was important to the forest and the world. A child who lived in the forest asked the man to look at the rain forest in a new way.

When the man woke up, the animals and the child were around him. Everything looked beautiful to him. The man stood up to chop again. Then he stopped and looked at the animals. He dropped the ax and walked out of the rain forest.

Spanish

El enorme árbol Capoc

Dos hombres llegaron a la selva del Amazonas. Uno de ellos señaló un enorme árbol Capoc y se fue. El otro comenzó a cortar el árbol. El hombre se sintió cansado y se acostó a dormir debajo del árbol.

Mientras estaba dormido, los animales se acercaron a él. Le dijeron que necesitaban el árbol para tener allí su hogar. Le dijeron que el árbol era importante para la selva y para el mundo. Un niño que vivía en la selva le pidió al hombre que mirara la selva de una manera nueva.

Cuando el hombre se despertó, los animales y el niño estaban alrededor de él. Todo le parecía hermoso. El hombre se levantó y comenzó a cortar el árbol otra vez. Después se detuvo y miró a los animales. Tiró el hacha y se marchó de la selva.

Multilingual Summaries

Chinese

巨大的木棉樹

有兩個人走進亞馬遜雨林，其中一個人對著一棵大木棉樹指了一下，然後就離開了，另外一個人留下來開始砍樹，砍著砍著他漸漸覺得有點累，於是就靠在樹下睡著了。

在他睡著的時候，動物們走過來求他不要砍樹，因為他們需要樹，沒有樹他們就沒有家。動物們還告訴他，樹對森林和整個世界都很重要。一個住在森林裡的小孩也請求他用一種新的方式來看待雨林。

那個人醒過來後，看見動物和小孩都圍在他身邊。森林裡的一景一物看起來都好漂亮呀！那個人站起來，又開始砍樹了，但是沒砍幾下，他就停下來看看動物們，不一會兒，他就扔開斧頭，走出了雨林。

Vietnamese

Cây Bông Gạo (Kapok) To Lớn

Hai người đàn ông đi vào trong khu rừng rậm Amazon. Một người chỉ cây bông gạo rồi bỏ đi. Người kia thì bắt đầu đốn cây ấy. Ông này mệt và ngủ thiếp dưới bóng cây.

Khi ông ngủ, các con thú đến. Chúng nói với ông là chúng cần cây này vì cây là nhà của chúng. Chúng bảo rằng cây quan trọng cho khu rừng và cho thế giới. Một đứa bé sống ở trong rừng kêu ông này hãy nhìn khu rừng rậm này với một lối suy nghĩ mới.

Khi ông này thức dậy, các con thú và đứa bé đang bao quanh ông. Mọi thứ đối với ông đều đẹp. Ông đứng lên tiếp tục đốn cây nữa. Rồi ông ngừng tay và nhìn các con thú. Ông bỏ cây rìu xuống và ra khỏi khu rừng.

Multilingual Summaries

Korean

커다란 판야 나무

두 사람이 아마존의 열대 우림으로 걸어 들어간다. 한 사람이 커다란 판야 나무를 가리킨 다음 가버리자 다른 사람이 그 나무를 자르기 시작한다. 그 사람은 일하다 지쳐 나무 아래에서 잠이 든다.

그가 잠을 자는 동안 동물들이 온다. 동물들은 그에게 자기들의 집으로 쓰이는 그 나무가 필요하다고 말한다. 그리고 그 나무는 숲과 세상을 위해 중요한 나무라고 말해준다. 숲에 사는 한 아이는 그 남자에게 새 방식으로 열대 우림을 봐 달라고 부탁한다.

남자가 잠에서 깨어났을 때 동물들과 그 아이가 그의 곁에 있다. 이제 그는 모든 것이 아름다워 보인다. 남자는 일어나서 다시 나무를 베기 시작하다가 멈추고 동물들을 바라본다. 그는 도끼를 내려 놓고 열대 우림 밖으로 걸어나간다.

Hmong

Tsob Ntoo Kapok uas Loj

Ob tug txiv neej tau mus hauv lub hav zoov nuj txeeg Amazon. Ib tug tau taw tes mus rau tsob ntoo Kapok uas loj heev thiab tau ncaim mus. Ho ib tug tau pib ntov tsob ntoo. Tus txiv neej ntawd tau nkee. Nws tau pw tsaug zog ntawm tsob ntoo.

Thaum nws tab tom pw, cov tsiaj txu tau los ntawm nws. Lawv los hais tias lawv yuav tsum tau tsob ntoo ua lawv lub tsev. Lawv hais tias tsob ntoo ntawd tseem ceeb rau lub hav zoov nuj txeeg thiab rau lub ntiaj teb. Ib tug me nyuam uas tau nyob hauv lub hav zoov tau thov kom tus neej ntsia lub hav zoov nuj txeeg txawv zog.

Thaum tus txiv neej sawv los, cov tsiaj txum thiab tus me nyuam tau nyob ib ncig nws. Txhua yam zoo nkauj rau nws heev. Tus txiv neej sawv rov los ntov tsob ntoo ntxiv. Ces nws tsum thiab ntsia cov tsiaj txu. Nws tso nws rab taus thiab tawv ntawm lub hav zoov nuj txeeg.

The Houdini Box

Student Edition pages 396–409

Week at a Glance	Customize instruction every day for your English Language Learners.				
	Day 1	**Day 2**	**Day 3**	**Day 4**	**Day 5**
Teacher's Edition	Use the ELL Notes that appear throughout each day of the lesson to support instruction and reading.				
ELL Poster 16	• Assess Prior Knowledge • Develop Concepts and Vocabulary	• Preteach Tested Vocabulary	• Tricks We Know	• Tricks on Us	• Monitor Progress
ELL Teaching Guide	• Picture It! Lesson, pp. 106–107 • Multilingual Summaries, pp. 110–112	• ELL Reader Lesson, pp. 242–243	• Vocabulary Activities and Word Cards, pp. 108–109 • Multilingual Summaries, pp. 110–112		
ELL Readers	• Reread *Happy Day*	• Teach *Two Master Magicians*	• Reread *Two Master Magicians* and other texts to build fluency		
ELL and Transition Handbook	Use the following as needed to support this week's instruction and to conduct alternative assessments: • Phonics Transition Lessons • Grammar Transition Lessons • Assessment				

Picture It! Comprehension Lesson

Compare and Contrast

Use this lesson to supplement or replace the skill lesson on pages 392–393 of the Teacher's Edition.

Teach

Distribute copies of the Picture It! blackline master on page 107.

- Have students look at the picture. Then read the paragraph aloud.
- Ask: *How was Harry Houdini different from other magicians?* (He performed real acts of escape.)
- Share the Skill Points (at right) with students.
- Have students describe how Houdini and David Copperfield were different and the same.

Skill Points

✓ When you **compare and contrast,** you tell how two or more things are the same and different.

✓ A chart or circle (Venn) diagram can help you compare and contrast.

Practice

Read aloud the directions on page 107. Have students fill in the Venn diagram. Have them keep their organizers for later reteaching.

Answers for page 107: *Both*: most famous magicians of their times, became interested in magic very young; *Houdini*: born in Hungary, escape artist, starred in movies, died in 1926; *Copperfield*: born in United States, illusionist, starred in TV shows, still alive

Name ______________________________

Compare and Contrast

Look at the picture. **Read** the paragraph.

- How are Harry Houdini and David Copperfield similar? **Write** your ideas in the middle section of the Venn diagram.
- How are they different? **Describe** Houdini in the left-hand side of the diagram. **Describe** Copperfield in the right-hand side of the diagram.

Famous Magicians of the Past and Present

Harry Houdini was born in Hungary in 1874. He came to the United States when he was four years old. When he was fifteen, he decided to be an escape artist. He became the most famous magician of his time. He starred in many movies. He died in 1926.

David Copperfield was born in New Jersey in 1956. He is an illusionist: he knows how to make things seem to disappear. He has starred in many television shows and is the most famous magician of his time. Like Houdini, he became interested in magic as a young boy.

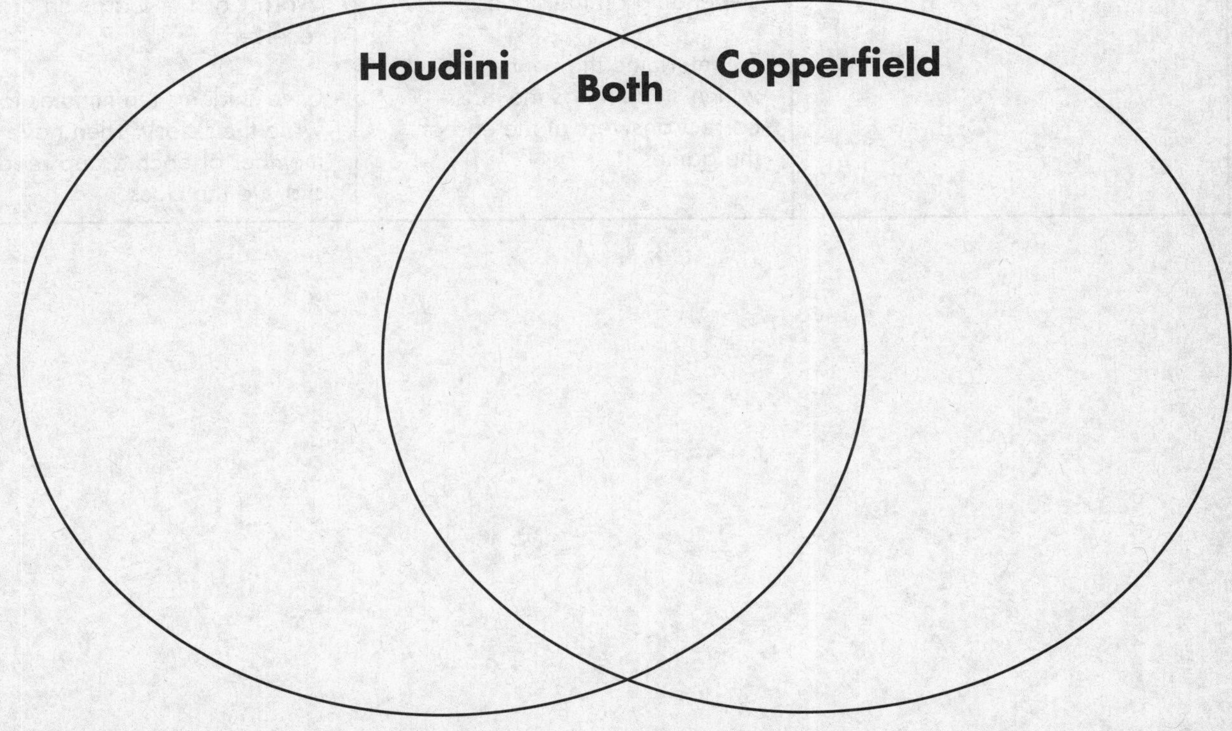

Vocabulary Activities and Word Cards

Copy the Word Cards on page 109 as needed for the following activities.
Use the blank card for an additional word that you want to teach.
Also see suggestions for teaching vocabulary in the ELL and Transition Handbook.

Charades	Synonym Game	Write a Story
• Divide the class into small groups, and give each group one Word Card. • Have each group discuss how to silently act out the meaning of its vocabulary word. • Allow time for the groups to practice their charades before performing them for the class. • When they are ready, have groups take turns acting out their charades while their classmates try to guess the word.	• Give each student a set of Word Cards. • Have each student write a synonym for each word on the back of the Word Cards. Remind students that synonyms are words with the same or similar meanings. If students are unable to think of a synonym for a vocabulary word, have them write a definition instead. • Ask students to form pairs and exchange their Word Cards with the synonym sides facing up. • Have students take turns looking at their partner's synonym and guessing the vocabulary word. Have them place each card in a correct or incorrect pile, depending on their guess. • To determine the winner, check which student has the most correct answers at the end of the game.	• Divide the class into small story-writing groups, and give each group a set of Word Cards. • Within each group, distribute the Word Cards so that each student has at least one card. • Have students select one member of the group to record the story, another to make sure that each student contributes at least one sentence to the story, and a third to read the story to the class. • Have each group brainstorm ideas for the story. Tell the students that the story can be silly or serious but must include all of the vocabulary words. Then have each student come up with a sentence for the story using the Word Card or Cards he or she received. • Give students ten minutes to write their story. Then have one member of each group read the story to the class.

appeared	**bustling**
crumbled	**escape**
magician	**monument**
vanished	

Multilingual Summaries

English

The Houdini Box

Victor wanted to be a magician like Houdini. He tried to perform Houdini's tricks, but he could not.

Victor saw Houdini one day. He asked him the secret of his tricks. Houdini said he would write Victor a letter. In the letter Houdini invited Victor to his house. Victor went that night. Houdini's wife told Victor that Houdini had died that day. She gave Victor a box with the initials E. W. on it. Victor thought it was not Houdini's, so he put it in his closet and forgot it.

Victor grew up. One night his son hit a baseball into a graveyard. It landed on Houdini's grave. Victor read Houdini's real name, Ehrich Weiss, on the gravestone. He realized that E. W. was Houdini! That night, he found the box in the attic and learned Houdini's secrets.

Spanish

La caja de Houdini

Víctor quería ser un mago como Houdini. Trató de hacer algunas de las magias que hacía Houdini, pero no lo logró.

Un día, Víctor vio a Houdini. Le preguntó el secreto de sus magias. Houdini dijo que le iba a escribir una carta a Víctor. En la carta, Houdini invitaba a Víctor a su casa. Víctor fue esa noche a la cita. La esposa de Houdini le dijo a Víctor que ese día Houdini había fallecido. También le dio a Víctor una caja que tenía inscritas las iniciales E. W. Víctor pensó que la caja no era de Houdini, así que la guardó en su armario y se olvidó de ella.

Víctor creció. Una tarde, su hijo bateó una pelota dentro del cementerio. La pelota cayó en la tumba de Houdini. Grabado sobre la lápida estaba el verdadero nombre de Houdini, Ehrich Weiss. ¡Víctor comprendió que E. W. era Houdini! Esa noche buscó la caja en el ático y aprendió los secretos de Houdini.

Multilingual Summaries

Chinese

胡迪尼的盒子

維特想變成像胡迪尼那樣的魔術師，他曾經試著表演胡迪尼的魔術，但是從來沒有成功過。

有一天，維特遇見胡迪尼，他問胡迪尼到底他的魔術有什麼秘密。胡迪尼說他會寫信給維特。信終於寄來了，胡迪尼在信裡邀請維特去他家。維特當天晚上就去了，可是胡迪尼的妻子告訴維特，胡迪尼已經在今天去世了。她給維特一個箱子，上面有個名字縮寫 E.W.。維特想，這不是胡迪尼的東西，所以他就把箱子放到衣櫥裡，不久之後就忘記有這樣東西了。

維特長大後結婚生了小孩。有一天晚上，他兒子把棒球打進墓園裡，球正好落在胡迪尼的墓碑上，墓碑上刻著胡迪尼真正的名字，維特讀了以後才知道胡迪尼就是艾利克・韋斯，這下子他懂了，E. W. 原來就是胡迪尼！當天晚上，他就從閣樓裡把箱子找出來，他終於知道胡迪尼的秘密了。

Vietnamese

Chiếc Hộp của Houdini

Victor muốn thành một nhà ảo thuật như Houdini. Cậu bé thử biểu diễn những trò ảo thuật của Houdini, nhưng cậu không làm được.

Một ngày kia Victor gặp Houdini. Cậu hỏi ông về bí mật của những trò ảo thuật của ông. Houdini nói là ông sẽ viết cho Victor một lá thư. Trong thư Houdini mời Victor đến nhà của ông. Victor đi ngay đêm đó. Vợ của Houdini cho Victor biết là Houdini đã qua đời cùng ngày đó. Bà đưa cho Victor một cái hộp với hai chữ tắt E. W. trên hộp. Victor nghĩ là hộp này không phải của Houdini, nên cậu để hộp vào trong tủ và quên bẵng đi chuyện này.

Victor lớn lên. Một tối nọ con trai của ông đánh quả bóng chày vào trong nghĩa địa. Quả bóng rớt trên mộ của Houdini. Victor đọc tên thật của Houdini trên tấm mộ bia là Ehrich Weiss. Ông mới nhận ra rằng E.W. là Houdini! Tối hôm đó, ông tìm thấy chiếc hộp trên gác xép và học những bí mật của Houdini.

Multilingual Summaries

Korean

후디니의 상자

빅터는 후디니 같은 마술사가 되고 싶어한다. 그는 후디니의 기술을 따라 하려고 했지만 할 수가 없었다.

빅터는 어느 날 후디니를 보고 그의 기술의 비밀에 대해 물어본다. 후디니는 빅터에게 편지를 쓰겠다고 말한다. 편지에는 후디니가 빅터를 집으로 초대한다고 되어 있었고 빅터는 그날 밤 후디니 집으로 간다. 하지만 후디니의 아내는 빅터에게 후디니가 그 날 죽었다고 말한다. 그녀는 빅터에게 E. W라는 머리 글자가 쓰여진 상자 하나를 준다. 빅터는 그것이 후디니의 것이 아니라고 생각하고 장롱에 넣어둔다. 그리고 그 상자에 대해 잊어버리고 만다.

빅터는 자라 어른이 된다. 어느 날 밤 그의 아들이 야구를 하다가 무덤에 공을 날려보낸다. 그 공이 후디니의 무덤에 떨어지고 빅터는 비석에 있는 후디니의 진짜 이름인 에리히・와이스를 보게 된다. 그리고 E.W가 후디니라는 것을 깨닫는다. 그날 밤 그는 다락방에서 후디니의 상자를 찾아 후디니의 비밀에 대해 알게 된다.

Hmong

Lub Npov Houdini

Victor xav ua ib tug neeg txawj khaws koob li Houdini. Nws txiav txim ua Houdini cov khaws koob, tiam sis nws tsis txawj.

Muaj ib hnub Victor pom Houdini. Nws nug Houdini txog nws tej khaws koob. Houdini hais tias nws mam sau Victor ib tsab ntawv. Hauv tsab ntawv Houdini caw Victor mus hauv nws lub tsev. Houdini tus poj niam tau qhia Victor tias Houdini taut as sim neej hnub ntawd. Nws muab Victor ib lub npov uas muaj ob tug ntawv E.W. Victor xav hais tias tej zaum tsis yog Houdini li, ces nws txawm muab cia hauv chaw rau khaub ncaws thiab tsis nco qab txog lub npov.

Victor tau loj hlob. Muaj ib hmo nws tus tub ntaus ib lub pob mus rau hauv ib lub toj ntxas. Nws poob mus rau Houdini lub qhov ntxa. Victor nyeem Houdini lub npe tiag tiag uas hu ua Ehrich Weiss ntawm daim pob zeb. Ces nws pom hais tias E.W. yog Houdini! Hmo ntawd, nws tau nrhiav lub npov saum qaum tsev thiab kawm tau Houdini tej txuj ci.

Encantado Student Edition pages 420–433

Week at a Glance	Customize instruction every day for your English Language Learners.				
	Day 1	**Day 2**	**Day 3**	**Day 4**	**Day 5**
Teacher's Edition	Use the ELL Notes that appear throughout each day of the lesson to support instruction and reading.				
ELL Poster 17	• Assess Prior Knowledge • Develop Concepts and Vocabulary	• Preteach Tested Vocabulary	• Marine Biologists	• Other Animal Behavior	• Monitor Progress
ELL Teaching Guide	• Picture It! Lesson, pp. 113–114 • Multilingual Summaries, pp. 117–119	• ELL Reader Lesson, pp. 244–245	• Vocabulary Activities and Word Cards, pp. 115–116 • Multilingual Summaries, pp. 117–119		
ELL Readers	• Reread *Two Master Magicians*	• Teach *Life in the Amazon Rain Forest*	• Reread *Life in the Amazon Rain Forest* and other texts to build fluency		
ELL and Transition Handbook	Use the following as needed to support this week's instruction and to conduct alternative assessments: • Phonics Transition Lessons • Grammar Transition Lessons • Assessment				

Picture It! Comprehension Lesson

Compare and Contrast

Use this lesson to supplement or replace the skill lesson on pages 416–417 of the Teacher's Edition.

Teach

Distribute copies of the Picture It! blackline master on page 114.

- Have students look at the two pictures and how they are alike and different. Then read the paragraph aloud.
- Ask: *How are rain forests and softwood forests different?*
- Share the Skill Points (at right) with students.

Practice

Read aloud the directions on page 114. Have students underline the clue words. Then ask them to fill in the Venn diagram. Have students keep their organizers for later reteaching.

Answers for page 114: *Both*: many trees, animals; wood used to make furniture; *Softwood forests*: in cold and temperate regions; trees have cones; wood used to make paper; bears, deer, beavers live there; *Tropical rain forests*: in hot, wet regions; many different kinds of trees; wood used to make boxes; parrots, monkeys, crocodiles live there

Skill Points

✓ To **compare** is to tell how two or more things are the same. To **contrast** is to tell how two or more things are different.

✓ Clue words such as *like* and *as* show a comparison. Clue words such as *but, instead,* and *unlike* show a contrast.

Name ______________________________

Look at the picture. **Read** the paragraph.

- How are tropical rain forests and softwood forests alike? **Write** your ideas in the section of the Venn diagram labeled *Both*.
- How are softwood forests and tropical rain forests different? **Write** about their differences in the two side sections of the diagram.

Two Kinds of Forests

Forests are places with many trees in them. Some forests in cold and temperate regions are softwood forests. Trees with cones grow there. The wood from these trees is used to make furniture and paper. Bears, deer, beavers, and other animals live in these forests. Tropical rain forests grow in hot, wet regions. Many different kinds of trees grow there. The wood from these trees is used to make furniture and wooden boxes. Parrots, monkeys, crocodiles, and many other animals live in rain forests.

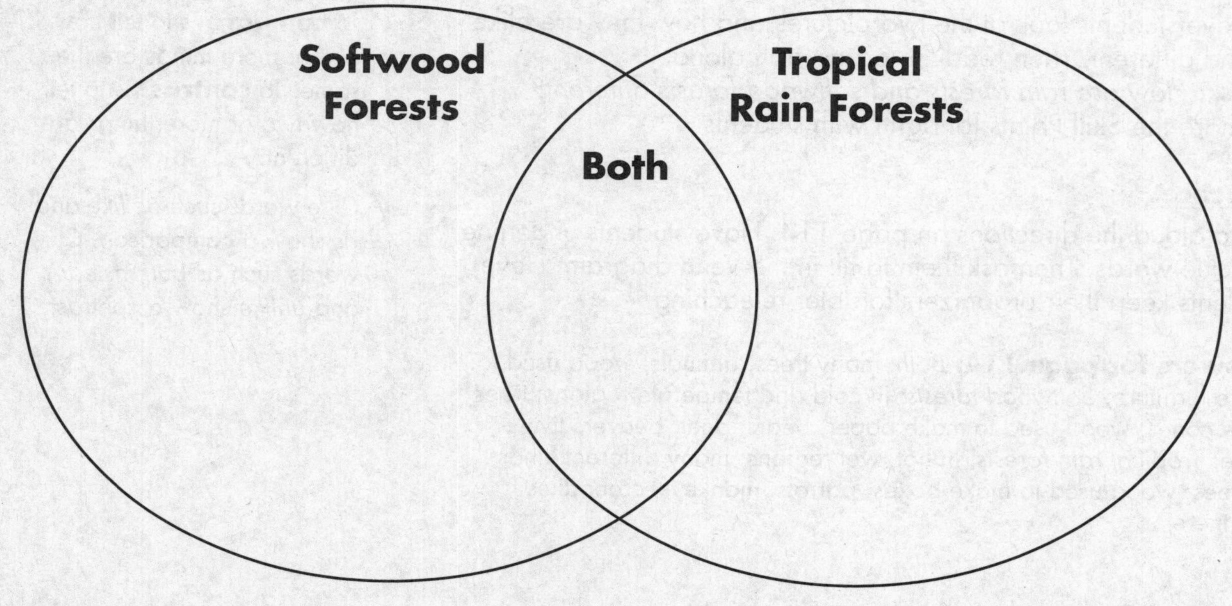

Vocabulary Activities and Word Cards

Copy the Word Cards on page 116 as needed for the following activities.
Use the blank card for an additional word that you want to teach.
Also see suggestions for teaching vocabulary in the ELL and Transition Handbook.

Definition Concentration	Tell a Story	Find Your Partner
• Create one set of Word Cards and seven blank cards for every pair of students. • Have pairs of students work together to write definitions for each word on the blank cards. Remind students that a definition tells what a word means. • Have students place the Word Cards and definition cards face down in rows on a table. • Instruct students to take turns turning over two cards and looking for a matched pair. A matched pair is a Word Card and its definition card. When a student finds a matched pair, the student keeps the cards. • To determine the winner, check which student has the most cards at the end of the game.	• Distribute one set of Word Cards to each student. • Gather the students in a circle and explain that the group will be telling a story together. • Begin the story with a sentence that uses a vocabulary word. • Have the student to your right continue the story, adding a sentence that uses any of the other vocabulary words. • Have each student continue the story, adding a sentence that uses a vocabulary word. • Let students help one another think of sentences that continue the story. • Encourage students to be creative and to try to make the story exciting or funny.	• Give one Word Card to each student, making sure that each student in the class has the same card as one other student. • Ask students to write definitions in their own words on the backs of their Word Cards. • Ask half of the students to place their cards on their desks word side up and half of the students to place their cards definition side up. • Have each student whose card has a definition facing up stand, one at a time, and read the definition to the class. • Have all students with word-side-up cards examine their cards to see if they match the definition. If a card matches, have that student stand up. Then have the two standing students exchange cards to see whether their cards match. • Continue the game until all students whose cards show definitions have read them to the class.

aquarium	**dolphins**
enchanted	**flexible**
glimpses	**pulses**
surface	

Multilingual Summaries

English

Encantado: Pink Dolphin of the Amazon

In the wet season, you might see pink dolphins, which live in the rivers of the Amazon. They are called encantados. Pink dolphins are different from ocean dolphins. They swim slowly and do not have a fin on their backs. Their bodies bend so they can swim around the plants in the rivers.

A guide takes you through the rain forest in a canoe. You are going to a lake to see pink dolphins. Along the way, you see huge spiders and stinging ants. There are trees with sharp spines and trees with sap that burns the skin.

At the lake, you can hear the dolphins. They are hard to see. The water is very dark. You can only see a head or a tail. The guide says encantados are mysterious.

Spanish

Encantado: El delfín rosado del Amazonas

En la estación de las lluvias puedes ver delfines rosados que viven en los ríos del Amazonas. Los llaman encantados. Los delfines rosados son diferentes a los delfines del océano. Nadan lentamente y no tienen una aleta en el dorso. Sus cuerpos se arquean para poder nadar entre las plantas de los ríos.

Un guía te lleva a través de la selva en una canoa. Vas al lago a ver los delfines rosados. A lo largo del trayecto ves enormes arañas y hormigas que pican. Allí hay árboles con espinas puntiagudas y árboles con savia que quema la piel.

En el lago puedes escuchar a los delfines. Es difícil verlos porque el agua es muy oscura. Puedes ver solamente una cabeza o una cola. El guía dice que los delfines encantados son misteriosos.

Multilingual Summaries

Chinese

恩肯塔多：亞馬遜河的粉紅海豚

在潮濕的季節裡，你或許可以在亞馬遜河看到粉紅海豚，大家都叫牠們「恩肯塔多」。粉紅海豚和生活在海洋裡的海豚不同，牠們游得很慢而且背上也沒有鰭，身體會彎曲，這樣游泳的時候就可以繞著河裡面的植物游過去。

導遊會帶你坐獨木舟穿過雨林，你們的目的地是一個湖，在那裡可以看到粉紅海豚。沿路上，你會看到巨型蜘蛛和會咬人的螞蟻，有些樹長有尖刺，有些樹的汁液還會灼傷人的皮膚。

在這個湖上，你可以聽到粉紅海豚的聲音，但是很難看得到牠們，因為湖水的顏色很深，故只能看見頭或者尾鰭的部分。導遊說恩肯塔多像謎一樣的非常神秘。

Vietnamese

Encantado: Cá Heo Màu Hồng của Vùng Amazon

Vào mùa mưa, bạn có thể thấy những con cá heo màu hồng, sống trong những con sông ở Amazon. Chúng được gọi là “encantados”. Cá heo màu hồng khác với cá heo đại dương. Cá heo màu hồng bơi chậm hơn và không có vây ở trên lưng. Thân hình có thể uốn cong để chúng có thể bơi quanh các thực vật dưới sông.

Một người hướng dẫn đưa bạn xuyên qua khu rừng rậm trong một chiếc ca-nô. Bạn sẽ đi đến một cái hồ để xem cá heo màu hồng. Trên đường đi bạn thấy những con nhện khổng lồ và các con kiến chích. Có cây có gai và cây có nhựa làm phỏng da.

Tại hồ, bạn có thể nghe được tiếng cá heo. Khó mà thấy được chúng. Nước có màu rất sậm. Bạn chỉ có thể thấy cái đầu hoặc cái đuôi. Người hướng dẫn nói rằng những con cá heo màu hồng là rất bí ẩn.

Multilingual Summaries

Korean

엔칸타도: 아마존의 핑크색 돌고래

습기가 많은 계절에는 아마존 강에 살고 있는 핑크색 돌고래를 볼 수 있을지도 모른다. 핑크색 돌고래는 엔칸타도라고 불린다. 핑크색 돌고래는 바다에 사는 돌고래와는 달리, 천천히 수영하며 등에 지느러미가 없고 몸을 굽혀 강에 서식하는 식물 주위를 수영할 수도 있다.

한 여행 안내자가 카누를 타고 열대 우림으로 안내한다. 호수에 가면 핑크색 돌고래를 볼 수 있다. 가는 도중엔 큰 거미와 독개미도 만난다. 날카로운 가시가 있는 나무와 살도 태워버리는 수액을 가진 나무도 있다.

호수에 가면 돌고래 소리를 들을 수 있지만 돌고래는 잘 보이지 않는다. 물은 매우 탁해서 단지 돌고래의 머리와 꼬리만 볼 수 있을 뿐이다. 여행 안내자는 엔칸타도가 신비롭다고 말한다.

Hmong

Encantado: Cov Dolphin Xim Liab Dawb Muag Hauv Amazon

Thaum lub ciaj los nag, tej zaum koj pom tau tej dolphine xim liab dawb muag, uas nyob hauv cov dej ntawm Amazon. Lawv hu ua encantados. Cov dolphine xim liab dawb muag yeej txawv cov dolphine hauv dej hiav txwv. Lawv ua luam dej qeeb zog thiab tsis muaj tus nqa txaj qaum saum lawv dab qaum. Lawv lub cev txawj lov kom lawv thiaj ua luam dej ib ncig tau ntawm tej hmab ntoov nyob hauv cov dej.

Ib tug coj kev coj koj mus hauv lub hav zoov nuj txeeg siv ib lub nkoj me me. Koj tam tom mus hauv lub pas dej mus saib cov dolphin xim liab dawb muag. Hauv koj txoj kev koj pom cov kab laug sab loj loj thiab cov ntsaum uas txawj plev. Muaj cov ntoo uas muaj muaj pos thiab cov ntoo uas muaj tej kua ua kom nqaij tawv khaus khuas.

Hauv lub pas dej, koj yeej hnov tau cov dolphin. Kom pom lawv mas yeej nyuaj. Cov dej tsaus tsaus heev. Koj tsuas pom tau lub taub hau los sis tusk o tw xwb. Tus coj kev hais tias neeg yeej tsis paub dab tsis txog cov encantados li.

The King in the Kitchen

Student Edition pages 444–461

Week at a Glance	Customize instruction every day for your English Language Learners.				
	Day 1	**Day 2**	**Day 3**	**Day 4**	**Day 5**
Teacher's Edition	Use the ELL Notes that appear throughout each day of the lesson to support instruction and reading.				
ELL Poster 18	• Assess Prior Knowledge • Develop Concepts and Vocabulary	• Preteach Tested Vocabulary	• Class Story	• How Our Mistakes Become Successes	• Monitor Progress
ELL Teaching Guide	• Picture It! Lesson, pp. 120–121 • Multilingual Summaries, pp. 124–126	• ELL Reader Lesson, pp. 246–247	• Vocabulary Activities and Word Cards, pp. 122–123 • Multilingual Summaries, pp. 124–126		
ELL Readers	• Reread *Life in The Amazon Rain Forest*	• Teach *Inventions*	• Reread *Inventions* and other texts to build fluency		
ELL and Transition Handbook	Use the following as needed to support this week's instruction and to conduct alternative assessments: • Phonics Transition Lessons • Grammar Transition Lessons • Assessment				

Picture It! Comprehension Lesson

Character and Setting

Use this lesson to supplement or replace the skill lesson on page 440–441 of the Teacher's Edition.

Teach

Distribute copies of the Picture It! blackline master on page 121.

- Have students describe what they see in the picture. Then read the paragraph.
- Ask: *Who are the people, or characters, in this play?* (the king, the princess, and the peasant)
- Share the Skill Points (at right) with students.
- Have students describe where the story takes place.

Skill Points

✓ **Characters** are people in a story or play. You can learn about characters by reading what they say and do.

✓ The **setting** is the time and place of a story or play.

Practice

Read aloud the directions on page 121. Have students fill in the graphic organizer. Have them keep their organizers for later reteaching.

Answers for page 121: *Setting*: royal palace; *Characters*: The king (foolish, uninterested in the world); the princess (wise, curious); the peasant (gentle, curious, rich)

Name ______________________________

Character and Setting

Look at the picture. **Read** the paragraph.

- What is the setting of the story? **Write** it below.
- Who are the characters in the story? **List** them in the chart.
- **Write** what you know about each character in the second column of the chart.

The King, the Princess, and the Peasant

Once there was a foolish king who had a smart daughter. Every month, a gentle peasant brought the two something new. The king paid the peasant well. One month he brought books. The king laughed, but his daughter learned to read. One month the peasant brought a pen and paper. The king fell asleep, but his daughter learned to write. One month the peasant brought a globe. The king played with it, but the princess learned the names of countries. The princess became a very wise queen. The peasant became a very rich man. But the king remained foolish.

Setting: ______________________________

Name of Character	Description of Character

Vocabulary Activities and Word Cards

Copy the Word Cards on page 123 as needed for the following activities.
Use the blank cards for additional words that you want to teach.
Also see suggestions for teaching vocabulary in the ELL and Transition Handbook.

Riddle Game	True or False?	Skits
• Divide the students into pairs, and give each pair a set of Word Cards. • Have students place the set of Word Cards face down in a pile. • Ask one partner to choose a card and make up a riddle about the word. Provide examples, such as: *I am not a king, but I am not just a regular person either;* or, *I am so smart that people use a special word to describe me.* Then have students tell their riddles to their partners. • Have the partner try to guess the word. Then have students switch roles. • Continue the activity until students have created riddles for every Word Card.	• Make one set of Word Cards. • Ask a student to select a card. • Make up a sentence using the vocabulary word, and ask the student if the sentence is true or false. For example: *A peasant is usually quite rich.* (false) • Ask the rest of the group whether they agree with the student's answer. • Repeat the exercise until all students have had a chance to choose a card.	• Have students form small groups, and give each group a set of Word Cards. • Ask each group to write a short skit that uses all the vocabulary words. Encourage students to be creative, making their skits interesting, exciting, funny, or silly. Allow them to improvise props and costumes from items in the classroom. • Invite each group to perform its skit for the class.

duke	**dungeon**
furiously	**genius**
majesty	**noble**
peasant	**porridge**

Multilingual Summaries

English

The King in the Kitchen

A guard in a castle enters the palace kitchen. He is taking a peasant to the prison because the peasant asked the princess to marry him. The cook says the princess must marry someone rich, like a duke.

The king comes into the kitchen. He is angry about the terrible soup the cook made. The king makes his own soup. But it does not look like soup. The king has a contest for people to guess what he made. The winner will marry the princess.

The duke guesses it is pudding, but he is wrong. The guard cannot guess because he is already married. Then the peasant guesses that it is very good glue. He says the king will be rich if he sells the glue. The peasant and the princess will get married.

Spanish

El Rey en la cocina

Un guardia entra a la cocina del palacio. Va llevando a un campesino a la prisión porque el campesino le pidió a la princesa que se casara con él. El cocinero dice que la princesa debería casarse con alguien rico, como un duque.

El rey llega a la cocina. Está furioso porque el cocinero hizo una sopa malísima. El rey hace su propia sopa, pero no parece sopa. El rey hace un concurso para que la gente adivine lo que hizo. El ganador se casará con la princesa.

El duque dice que es un pudín, pero está equivocado. El guardia no puede participar en el concurso porque es casado. Entonces, el campesino adivina que es un pegamento muy bueno. Le dice al rey que se hará rico vendiéndolo como pegamento. El campesino y la princesa se casarán.

Multilingual Summaries

Chinese

廚房裡的國王

城堡的守衛進了宮殿廚房，他正要帶一個農夫去關在監獄裡，因為這個農夫要公主跟他結婚，實在是太大膽了。廚師說公主要嫁像公爵那樣的有錢人。

國王也進了廚房，他很生氣，因為廚師做的湯很難喝，國王要自己做湯喝。但是做出來的東西看起來不像湯。國王靈機一動，他要辦個比賽，讓大家猜猜他做了什麼東西，猜對的人可以和公主結婚。

公爵猜是布丁，不對；守衛不能猜，因為他已經結婚了；農夫猜做出來的東西是很好的漿糊，要是拿出去賣，一定可以賣得很好，這樣子國王就會變得很富有。農夫猜對了，他終於可以和公主結婚了。

Vietnamese

Vua Bếp

Một lính canh tòa lâu đài đi vào trong bếp của cung điện. Lính canh này đưa một người nông dân vào tù vì người này đã cầu hôn công chúa. Ông đầu bếp nói rằng công chúa phải có một người chồng giàu, như một Công Tước chẳng hạn.

Đức vua đi vào trong bếp. Vua giận dữ vì món canh dở tệ mà người đầu bếp đã nấu. Vua tự mình nấu món canh. Nhưng món này nhìn không giống canh. Nhà vua mở cuộc thi cho người ta đoán xem vua đã nấu món gì. Kẻ thắng cuộc sẽ được cưới công chúa.

Vị Công Tước đoán đó là món bánh ngọt, nhưng ông đoán sai. Tay lính canh không thể đoán vì tay này đã có vợ. Rồi đến người nông dân đoán đó là một chất keo rất tốt. Anh nói rằng nhà vua sẽ làm giàu nếu vua bán keo này. Anh nông dân và công chúa sẽ được kết hôn.

Multilingual Summaries

Korean

부엌에 들어온 왕

성을 지키는 한 호위병이 궁전의 부엌에 들어간다. 그는 공주에게 청혼을 한 농부에게 독을 갖다 주고 있다. 요리사는 공주가 공작처럼 부자인 사람과 결혼해야 된다고 말한다.

왕이 부엌으로 들어온다. 왕은 요리사가 만든 맛없는 스프때문에 화가 나 있다. 왕은 직접 스프를 만들어 보지만 스프처럼 보이지 않는다. 왕은 사람들에게 그가 만든 것을 알아 맞추게 하는 대회를 열고 대회의 우승자는 공주와 결혼하게 된다.

공작은 그게 푸딩일 거라고 추측하지만 틀린다. 호위병은 이미 결혼했기 때문에 대회에 참가할 수 없다. 그때 그 농부가 그것이 아주 좋은 접착제라고 생각하고 접착제를 팔면 왕이 부자가 될 것이라고 말한다. 나중에 농부와 공주는 결혼하게 된다.

Hmong

Tus Vaj Ntxwv Hauv Chaw Tsev Ua Mov Noj

Ib tug tub zov lub loog vaj tau nkag mus rau hauv chaws tsev ua mov noj hauv lub tsev vaj ntxwv. Nws tab tom coj ib tug neeg ua liaj ua teb mus kaw vim tus neeg ua liaj ua teb tau hais kom tus ntxhais vaj ntxwv yuav nws. Tus ua mov noj hais tias tus ntxhais vaj ntxwv yuav tsum yuav ib tug neeg muaj nyiaj muaj txiaj, zoo li ib tug Duke.

Tus vaj ntxwv los rau hauv chaw ua mov noj. Nws npau taws txog cov kua nqaij uas tus ua mov noj tau ua. Tus vaj ntxwv ua rau nws tus kheej ib cov kau nqaij. Tiam sis nws tsis zoo li ib cov kua nqiaj. Tus vaj ntxwv muaj ib qho sib tw seb nws tau ua tau hom mov dab tsi. Tus yeej yuav yuav taut us ntxhais vaj ntxwv.

Tus Duke tw hais tias yog ib cov kua dis, tiam sis tsis yog. Tus tub zov lub loog vaj tw tsis tau vim nws twb muaj poj niam lawm. Ces tus neeg ua liaj ua teb tw hais tias cov kua nqaij yog ib cov kua uas nplaum zoo zoo heev. Nws hais tias tus vaj ntxwv yuav muaj nyiaj heev yog nws muag cov kua nplaum. Tus neeg ua liaj ua teb thiab tus ntxhias vaj ntxwv yuav sib yuav.

Seeker of Knowledge Student Edition pages 470–481

Week at a Glance	Customize instruction every day for your English Language Learners.				
	Day 1	**Day 2**	**Day 3**	**Day 4**	**Day 5**
Teacher's Edition	Use the ELL Notes that appear throughout each day of the lesson to support instruction and reading.				
ELL Poster 19	• Assess Prior Knowledge • Develop Concepts and Vocabulary	• Preteach Tested Vocabulary	• I See a . . .	• Act It Out	• Monitor Progress
ELL Teaching Guide	• Picture It! Lesson, pp. 127–128 • Multilingual Summaries, pp. 131–133	• ELL Reader Lesson, pp. 248–249	• Vocabulary Activities and Word Cards, pp. 129–130 • Multilingual Summaries, pp. 131–133		
ELL Readers	• Reread *Inventions*	• Teach *Alphabets and Other Writing Systems*	• Reread *Alphabets and Other Writing Systems* and other texts to build fluency		
ELL and Transition Handbook	Use the following as needed to support this week's instruction and to conduct alternative assessments: • Phonics Transition Lessons • Grammar Transition Lessons • Assessment				

Picture It! Comprehension Lesson

Graphic Sources

Use this lesson to supplement or replace the skill lesson on pages 466–467 of the Teacher's Edition.

Teach

Distribute copies of the Picture It! blackline master on page 128.

- Have students look at and discuss the hieroglyphics. Then read the paragraph aloud.
- Ask: *What are hieroglyphics?*
- Share the Skill Points (at right) with students.
- Have students discuss how the graphic helps them understand what hieroglyphics are.

Practice

Read aloud the directions on page 128. Have students write short answers to the questions. Have students keep their work for later reteaching.

Answers for page 128: 1. pictures used for writing **2.** their lives, their gods, their kings **3.** Possible response: It illustrates what hieroglyphics are.

Skill Points

✓ A **graphic source** is a picture, map, chart, or time line.

✓ Graphic sources organize information and make it easy to see.

✓ You can use graphic sources to help you understand what you read.

Name ______________________________

Look at the picture. **Read** the paragraph.

- **Use** the information in the picture and the paragraph.
- **Answer** the questions below.

Ancient Egyptian Writing

Thousands of years ago, people in Egypt used pictures instead of letters to write. This kind of writing is called *hieroglyphics*. The Egyptians used hieroglyphics to write about their lives, their gods, and their kings. Today, we can read these hieroglyphics to learn about the ancient Egyptian world. What do you think the wavy line stood for? What do you think the bird meant?

1. What are hieroglyphics?

____

____

____

2. What are some of the things Egyptians wrote about?

____

____

____

3. How does the picture help you understand the paragraph?

____

____

____

Vocabulary Activities and Word Cards

Copy the Word Cards on page 130 as needed for the following activities.
Use the blank cards for additional words that you want to teach.
Also see suggestions for teaching vocabulary in the ELL and Transition Handbook.

Context Game	Write a Story	Poster Clues
• Give a set of Word Cards to each student. • Have each student write a context sentence for each word on the back of each card. Remind students that context sentences are sentences that show the meaning of the word. Instruct students not to include the vocabulary word in the context sentence but to leave a blank where the word belongs. • Have students form pairs and exchange their cards with the context sides up. • Have students take turns looking at their partner's context sentence and guessing the vocabulary word. Have them discard each card into a correct or incorrect pile, depending on their guess. • To determine the winner, check which student has the most cards in the correct pile at the end of the game.	• Divide the class into small story-writing groups, and give each group a set of Word Cards. • Within each group, distribute the Word Cards so that each student has at least one card. • Have students select one member of the group to record the story, another to make sure that each student contributes at least one sentence to the story, and a third to read the story to the class. • Have each group brainstorm ideas for the story. Tell the student that the story can be silly or serious but must include all of the vocabulary words. Then have each student come up with a sentence for the story using the Word Card or Cards he or she received. • Give students ten minutes to write their story. Then have one member of each group read the story to the class.	• Distribute sets of Word Cards to students. Then, from your own set of Word Cards, have one student pick a card without letting the others see it. • The student stands at the ELL Poster, points to the relevant area on it, and uses the information on the Poster to give hints about the vocabulary word. • Other students should try to guess which vocabulary word the student has. The first person to guess correctly may choose the next Word Card and make up clues about it. • Continue until all of the vocabulary words have been used.

ancient	**link**
scholars	**seeker**
temple	**translate**
triumph	**uncover**

Multilingual Summaries

English

Seeker of Knowledge

In the 1790s in Grenoble, France, a boy named Jean-François Champollion went with his brother to visit a scientist's home. The home was filled with things from ancient Egypt. The scientist told him that no one could read the writings of the ancient Egyptians, called hieroglyphics. Jean-François read many books about Egypt and the hieroglyphics. He claimed he would read them someday.

When he finished school, he went to Paris to study hieroglyphics with historians. They turned him away. Jean-François returned to Grenoble and began to teach. He often spoke about ancient Egypt. Even Napoleon came to listen to Jean-François speak.

Years later, Jean-François returned to Paris. He was determined to translate the hieroglyphics. After years of study, Jean-François became the first modern person to translate ancient Egyptian writing. He finally got to go to Egypt.

Spanish

El buscador de conocimiento

En la década de 1790, en Grenoble, Francia, un niño llamado Jean-François Champollion fue con su hermano a visitar la casa de un científico. La casa estaba llena de cosas del antiguo Egipto. El científico le dijo que nadie podía leer los escritos de los antiguos egipcios, llamados jeroglíficos. Jean-François leyó muchos libros sobre Egipto y los jeroglíficos. Dijo que él los leería algún día.

Cuando terminó la escuela, fue a París a estudiar jeroglíficos con los historiadores. Ellos no le hicieron caso. Jean-François volvió a Grenoble y comenzó a enseñar. A menudo hablaba del antiguo Egipto. Hasta Napoleón fue a escuchar las charlas sobre Egipto de Jean-François.

Años después, Jean-François regresó a París. Estaba decidido a traducir los jeroglíficos. Después de años de estudio, Jean-François se convirtió en la primera persona de este tiempo que tradujo la escritura egipcia antigua. Finalmente, pudo viajar a Egipto.

Multilingual Summaries

Chinese

追求知識的人

1790 年代在法國格勒諾伯這個地方，有個男孩名字叫做向波倫。有一天，向波倫和他的兄弟一起去拜訪一位科學家，那科學家的家裡到處都是古埃及的東西。科學家告訴他，世界上沒有人看得懂古埃及人寫的文字，那種文字叫做象形文字。向波倫看了很多跟埃及和象形文字有關的書，他說有一天他一定會看得懂埃及象形文字。

在學校畢業以後，向波倫出發往巴黎，想跟史學家學習象形文字，可是被拒絕了，所以他就回格勒諾伯，然後開始教書。向波倫經常談到古埃及，後來連拿破崙都跑來聽向波倫講有關古埃及的事。

幾年後，向波倫又回到巴黎，這次他決定要翻譯埃及象形文字。經過好幾年的研究之後，向波倫終於成為現代第一個翻譯古埃及文字的人，最後他還去了埃及。

Vietnamese

Người Tìm Kiến Thức

Trong những thập niên 1790 ở Grenoble, nước Pháp, một cậu bé tên Jean-François Champollion đi với anh mình đến thăm nhà của một khoa học gia. Ngôi nhà đầy các vật từ thời Ai Cập cổ xưa. Nhà khoa học nói với cậu bé rằng không ai có thể đọc những chữ viết của những người Ai Cập cổ xưa, được gọi là chữ viết tượng hình (hieroglyphics). Jean-François Champollion đã đọc nhiều sách về Ai Cập và kiểu chữ viết tượng hình. Cậu tuyên bố rằng một ngày nào đó cậu sẽ đọc được những chữ này.

Khi học xong, cậu đi đến Paris để học chữ viết tượng hình với các sử gia. Họ từ chối không nhận cậu. Jean-François Champollion trở về Grenoble và bắt đầu dạy học. Cậu thường nói về Ai Cập cổ xưa. Ngay cả Napoleon cũng đến nghe Jean-François giảng thuyết.

Nhiều năm trôi qua, Jean-François trở lại Paris. Ông cương quyết dịch ra những chữ viết tượng hình. Sau nhiều năm nghiên cứu, Jean-François trở thành người đầu tiên của thời hiện đại có thể dịch chữ viết của người Ai Cập cổ xưa. Cuối cùng ông được đi sang Ai Cập.

Multilingual Summaries

Korean

지식 탐구자

1790년대 프랑스의 그르노블에서 장 프랑수아 샹폴리옹이라는 한 남자 아이가 동생과 함께 한 과학자의 집으로 갔다. 그 집은 고대 이집트 물건들로 가득했는데 그 과학자는 아이에게 상형문자라고 하는 고대 이집트 사람들의 글자를 읽을 수 있는 사람은 아무도 없다고 말했다. 장 프랑수아는 이집트와 상형문자에 관한 많은 책을 읽었고, 언젠가 그는 상형문자를 읽을 수 있게 될 것이라고 주장했다.

그는 학교를 마치고 파리로 가서 역사학자들과 함께 상형문자를 공부하려 했지만 역사학자들은 그를 돌려보냈다. 장 프랑수아는 그르노블로 돌아와 선생님이 되었다. 그는 종종 고대 이집트에 대한 이야기를 했고 심지어 나폴레옹도 장 프랑수아의 연설을 들으러 왔다.

몇 년 후 장 프랑수아는 파리로 돌아왔고 상형문자를 해석하기로 결심한다. 몇 년 간의 연구 후 장 프랑수아는 고대 이집트 문자를 해석한 최초의 현대인이 되었고 그는 결국 이집트로 갔다.

Hmong

Tus Neeg Nrhiav Kev Txawj Kev Ntse

Thaum xyoo 1790 hauv lub zos Grenoble, France, ib tug me nyuam tub uas muaj lub npe hu ua Jean-Francois Champollion tau mus nrog nws tus tij laug mus xyuas ib tug neeg txawj ntse lub tsev. Lub tsev muaj ntau yam khoom qub qub uas tau hauv nyob I-yiv. Tus neeg txawj ntse hais tias tsis muaj leej twg uas nyeem tau I-yiv cov ntawv txheej puag thaum ub uas hu ua cov ntawv hieroglyphics. Jean-Francois tau nyeem ntau phau ntawv txog I-yiv thiab cov ntawv hieroglyphics. Nws hais tias yuav muaj ib hnub nws yuav nyeem tau cov ntawv no.

Thaum nws kawm ntawv tas, nws tau mus hauv Paris mus kawm cov ntawv hieroglyphics nrog cov neeg paub keeb kwm. Lawv tsis kam nws nrog lawv. Jean-Francois rov qab mus rau Grenoble thiab pib qhia ntawv. Ntau zaus nws yeej hais txog I-yiv txheej puag thuam ub. Napoleon los kuj tau tuaj mloog Jean-Francois hais lus thiab.

Ntau xyoo dhau mus, Jean-Francois tau rov qab mus hauv Paris. Nws muaj siab xav txhais cov ntawv hieroglyphics. Tom qab ntau xyoo uas nws kawm cov ntawv no, Jean-Francois tau los yog thawj tug neeg niaj hnub nim no uas txhais tau I-yiv cov ntawv txheej puag thaum ub. Ces thaum kawg nws tau mus hauv I-yiv.

Encyclopedia Brown and the Case of the Slippery Salamander

Student Edition pages 492–500

<table>
<tr><th rowspan="2">Week at a Glance</th><th colspan="5">Customize instruction every day for your English Language Learners.</th></tr>
<tr><th>Day 1</th><th>Day 2</th><th>Day 3</th><th>Day 4</th><th>Day 5</th></tr>
<tr><td>Teacher's Edition</td><td colspan="5">Use the ELL Notes that appear throughout each day of the lesson to support instruction and reading.</td></tr>
<tr><td>ELL Poster 20</td><td>• Assess Prior Knowledge
• Develop Concepts and Vocabulary</td><td>• Preteach Tested Vocabulary</td><td>• Tell the Story</td><td>• Another Mystery</td><td>• Monitor Progress</td></tr>
<tr><td>ELL Teaching Guide</td><td>• Picture It! Lesson, pp. 134–135
• Multilingual Summaries, pp. 138–140</td><td>• ELL Reader Lesson, pp. 250–251</td><td colspan="3">• Vocabulary Activities and Word Cards, pp. 136–137
• Multilingual Summaries, pp. 138–140</td></tr>
<tr><td>ELL Readers</td><td>• Reread Alphabets and Other Writing Systems</td><td>• Teach The Case of the Disappearing Sugar</td><td colspan="3">• Reread The Case of the Disappearing Sugar and other texts to build fluency</td></tr>
<tr><td>ELL and Transition Handbook</td><td colspan="5">Use the following as needed to support this week's instruction and to conduct alternative assessments:
• Phonics Transition Lessons
• Grammar Transition Lessons
• Assessment</td></tr>
</table>

Picture It! Comprehension Lesson

Plot

Use this lesson to supplement or replace the skill lesson on pages 488–489 of the Teacher's Edition.

Teach

Distribute copies of the Picture It! blackline master on page 135.

- Have students look at the picture. Then read the story aloud.
- Ask: *What is Katie's problem?* (She can't find Leo, her pet lizard.)
- Share the Skill Points (at right) with students.
- Have students discuss the plot of the story.

Practice

Read aloud the directions on page 135. Have students answer the questions at the bottom of the page. Have them keep their work for later reteaching.

Answers for page 135: 1. Katie can't find Leo, her pet lizard. **2.** Katie looks around the cage and under her bed. **3.** Carlos **4.** Carlos finds Leo sleeping under a log in his cage.

Skill Points

✓ The **plot** is the structure, or plan of events, of a story.

✓ A plot is often based on a problem that someone in the story has.

✓ The problem gets bigger during the rising action.

✓ The highest point of the action is the climax.

✓ The action ends with the resolution, or solving, of the problem.

Name ____________________

Look at the picture. **Read** the story.

- **Answer** the questions below.

Leo the Lost Lizard

Katie looked everywhere for her pet lizard, Leo. She couldn't find him anywhere. She looked around the cage and under her bed. Where could Leo be? Finally, Katie asked her friend, Carlos, to help her find her lizard. Carlos looked in Leo's cage for clues. Then he laughed out loud. "Katie," Carlos said, "Leo isn't lost! He's sleeping under his log!" Katie thanked Carlos for his good detective work.

1. What is Katie's problem?

____

____

2. What does Katie do to try to solve the problem?

____

____

3. Who helps Katie?

____

____

4. What is the resolution of the problem?

____

____

Vocabulary Activities and Word Cards

Copy the Word Cards on pages 136–137 as needed for the following activities.
Use the blank card for an additional word that you want to teach.
Also see suggestions for teaching vocabulary in the ELL and Transition Handbook.

Definition Concentration	Clue Game	Home Language Clues
• Create one set of Word Cards and nine blank cards for every pair of students. • Have pairs of students work together to write definitions for each word on the blank cards. Remind students that a definition tells what a word means. • Have students place the Word Cards and definition cards face down in rows on a table. • Instruct students to take turns turning over two cards and looking for a matched pair. A matched pair is a Word Card and its definition card. When a student finds a matched pair, the student keeps the cards. • To determine the winner, check which student has the most cards at the end of the game.	• Write the definition of each vocabulary word on the back of a set of Word Cards. • Have one student read the definition and the others try to guess the word. • Once the students correctly identify the word, ask several students to create sentences using the word.	• Pair students who have writing proficiency in the same home language, and give each student a set of Word Cards. • Have students work together to write translations of the vocabulary words in their home language on the back of each card. (See the Multilingual Lesson Vocabulary beginning on page 272 for suggested translations.) • Have partners lay out the cards with the home language sides facing up. • Invite students to generate synonyms for each word in their home language. Then ask them to name the English vocabulary word with the same meaning. They can flip the cards over to check their answers.

amphibians	**baffled**

crime	**exhibit**
lizards	**reference**
reptiles	**salamanders**
stumped	

Multilingual Summaries

English

Encyclopedia Brown and the Case of the Slippery Salamander

No one got away with breaking the law in the town of Idaville. The police chief's son was called Encyclopedia Brown because he knew so many things. He was a great detective and helped his father solve crimes.

One night the police chief was upset. That day a salamander had been stolen from the town's aquarium. Encyclopedia Brown asked his father many questions about that. They talked about the suspects, Doctor Donnell, Mrs. King, and Sam Maine. Sam Maine, the new caretaker, had told Chief Brown that he had worked with salamanders and other lizards for many years. Encyclopedia said Sam was lying, because salamanders are not lizards. Lizards are reptiles, and salamanders are amphibians. Sam admitted to stealing the salamander, gave the salamander back, and was fired from his job.

Spanish

Enciclopedia Brown y el caso de la escurridiza salamandra

En el pueblo de Idaville nadie se escapaba si traspasa la ley. Al hijo del jefe de la policía le decían Enciclopedia Brown porque sabía muchas cosas. Era un gran detective y le ayudaba a su padre a resolver muchos crímenes.

Una noche, el jefe de la policía estaba preocupado. Ese día se habían robado una salamandra del acuario del pueblo. Enciclopedia Brown le hizo a su padre muchas preguntas relacionadas con el robo. Hablaron de los sospechosos, como el Doctor Donnell, la Sra. King y Sam Maine. Sam Maine, el nuevo conserje, le había dicho al Jefe Brown que él había trabajado con salamandras y otros lagartos durante muchos años. Enciclopedia dijo que Sam estaba mintiendo porque las salamandras no son lagartos. Los lagartos son reptiles, y las salamandras son anfibios. Sam admitió que se había robado la salamandra, devolvió la salamandra y fue despedido de su trabajo.

Multilingual Summaries

Chinese

「萬事通」布朗與狡猾的火蜥蜴賊

在印達維爾鎮，所有違法的人都不可能逍遙法外，因為警長的兒子一「萬事通」布朗知道很多事，是一個非常厲害的偵探，他還會幫助他父親打擊犯罪。

有一天晚上，警長很不高興，因為那天有人偷了水族館裡的火蜥蜴。「萬事通」布朗問了父親很多有關的問題。兩人討論到最後，覺得嫌疑犯有三個人：唐奈醫生、金太太，和薩姆・緬因。薩姆・緬因是水族館裡新來的動物管理員，他告訴布朗警長，他照顧火蜥蜴和其他蜥蜴已經有好多年了。「萬事通」布朗說薩姆說謊，因為火蜥蜴不是蜥蜴，而是兩棲類動物。薩姆最後終於承認偷了火蜥蜴，他把火蜥蜴還給水族館，不過也被辭退了。

Vietnamese

Cậu Bé Brown Bách Khoa Thư và Vụ Kỳ Nhông Nan Giải

Không ai có thể chạy tội khi phạm luật ở thành phố Idaville. Con trai của viên cảnh sát trưởng được gọi là Brown Bách Khoa Thư vì cậu bé biết rất nhiều điều. Cậu là một thám tử giỏi và đã giúp ba giải quyết nhiều vụ tội phạm.

Một tối nọ viên cảnh sát trưởng buồn bực. Hôm đó một con kỳ nhông đã bị ăn cắp từ tòa nhà có bể nuôi cá của thành phố. Brown Bách Khoa Thư hỏi ba nhiều câu hỏi về việc này. Hai cha con nói về những kẻ bị tình nghi, Bác sĩ Donnell, Bà King, và Sam Maine. Sam Maine, người mới nhận việc chăm sóc kỳ nhông, đã nói với Cảnh Sát Trưởng Brown là ông ta đã làm việc nhiều năm với các kỳ nhông và thằn lằn. Bách Khoa Thư bảo là Sam nói dối, vì kỳ nhông không thuộc giống thằn lằn, mà thuộc loại động vật lưỡng cư. Sam thừa nhận đã ăn cắp con kỳ nhông, giao trả con kỳ nhông lại, và bị đuổi việc.

Multilingual Summaries

Korean

브라운 백과사전과 미끌미끌 도롱뇽 사건

아이다빌이라는 마을에서는 법을 어기면 누구나 처벌을 받는다. 경찰서장의 아들은 지식이 해박하여 브라운 백과사전이라고 불린다. 그는 훌륭한 탐정이고 아버지가 범죄를 해결하도록 도와준다.

어느 날 밤 경찰서장이 매우 화가 났다. 그날 도롱뇽 한 마리가 마을의 수족관에서 도난 당한 것이다. 브라운 백과사전은 아버지에게 그 사건에 대해 이것저것을 물어보고 용의자인 도넬 의사, 킹 아줌마, 그리고 샘 메인에 대해 얘기한다. 새로운 관리자인 샘 메인은 브라운 서장에게 자신은 수년 동안 도롱뇽뿐만 아니라 다른 도마뱀과 함께 일해왔다고 말한다. 브라운 백과사전은 도롱뇽은 도마뱀이 아니고 양서류이기 때문에 샘이 거짓말을 한다고 말한다. 샘은 도롱뇽을 훔친 것을 인정하고 도롱뇽을 돌려주지만 직장에서 해고된다.

Hmong

Encyclopedia Brown thiab Zaj Uas Muaj Tus Salamander Nplua Nplua

Tsis muaj leej twg uas mus dawb thaum lawv tau ua txhaum txoj cai hauv lub zos Idaville. Tus thawj tub ceev xwm tus tub uas muaj lub npe hu ua Encyclopedia Brown vim nws paub txhua yam txhua tsav. Nws yog ib tug tub ceev xwm siv tswv yim zoo heev thiab nws pab nws txiv nrhiav tau cov neeg phem.

Muaj ib hmo tus thawj tub ceev xwm tau chim. Hnub ntawd tau muaj leej twg uas nyiag ib tug salamander hauv qhov chaw rau cov salamander. Encyclopedia Brown nug nws txiv ntau yam txog qhov ntawd. Nkawd sib tham ntau txog cov neeg uas tej zaum tau nyiag tus salamander, xws li Doctor Donnel, Mrs. King, thiab Sam Maine. Sam Maine, tus neeg tshiab saib xyuas qhov chaw yug salamander, tau qhia Chief Brown tias nws tau ua hauj lwm nrog cov salamander thiab lwm cov nab qa tau ntau xyoo los lawm. Encyclopedia tau hais tias Sam dag xwb, vim cov salamander tsis nab qa, tiam sis yog amphibians. Sam tau lees hais tias nws tau nyiag tus salamander, rov muab tus salamander los, thiab tau raug ntiab tawv hauj lwm.

Sailing Home Student Edition pages 520–533

Week at a Glance	Customize instruction every day for your English Language Learners.				
	Day 1	**Day 2**	**Day 3**	**Day 4**	**Day 5**
Teacher's Edition	Use the ELL Notes that appear throughout each day of the lesson to support instruction and reading.				
ELL Poster 21	• Assess Prior Knowledge • Develop Concepts and Vocabulary	• Preteach Tested Vocabulary	• Let's Pack!	• Categorize	• Monitor Progress
ELL Teaching Guide	• Picture It! Lesson, pp. 141–142 • Multilingual Summaries, pp. 145–147	• ELL Reader Lesson, pp. 252–253	• Vocabulary Activities and Word Cards, pp. 143–144 • Multilingual Summaries, pp. 145–147		
ELL Readers	• Reread *The Case of the Disappearing Sugar*	• Teach *The Treasure Fleet*	• Reread *The Treasure Fleet* and other texts to build fluency		
ELL and Transition Handbook	Use the following as needed to support this week's instruction and to conduct alternative assessments: • Phonics Transition Lessons • Grammar Transition Lessons • Assessment				

Picture It! Comprehension Lesson

Author's Purpose

Use this lesson to supplement or replace the skill lesson on pages 516–517 of the Teacher's Edition.

Teach

Distribute copies of the Picture It! blackline master on page 142.

- Have students look at the picture and describe what they see. Then read the paragraph aloud.
- Ask: *Why do you think the author wrote this paragraph?* (to tell people what life on a ship is like)
- Share the Skill Points (at right) with students.
- Have students discuss the author's purpose and explain what the author did to achieve it.

Skill Points

✓ Authors have different **purposes**, or reasons, for writing. Four common reasons are to persuade, to inform, to express ideas or feelings, and to entertain.

✓ An author may have more than one reason for writing.

Practice

Read aloud the directions on page 142. Have students answer the questions. Have students keep their work for later reteaching.

Answers for page 142: 1. c **2.** a

Name ________________________________

Look at the picture. **Read** the paragraph.

- **Read** each question and the four answer choices given.
- **Circle** the letter of the correct answer.

Life on a Sailing Ship

There is always something to do on a ship. The crew makes sure that the ship moves safely through the water. They also clean the ship. If a sail tears, they sew it. The ship's cook makes meals for everyone on the ship. Other people on the ship watch for signs of bad weather. The captain of the ship tells everyone what do to.

1. What is the author's purpose in writing this paragraph?

a. to make the reader laugh
b. to frighten the reader
c. to explain to the reader what life on a ship is like
d. to convince the reader that working on a ship is boring

2. How does the author meet this purpose?

a. by providing facts
b. by providing opinions
c. by telling funny stories
d. by confusing the reader

Vocabulary Activities and Word Cards

Copy the Word Cards on page 144 as needed for the following activities.
Use the blank cards for additional words that you want to teach.
Also see suggestions for teaching vocabulary in the ELL and Transition Handbook.

Cloze Sentences	Part-of-Speech Word Sort	True or False?
• Give each student a set of Word Cards and two pieces of paper. • Have students write one sentence using each vocabulary word. • On a second sheet of paper, have students rewrite each sentence, replacing the vocabulary word with a line. • Divide the class into pairs. Have each pair exchange the papers with their cloze sentences and try to fill in the missing vocabulary words. Have partners check one another's work.	• Divide the students into pairs. Give each pair a set of Word Cards and two sheets of paper. • Have each pair prepare a three-column chart with *Nouns, Verbs,* and *Adjectives* as the headings. • Have students sort the Word Cards, discussing where to put each word. • Then have each pair of students write sentences that use words from each column.	• Ask a student to select a card from a set of Word Cards. • Make up a sentence using the vocabulary word, and ask the student if the sentence is true or false. For example: *Things that are celestial are in the sky.* (true) • Ask the rest of the group whether they agree with the student's answer. • Repeat the exercise until all students have had a chance to choose a card.

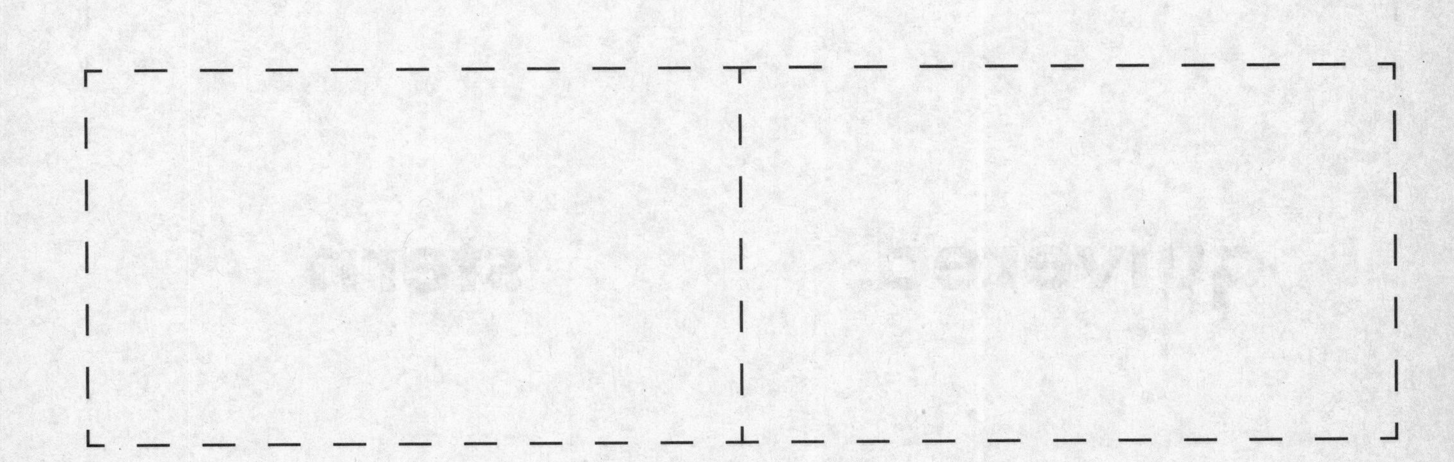

bow	**cargo**
celestial	**conducted**
dignified	**navigation**
quivered	**stern**

Multilingual Summaries

English

Sailing Home: The Story of a Childhood at Sea

Matilda and her family lived on a big sailing ship. Her father was the ship's captain. The family had pets and farm animals on the ship. The children played games on the deck or inside in the main saloon. They learned to send messages with flags. They went to school at the dining table. Their teacher lived on the ship too.

One year, they almost didn't have Christmas. There was a very bad storm. The ship almost sank, but the storm passed. The ship and the family were safe. They had a big Christmas party with good food and presents.

Spanish

Casa de velas: La historia de una niñez en el mar

Matilda y su familia vivían en un gran barco de vela. Su papá era el capitán del barco. La familia tenía mascotas y animales de granja en el barco. Los niños jugaban en la cubierta o en el salón principal. Ellos aprendieron a enviar señales con banderas. Iban a la escuela a mesa del comedor. Su maestra también vivía en el barco.

Un día casi se quedan sin su fiesta de Navidad. Había una tormenta muy fuerte. El barco por poco se hunde. Pero la tormenta pasó. El barco y la familia estaban a salvo. Entonces hicieron una gran fiesta de Navidad con comida deliciosa y muchos regalos.

Multilingual Summaries

Chinese

海上之家

瑪蒂爾達和家人住在一艘帆船上，她的父親是船長。一家人在船上養了很多寵物與牲畜。孩子們都愛在甲板上和大廳裏玩耍，他們還會用旗發信號。餐桌是他們的課堂，老師也住在船上。

可有一年，他們差點過不上聖誕節。猛烈的暴風雨幾乎要淹沒船。不過，他們克服了種種困難，家人和帆船都安全度過了暴風雨。大家準備了許多美味的食物和漂亮的禮物，開了一個非常熱鬧的聖誕晚會。

Vietnamese

Giương Buồm Trở Về

Matilda và gia đình cô sống trên một chiếc thuyền buồm to lớn. Ba của cô là thuyền trưởng. Gia đình có nuôi những con thú nhỏ và những thú vật của nông trại trên thuyền. Các trẻ em chơi các trò chơi trên boong tàu hoặc bên trong phòng khách chính. Các em học cách gửi lời nhắn bằng những lá cờ. Các em đến lớp học ở tại bàn ăn. Thầy giáo của các em cũng sống trên chiếc thuyền này.

Có một năm họ suýt không được mừng lễ Giáng Sinh. Có một cơn bão rất lớn. Chiếc thuyền suýt bị đắm, nhưng cơn bão qua đi. Chiếc thuyền và gia đình được an toàn. Họ có một tiệc Giáng Sinh thịnh soạn với thức ăn ngon và những món quà.

Multilingual Summaries

Korean

항해하는 가족

마틸다의 가족은 커다란 범선에서 산다. 그녀의 아버지는 배의 선장이고 가족은 배 위에서 애완동물과 가축을 키운다. 아이들은 갑판 위나 중앙 홀 안에서 게임을 하며 놀고 깃발을 사용해서 메시지를 보내는 법을 배운다. 그들은 식당 테이블에서 학교 공부를 배우는데 선생님도 그들과 마찬가지로 배 위에서 함께 살고 있다.

어느 해 그들은 크리스마스를 거의 맞지 못할 뻔 한다. 매우 사나운 폭풍이 불었기 때문이다. 배가 거의 가라앉을 뻔했지만 폭풍우는 지나갔고 배와 가족은 이제 모두 무사하다. 그들은 맛있는 음식 및 선물들과 함께 성대한 크리스마스 파티를 벌인다.

Hmong

Caij Nkoj Mus Tsev

Matilda thiab nws tsev neeg nyob saum ib lub nkoj loj loj. Nws txiv yog tus coj saum lub nkoj. Nws tsev neeg muaj aub muaj mov thiab muaj tsiaj txu saum lub nkoj thiab. Cov menyuam ua si nyob rau lub nkoj sab saud thiab hauv qhov chaws nyob loj. Lawv kawm co tus chim kom xa tau xov mus rau luag tej. Lawv kawm ntawv saum lub rooj noj mov. Lawv tus nais khu nyob saum nkoj thiab.

Muaj ib xyoo uas lawv yuav luag tsis tau noj Christmas. Muaj cua daj cua dub thiab loj nag heev. Lub nkoj yuav luag tog tiam si nag cia li tu lawm. Lub nkoj thiab tsev neeg tsis muaj kev txhawj kev ntshai lawm. Lawv tau noj Christmas loj loj nrog zaub mov qab qab thiab tau muaj khoom plig.

Lost City
Student Edition pages 542–553

Week at a Glance	Customize instruction every day for your English Language Learners.				
	Day 1	**Day 2**	**Day 3**	**Day 4**	**Day 5**
Teacher's Edition	Use the ELL Notes that appear throughout each day of the lesson to support instruction and reading.				
ELL Poster 22	• Assess Prior Knowledge • Develop Concepts and Vocabulary	• Preteach Tested Vocabulary	• Our Expedition	• Acting Surprised	• Monitor Progress
ELL Teaching Guide	• Picture It! Lesson, pp. 148–149 • Multilingual Summaries, pp. 152–154	• ELL Reader Lesson, pp. 254–255	• Vocabulary Activities and Word Cards, pp. 150–151 • Multilingual Summaries, pp. 152–154		
ELL Readers	• Reread *The Treasure Fleet*	• Teach *Mexico's Mother Culture*	• Reread *Mexico's Mother Culture* and other texts to build fluency		
ELL and Transition Handbook	Use the following as needed to support this week's instruction and to conduct alternative assessments: • Phonics Transition Lessons • Grammar Transition Lessons • Assessment				

Picture It! Comprehension Lesson

Compare and Contrast

Use this lesson to supplement or replace the skill lesson on pages 538–539 of the Teacher's Edition.

Teach

Distribute copies of the Picture It! blackline master on page 149.

- Have students describe what they see in the illustration. Then read the paragraph aloud.
- Ask: *How was Pompeii different from Herculaneum?*
- Share the Skill Points (at right) with students.
- Have students discuss how Pompeii and Herculaneum were different and alike.

Practice

Read aloud the directions on page 149. Have students fill in the Venn diagram. Have students keep their organizers for later reteaching.

Answers for page 149: *Pompeii*: busy important city, buried by ash and rock; *Both*: ancient cities in what is now Italy, located at bottom of a mountain, buried by eruption, dug up in 1700s; Tourists visit today to see how people lived 2,000 years ago; *Herculaneum*: small, rich town; buried by mud

Skill Points

✓ To **compare** means to tell how two or more things are the same. To **contrast** means to tell how two or more things are different.

✓ Authors may use clue words such as *like, as,* and *same* to show comparisons. They may use clue words such as *but, unlike,* and *different* to show contrasts.

Name ______________________________

Look at the picture. **Read** the paragraph.

- How are Pompeii and Herculaneum alike? **Write** your ideas in the middle section of the Venn diagram.
- How are Pompeii and Herculaneum different? **Write** about their differences in the two side sections of the diagram.

Pompeii and Herculaneum—Ancient Italian Places

Two thousand years ago, Pompeii was a busy, important city in what is now Italy. Herculaneum was a small, rich town nearby. Both were at the bottom of a beautiful mountain. The mountain was a volcano. One day in the year 79, the volcano erupted. Ash and small pieces of rock fell down on Pompeii. Mud covered Herculaneum. Both places were buried. In the 1700s, people discovered the towns. Today, tourists visit them to learn how people lived 2,000 years ago.

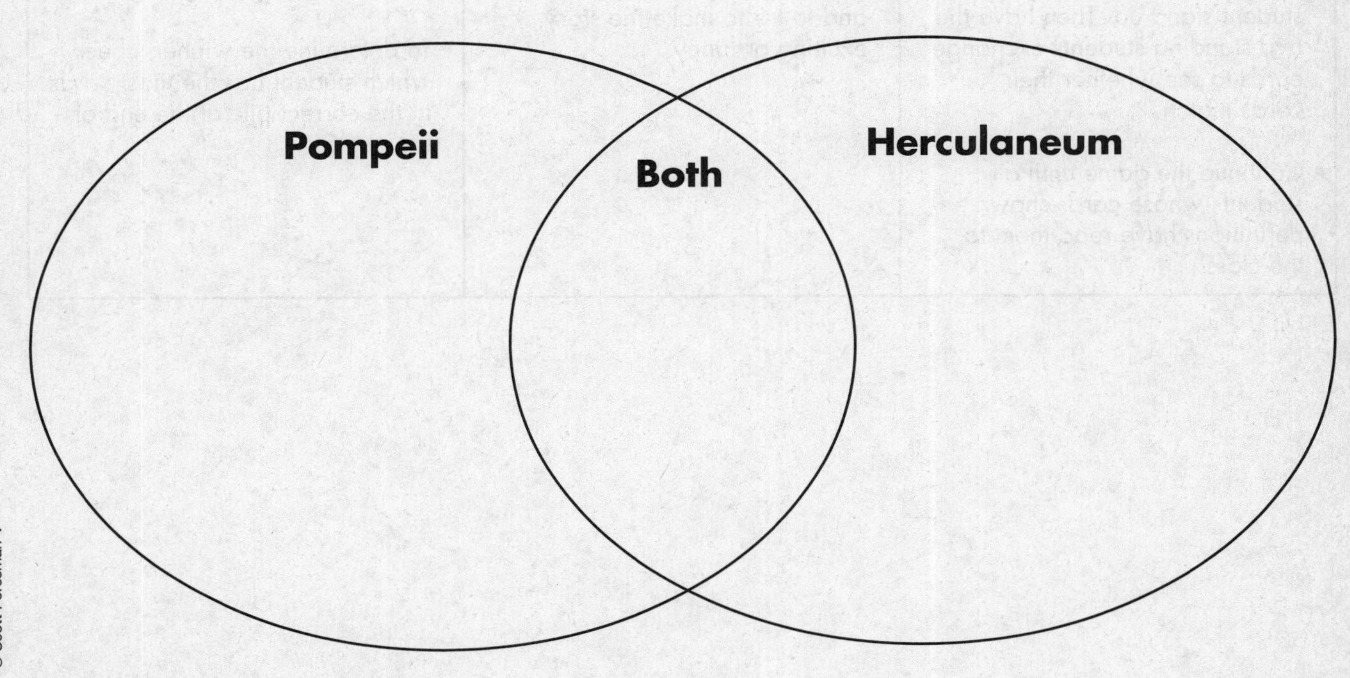

Vocabulary Activities and Word Cards

Copy the Word Cards on page 151 as needed for the following activities.
Use the blank card for an additional word that you want to teach.
Also see suggestions for teaching vocabulary in the ELL and Transition Handbook.

Find Your Partner	Tell a Story	Context Game
• Give one Word Card to each student, making sure that each student in the class has the same card as one other student. • Ask students to write definitions in their own words on the backs of their Word Cards. • Ask half of the students to place their cards on their desks word side up and half of the students to place their cards definition side up. • Have each student whose card has a definition facing up stand, one at a time, and read the definition to the class. • Have all students with word-side-up cards examine their cards to see if they match the definition. If the card matches, have that student stand up. Then have the two standing students exchange cards to see whether their cards match. • Continue the game until all students whose cards show definitions have read them to the class.	• Distribute one set of Word Cards to each student. • Gather the students in a circle and explain that the group will be telling a story together. • Begin the story with a sentence that uses a vocabulary word. • Have the student to your right continue the story, adding a sentence that uses any of the other vocabulary words. • Have each student continue the story, adding a sentence that uses a vocabulary word. • Let students help one another think of sentences that continue the story. • Encourage students to be creative and to try to make the story exciting or funny.	• Give a set of Word Cards to each student. • Have each student write a context sentence for each word on the back of each card. Remind students that context sentences are sentences that show the meaning of the word. Instruct students not to include the vocabulary word in the context sentence but to leave a blank where the word belongs. • Have students form pairs and exchange their cards with the context sides up. • Have students take turns looking at their partner's context sentence and guessing the vocabulary word. Have them discard each card into a correct or incorrect pile, depending on their guess. • To determine the winner, check which student has the most cards in the correct pile at the end of the game.

curiosity

glorious

granite

ruins

terraced

thickets

torrent

Multilingual Summaries

English

Lost City:
The Discovery of Machu Picchu

In 1911, Professor Hiram Bingham went to Peru. He hoped to find the lost city of Vilcapampa. He started in Cusco. There, he saw old stone walls and a stone temple. He knew the lost city would have stones like those.

Bingham went to the village of Ollantaytambo. No one knew about the lost city or about any ruins. Bingham was discouraged. Then he met a farmer who knew of ruins on top of a mountain. He took Bingham to the ruins.

After a long climb through the jungle, Bingham and the farmer met a young boy. The boy took them to an old city covered with vines. It was not Vilcapampa. Bingham had found the lost city of Machu Picchu.

Spanish

La ciudad perdida:
El descubrimiento de Machu Picchu

En 1911, el profesor Hiram Bingham viajó a Perú. Esperaba encontrar la ciudad perdida de Vilcapampa. Comenzó su viaje en Cuzco. Allí vio unas paredes de piedra antiguas y un templo de piedra. Él sabía que la ciudad perdida tendría piedras como ésas.

Bingham fue al pueblo de Ollantaytambo. Nadie sabía nada sobre la ciudad perdida o sobre ningunas ruinas. Bingham estaba desanimado. Luego conoció a un campesino que le dio información sobre unas ruinas en la cima de una montaña. Él llevó a Bingham a las ruinas.

Después de subir a través de la selva, Bingham y el campesino se encontraron con un muchacho. El muchacho los llevó a una antigua ciudad cubierta de enredaderas. No era Vilcapampa. ¡Bingham había encontrado la ciudad perdida de Machu Picchu!

Multilingual Summaries

Chinese

失落之城

1911年，希蘭姆· 賓漢教授前往秘魯，希望找到失落之城韋可帕母帕。他在庫斯科發現了古代的石墻和石廟，他知道韋可帕母帕也有一樣的石塊。

賓漢教授來到歐陽戴丹坡村。可是沒有人知道失落之城，也沒見過殘留的廢墟。賓漢教授非常失望。這時有一個農夫說，他知道山頂上有廢墟，可以帶賓漢教授去考察。

他們穿越叢林爬上了山頂，遇到一個小男孩，領他們去看野藤覆蓋的古代城市。原來它不是韋可帕母帕，而是另一個失落之城馬丘比丘。

Vietnamese

Thành Phố Diệt Vong

Vào năm 1911, Giáo Sư Hiram Bingham đi đến nước Peru. Ông ấy hy vọng tìm ra một thành phố đã diệt vong tên Vilcapampa. Ông bắt đầu ở Cusco. Ở đó, ông thấy những bức tường đá cổ và một đền thờ bằng đá. Ông biết là thành phố bị diệt vong cũng có những viên đá giống như vậy.

Bingham đi đến ngôi làng Ollantaytambo. Không ai biết về thành phố bị diệt vong, hoặc về những tàn tích của thành phố này. Bingham bị nản lòng. Rồi ông gặp một ông nông phu, ông này biết về những tàn tích trên một ngọn núi. Ông dẫn Bingham đến tàn tích này.

Sau một cuộc leo trèo xa xôi xuyên qua rừng, Bingham và bác nhà nông gặp một cậu thiếu niên. Cậu này đưa họ đến thành phố cổ phủ đầy dây leo. Không phải Vilcapampa. Bingham đã tìm ra thành phố diệt vong tên Machu Picchu.

Multilingual Summaries

Korean

잃어버린 도시

1911년 하이램 빙엄 교수는 페루에 갔다. 그는 그곳에서 빌까밤바의 잃어버린 도시를 발견하길 바랬다. 그는 쿠스코에서부터 발굴을 시작했고 거기서 오래된 돌 벽과 돌로 된 신전을 발견했다. 그는 잃어버린 도시에 그와 비슷한 돌들이 있을 것이라고 생각했다.

빙엄은 올란타이탐보의 마을로 갔지만 아무도 잃어버린 도시나 유적에 관해서 알지 못했다. 실망한 빙엄은 그리고 나서 산꼭대기에 있는 유적지에 대해 알고 있던 한 농부를 만났다. 농부는 빙엄을 그 유적지로 데리고 갔다.

정글을 지나 한참을 오른 후 빙엄과 그 농부는 한 어린 소년을 만났다. 그 소년은 덩굴로 뒤덮인 어느 고대 도시로 그들을 데리고 갔다. 하지만 그것은 빌까밤바가 아니었다. 빙엄은 잃어버린 도시인 마추피추를 발견한 것이었다.

Hmong

Lub Zos Uas Xiam Lawm

Nyob rau xyoo ib txhiab cuaj pua kaum ib, tus xibhwb hu ua Hiram Bingham mus rau Peru. Nws cia siab yuav mus nrhiav kom tau lub zos uas xiam lawm uas hu ua Vilcapampa. Nws xub pib nyob rau Cusco. Ntawd, nws pom ib cov phab ntsa pobzeb qub qub thiab ib lub tuam tsev pobzeb. Nws paub tias lus zos uas xiam lawm yuav muaj pobzeb zoo li ntawd thiab.

Bingham mus rau lus zos me me hu ua Ollantaytambo. Tsis muaj leej twg paub txog lub zos ua xiam ntawd lawm, lossis paub txog tej qub zog ntawd li. Bingham tsis muaj siab tag. Ces nws cia li ntsib ib tug neeg ua liaj ua teb uas paub txog ib lub qub zog nyob puag saum ib lub roob. Nws coj Bingham mus rau lub qub zog ntawd.

Tom qab nkawd nce mus siab siab rau puag hauv hav zoov lawm, Bingham thiab tus neeg ua liaj ua teb ntawd ntsib ib tug menyuam tub. Tus menyuam tub ntawd coj nkawd mus rau ib lub qub zog uas hmab ntoo tej muab vov tag lawm. Kuj tsis yog Vilcapampa thiab. Bingham nrhiav tau lub zos xiam lawm uas hu ua Machu Picchu.

Amelia and Eleanor Go for a Ride

Student Edition pages 564–575

Week at a Glance	Customize instruction every day for your English Language Learners.				
	Day 1	**Day 2**	**Day 3**	**Day 4**	**Day 5**
Teacher's Edition	Use the ELL Notes that appear throughout each day of the lesson to support instruction and reading.				
ELL Poster 23	• Assess Prior Knowledge • Develop Concepts and Vocabulary	• Preteach Tested Vocabulary	• A Time Line	• Act Out an Event	• Monitor Progress
ELL Teaching Guide	• Picture It! Lesson, pp. 155–156 • Multilingual Summaries, pp. 159–161	• ELL Reader Lesson, pp. 256–257	• Vocabulary Activities and Word Cards, pp. 157–158 • Multilingual Summaries, pp. 159–161		
ELL Readers	• Reread *Mexico's Mother Culture*	• Teach *Women Who Dared to Fly*	• Reread *Women Who Dared to Fly* and other texts to build fluency		
ELL and Transition Handbook	Use the following as needed to support this week's instruction and to conduct alternative assessments: • Phonics Transition Lessons • Grammar Transition Lessons • Assessment				

Picture It! Comprehension Lesson

Sequence

Use this lesson to supplement or replace the skill lesson on pages 560–561 of the Teacher's Edition.

Teach

Distribute copies of the Picture It! blackline master on page 156.

- Have students look at and describe the pictures. Then read the paragraph aloud.
- Ask: *What do the two pictures show?* (Earhart walking in a parade in 1928; Earhart setting off on her trip around the world in 1937)
- Share the Skill Points (at right) with students.
- Have students discuss the sequence of events in Amelia Earhart's life.

Skill Points

✓ **Sequence** is the order in which events happen in a story.

✓ Sometimes sequence is shown by clue words such as *first, next, then,* and *last*.

✓ Sometimes dates and times are used to show sequence.

✓ Some events may happen at the same time as other events.

Practice

Read aloud the directions on page 156. Have students fill in the time line. Have them keep their time lines for later reteaching.

Answers for page 156: 1897: Amelia Earhart born; 1921: takes first flying lesson; 1928: becomes first woman to fly across Atlantic; 1935: becomes first person to fly solo from Hawaii to California; 1937: tries to become first woman to fly around the world

Name ______________________________

Look at the picture. **Read** the paragraph.

- **Complete** the time line with five dates and events from the life of Amelia Earhart. Be sure to write the dates and events in the order they happened.

Amelia Earhart's Life

Amelia Earhart was born in Kansas in 1897. In 1921, when she was 24 years old, she took her first flying lesson. Just six months later she bought her own plane. In 1928 she joined two men in a flight across the Atlantic Ocean. This made her the first woman ever to cross the ocean in a plane. When they returned, they were greeted by a huge parade in New York City. In 1935 she became the first person to fly solo from Hawaii to California. Two years later she tried to become the first woman to fly around the world.

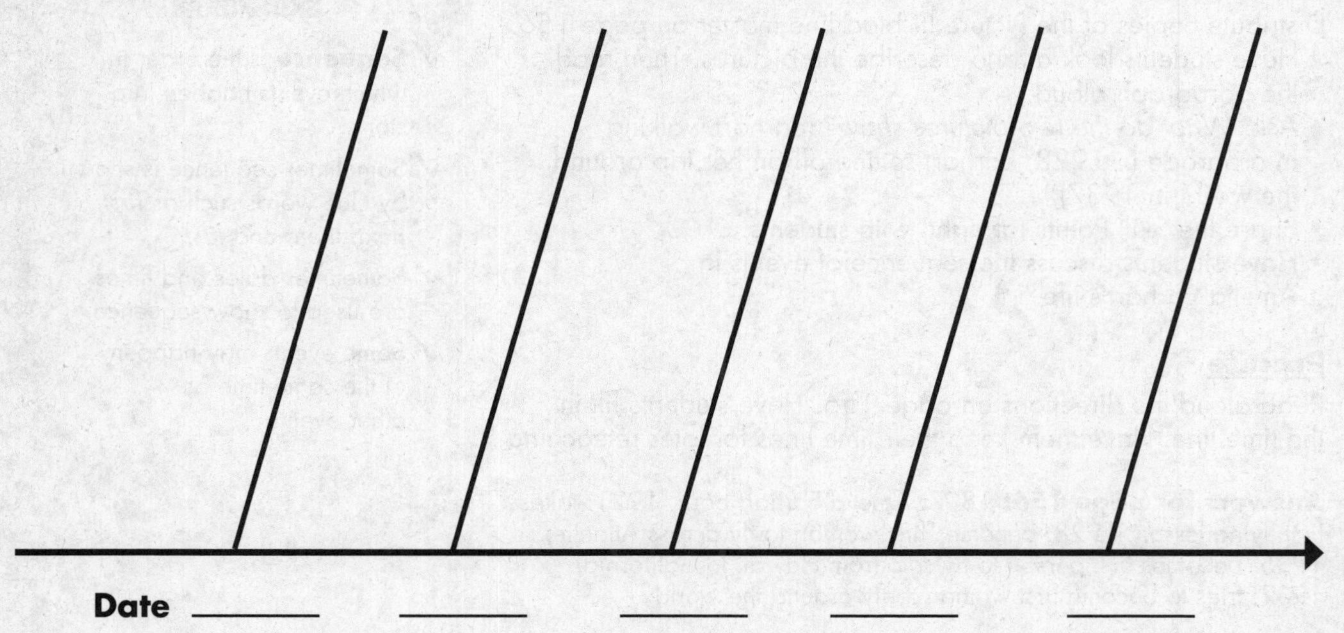

Date ________ ________ ________ ________ ________

Vocabulary Activities and Word Cards

Copy the Word Cards on page 158 as needed for the following activities.
Use the blank card for an additional word that you want to teach.
Also see suggestions for teaching vocabulary in the ELL and Transition Handbook.

Riddle Game	Skits	Poster Clues
• Divide the students into pairs, and give each pair a set of Word Cards. • Have students place the set of Word Cards face down in a pile. • Ask one partner to choose a card and make up a riddle about the word. Provide examples, such as: *I love my job because I always wanted to fly airplanes;* or, *When I have something to say, I say it.* Then have students tell their riddles to their partners. • Have the partner try to guess the word. Then have students switch roles. • Continue the activity until students have created riddles for every vocabulary word.	• Have students form small groups, and give each group a set of Word Cards. • Ask each group to write a short skit that uses all of the vocabulary words. Encourage students to be creative, making their skits interesting, exciting, funny, or silly. Allow them to improvise props and costumes from items in the classroom. • Invite each group to perform its skit for the class.	• Distribute sets of Word Cards to students. Then, from your own set of Word Cards, have one student pick a card without letting the others see it. • The student stands at the ELL Poster, points to the relevant area on it, and uses the information on the Poster to give hints about the vocabulary word. • Other students should try to guess which vocabulary word the student has. The first person to guess correctly may choose the next Word Card and make up clues about it. • Continue until all of the vocabulary words have been used.

aviator

brisk

cockpit

daring

elegant

outspoken

solo

Multilingual Summaries

English

Amelia and Eleanor Go for a Ride

Amelia Earhart and Eleanor Roosevelt were good friends. They both enjoyed adventure. One evening, Eleanor invited Amelia and her husband to a dinner party at the White House.

At dinner, they talked about flying planes. People asked Amelia what it was like to fly at night. Eleanor asked what the capital city looked like at night. Amelia asked Eleanor to take a short flight that night to see. Eleanor agreed.

It was a beautiful flight. Both women enjoyed it. When they got back to the White House, they decided to take Eleanor's new car for a drive around the city. They came back for dessert.

Spanish

Amelia y Eleanor dan un paseo

Amelia Earhart y Eleanor Roosevelt eran buenas amigas. Las dos disfrutaban la aventura. Una tarde, Eleanor invitó a Amelia y a su esposo a una cena en la Casa Blanca.

En la cena, hablaron sobre pilotear aviones. La gente le preguntó a Amelia qué se sentía al volar de noche. Eleanor le preguntó cómo se veía la ciudad capital en la noche. Amelia invitó a Eleanor a volar un poco esa noche para saberlo. Eleanor estuvo de acuerdo.

Fue un viaje maravilloso. Las dos mujeres lo disfrutaron. Cuando regresaron a la Casa Blanca, decidieron ir en el auto nuevo de Eleanor para dar una vuelta por la ciudad. Regresaron a la hora del postre.

Multilingual Summaries

Chinese

阿米莉亞和埃莉諾一起飛行

阿米莉亞和埃莉諾是好朋友，她們都非常喜歡冒險。一天晚上，埃莉諾邀請阿米莉亞和她丈夫參加白宮的宴會。

宴會上，她們談到飛機。人們都問阿米莉亞，夜間飛行是什麼感覺？埃莉諾還問，從空中俯視夜晚的首都是什麼樣子的？阿米莉亞請埃莉諾一起飛行，親自去體驗一番。埃莉諾高興地同意了。

這真是一次美妙的飛行，兩人都非常快樂。返回白宮前，她們還決定乘埃莉諾的新車周游全城。回來時正好趕上吃甜點呢！

Vietnamese

Amelia và Eleanor Đi Chơi

Amelia Earhart và Eleanor Roosevelt là bạn thân. Cả hai người đều thích phiêu lưu mạo hiểm. Một tối nọ, Eleanor mời Amelia và chồng của bà ấy đến một bữa tiệc ăn tối tại Tòa Bạch Ốc.

Trong bữa ăn, họ nói chuyện về việc bay các máy bay. Người ta hỏi Amelia về việc bay trong đêm tối. Eleanor hỏi thủ đô trông như thế nào vào ban đêm. Amelia mời Eleanor bay một chuyến bay ngắn vào tối hôm đó để được xem. Eleanor đồng ý.

Đó là một chuyến bay tuyệt đẹp. Cả hai phụ nữ đều thích thú. Khi họ trở về Tòa Bạch Ốc, họ quyết định lái chiếc xe mới của Eleanor đi vòng quanh thành phố. Họ quay trở về để ăn tráng miệng.

Multilingual Summaries

Korean

드라이브하는 아멜리아와 엘레노어

아멜리아 에어하트와 엘레노어 루즈벨트는 친한 친구 사이였고 둘 다 모험을 즐겼다. 어느 날 저녁 엘레노어는 아멜리아 부부를 백악관의 저녁 파티에 초대했다.

저녁을 먹으며 그들은 비행기를 모는 것에 대해서 이야기를 나누었다. 사람들은 아멜리아에게 야간 비행이 어떤 것과 같으냐고 물었고 엘레노어는 밤에 수도가 어떻게 보이냐고 물었다. 아멜리아는 엘레노어에게 그 날 밤 짧은 야간 비행을 하자고 요청했고 엘레노어는 수락했다.

참으로 아름다운 비행이었고 두 여인 모두 즐겁게 비행했다. 그들이 백악관으로 돌아왔을 때 그들은 엘레노어의 새 차를 타고 도시 주변을 드라이브하기로 했다. 나중에 그들은 디저트를 먹기 위해 백악관으로 돌아왔다.

Hmong

Amelia thiab Eleanor Mus Caij Tsheb Ua Si

Amelia Earhart thiab Eleanor Roosevelt nkawd yog ob tug phooj ywg zoo heev. Nkawd ob leeg nyiam mus ua si mus xyuas tej yam tshiab. Muaj ib hmo, Eleanor caw Amelia thiab nws tus txiv tuaj noj hmo pem Lub Tsev Dawb.

Thaum lawm noj mov, lawv tham txog kev ya nyoj hoom. Neeg nug Amelia tias seb ya nyoj hoom thaum tsaus ntuj zoo li cas. Eleanor nug nws tias seb lub nroog capital zoo li cas thaum tsaus ntuj. Amelia nug kom Eleanor kav tsij mus caij nyoj hoom ib pliag hmo ntawd kom nws pom seb zoo li cas. Eleanor kam kiag.

Caij nyoj hoom hmo ntawd mas zoo nkauj heev. Ob tug poj niam ntawd nyiam kawg. Thaum nkawd rov qab los txog pem Tsev Dawb, nkawd txiav txim siab mus caij Eleanor lub tsheb tshiab ncig zos. Nkawd rov qab los noj qhob noom.

Antarctic Journal Student Edition pages 586–601

Week at a Glance	Customize instruction every day for your English Language Learners.				
	Day 1	**Day 2**	**Day 3**	**Day 4**	**Day 5**
Teacher's Edition	Use the ELL Notes that appear throughout each day of the lesson to support instruction and reading.				
ELL Poster 24	• Assess Prior Knowledge • Develop Concepts and Vocabulary	• Preteach Tested Vocabulary	• Interviews	• Moving Is Like Exploring	• Monitor Progress
ELL Teaching Guide	• Picture It! Lesson, pp. 162–163 • Multilingual Summaries, pp. 166–168	• ELL Reader Lesson, pp. 258–259	• Vocabulary Activities and Word Cards, pp. 164–165 • Multilingual Summaries, pp. 166–168		
ELL Readers	• Reread *Women Who Dared to Fly*	• Teach *Antarctica*	• Reread *Antarctica* and other texts to build fluency		
ELL and Transition Handbook	Use the following as needed to support this week's instruction and to conduct alternative assessments: • Phonics Transition Lessons • Grammar Transition Lessons • Assessment				

Picture It! Comprehension Lesson

Main Idea and Details

Use this lesson to supplement or replace the skill lesson on pages 582–583 of the Teacher's Edition.

Teach

Distribute copies of the Picture It! blackline master on page 163.

- Have students look at and describe the picture. Then read the paragraph aloud.
- Ask: *What is the main idea of this paragraph?* (It was hard to survive on Earth 20,000 years ago, because it was very cold.)
- Share the Skill Points (at right) with students.
- Have students find the details that support the main idea.

Practice

Read aloud the directions on page 163. Have students complete the graphic organizer. Have them keep their organizers for later reteaching.

Answers for page 163: Possible response: *Main Idea:* It was hard to survive on Earth 20,000 years ago, because it was very cold. *Supporting Details:* Ice covered the northern part of the Earth. Only short grass and trees could grow. Only strong people and animals with thick fur coats could survive.

Skill Points

✓ A **topic** is what a text is about.

✓ The **main idea** is the most important idea about the topic.

✓ **Supporting details** give small pieces of information about the main idea.

Name ______________________________

Main Idea and Details

Look at the picture. **Read** the paragraph.

- What is the main idea of this paragraph? **Write** the main idea in the box below.
- What details support the main idea? **Write** the details in the boxes below.

An Age of Ice

Twenty thousand years ago, ice sheets, called glaciers, covered the northern parts of the Earth. The Earth was so cold that it was hard for plants and animals to survive. Only short grasses and trees could grow. Only strong people and animals could survive. Early humans, wolves, bears, and long-toothed tigers lived during this time. They had thick fur coats to help them survive in the icy world.

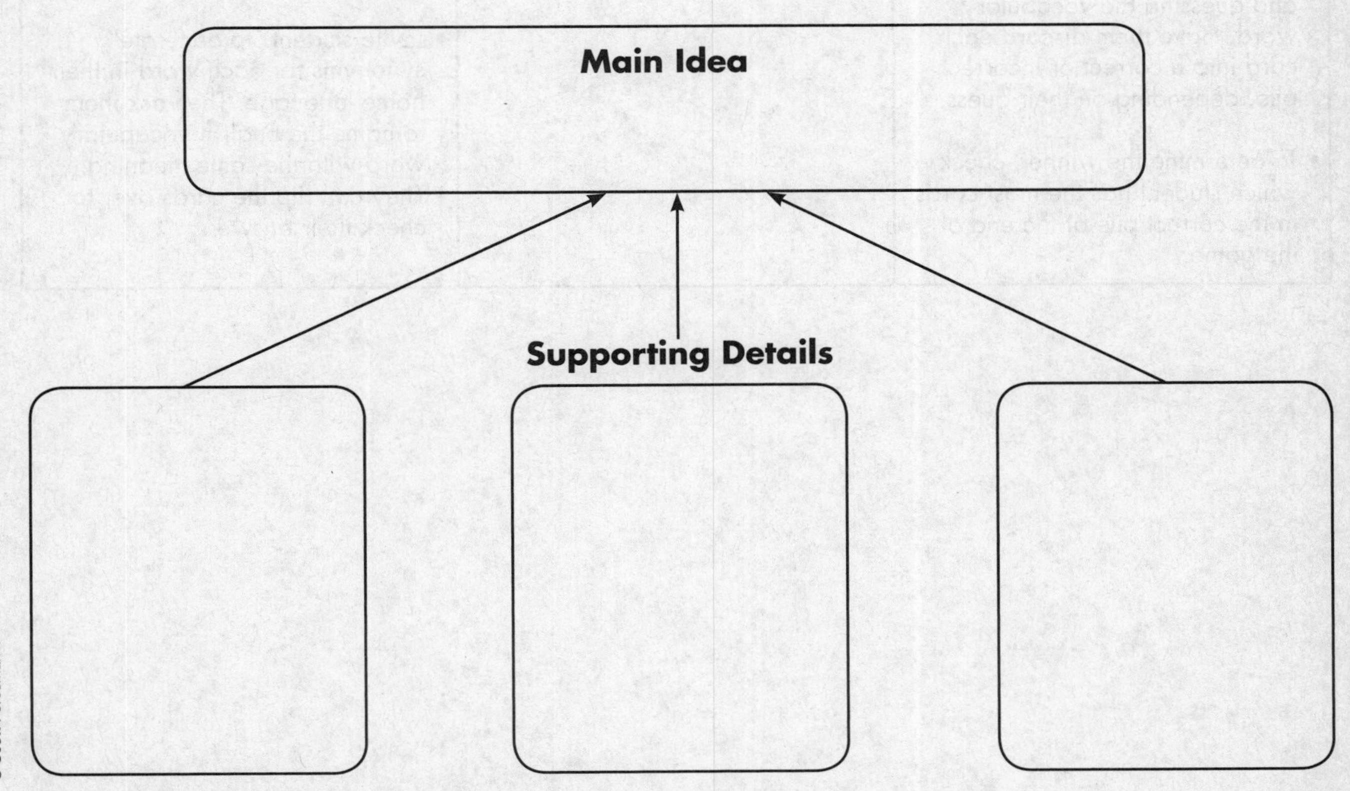

Vocabulary Activities and Word Cards

Copy the Word Cards on page 165 as needed for the following activities.
Use the blank card for an additional word that you want to teach.
Also see suggestions for teaching vocabulary in the ELL and Transition Handbook.

Context Game	What Is This?	Home Language Clues
• Give a set of Word Cards to each student. • Have each student write a context sentence for each word on the back of each card. Remind students that context sentences are sentences that show the meaning of the word. Instruct students not to include the vocabulary word in the context sentence, but to leave a blank where the word belongs. • Have students form pairs and exchange their cards with the context side up. • Have students take turns looking at their partner's context sentence and guessing the vocabulary word. Have them discard each card into a correct or incorrect pile, depending on their guess. • To determine the winner, check which student has the most cards in the correct pile at the end of the game.	• Divide the class into pairs, and reproduce several sets of Word Cards. • Give two or three Word Cards to each pair of students. • Have pairs write definitions or draw simple illustrations on the back of each card. • Then, have each pair of students show their pictures or read their definitions to the other pairs and ask them to guess the words.	• Create one set of Word Cards for each student. • Pair students who have writing proficiency in the same home language, and give each student a set of Word Cards. • Have students work together to write translations of the vocabulary words in their home language on the back of each card. (See the Multilingual Lesson Vocabulary beginning on page 272 for suggested translations.) • Have partners lay out the cards with the home language side facing up. • Invite students to generate synonyms for each word in their home language. Then ask them to name the English vocabulary word with the same meaning. They can flip the cards over to check their answers.

anticipation

continent

convergence

depart

forbidding

heaves

icebergs

Multilingual Summaries

English

Antarctic Journal

Jennifer Owings Dewey kept a journal during her trip to Antarctica. She flew in a plane to Chile. Then she took a boat to Palmer Station. During the trip, the boat stopped to let whales pass by.

The camp was cold. The weather was often dangerous. Everyone followed safety rules.

Dewey spent time exploring. She visited islands and old base camps. At one of the old camps, she watched a colony of penguins. She saw orca whales hunting for food.

The sun never sets in Antarctica. The sun keeps many people awake. When she could not sleep, she wrote letters. She ate krill, a kind of plankton, with the other people in her camp.

Early one morning, she climbed a glacier. The summer sun had made cracks in the glacier. She almost fell through. But she made it back to camp. Jennifer Owings Dewey had many wonderful adventures to remember.

Spanish

El diario de la Antártida

Jennifer Owings Dewey escribió un diario del viaje que hizo a la Antártida. Primero voló en un avión a Chile y después tomó un bote para llegar a la estación Palmer. Durante el viaje, el bote se detuvo para dejar pasar a las ballenas.

El campamento era frío. Con frecuencia, el tiempo era peligroso. Todos seguían las reglas de seguridad.

Dewey dedicó tiempo a explorar. Visitó las islas y los viejos campamentos. En uno de los viejos campamentos vio una colonia de pingüinos. Vio ballenas orca cazando para comer.

En la Antártida el sol nunca se pone. El sol mantiene a mucha gente despierta. Cuando no podía dormir, Jennifer escribía cartas. Comió kril, un tipo de plancton, con la otra gente del campamento.

Una mañana, temprano, la autora escalaba un glaciar. El sol del verano había hecho grietas al glaciar y ella casi se cae, pero pudo regresar al campamento sin problemas. La autora tenía muchas aventuras maravillosas para recordar.

Multilingual Summaries

Chinese

南極日誌
四個月的極地生活

作家杜薇去南極旅行時，把每天的活動都記在日誌上。她先是乘飛機到智利，然後坐船去帕默研究站。途中，船還停下來讓大鯨魚先通過。

研究站的天氣非常寒冷，經常會有各種危險，因此每個人都要嚴格遵守安全規定。

杜薇經常尋訪南極各地，看過許多島嶼與以前留下的舊營地。還曾在那裏觀察一群企鵝，看見逆戟鯨獵食。

南極的太陽永遠不下山，令許多人睡不著。難以入睡時，杜薇經常寫寫書信。她和研究站裏的人一樣也吃磷蝦，這是一種浮游生物。

有一天清晨，她去爬冰川。夏季的陽光融化出許多冰縫，杜薇差點掉進去，但她還是努力克服困難返回營地。南極的經歷真是非常奇妙令人難忘！

Vietnamese

Nhật Ký ở Nam Cực
Bốn Tháng ở Tận Cùng Thế Giới

Jennifer Owings Dewey viết nhật ký trong suốt chuyến đi của cô đến Nam Cực. Cô bay đến Chilê. Rồi cô đi bằng thuyền đến Trạm Palmer. Trong chuyến đi này, chiếc thuyền ngừng để cho các cá voi đi qua.

Trại lạnh. Thời tiết thường nguy hiểm. Mọi người đều tuân theo các quy định an toàn.

Dewey dành thì giờ để thám hiểm. Cô tham quan các đảo và các trại căn cứ cũ. Tại một trong những trại cũ, cô quan sát bầy chim cánh cụt. Cô thấy những con cá voi orca đi săn mồi.

Mặt trời không bao giờ lặn ở Nam Cực. Mặt trời làm cho nhiều người không ngủ được. Khi cô không ngủ được, cô viết những lá thư. Cô ăn những con tôm nhỏ tí, một loại sinh vật phù du, với những người khác ở trại.

Một buổi sáng sớm, cổ trèo lên một khối băng. Trời mùa hè làm khối băng nứt nhiều chỗ. Cô suýt bị lọt vào trong khối băng. Nhưng cô ấy trở về trại được. Jennifer Owings Deweỷ có nhiều cuộc phiêu lưu tuyệt vời để ghi nhớ.

Multilingual Summaries

Korean

남극 일기
지구 최남단에서의 4개월

제니퍼 오잉스 듀이는 남극 여행 동안 일기를 적었다. 그녀는 비행기를 타고 칠레에 갔고 거기서 또 배를 타고 팔머 스테이션으로 갔다. 항해 중 고래들이 지나가도록 배가 멈추기도 했다.

캠프는 추웠다. 날씨는 가끔 위험스러울 정도였고 모든 이들이 안전 수칙을 따랐다.

듀이는 탐험을 하며 시간을 보냈고 주변 섬들과 오래된 베이스 캠프을 방문했다. 오래된 캠프 중 한 곳에서 그녀는 펭귄들의 서식지와 먹이를 사냥하는 범고래를 보았다.

남극에서의 태양은 결코 지지 않으며 많은 사람들을 깨어있게 한다. 잠을 이룰 수 없을 때 그녀는 작가가 되어 편지를 썼다. 그녀는 캠프에서 다른 사람들과 함께 플랑크톤의 일종인 크릴새우를 먹었다.

어느 날 아침 일찍 작가는 빙하를 올라갔다. 여름의 태양이 빙하에 균열을 내 놓았다. 그녀는 갈라진 틈 사이로 떨어질 뻔했지만 가까스로 캠프로 다시 돌아왔다. 작가는 잊지 못할 멋진 경험들을 많이 갖게 됐다.

Hmong

Phaum Ntawv Sau Txog Antartic
Plaub Hlis Nyob Rau Sab Hauv Qab Ntiaj Teb No

Jennifer Owings Dewey khaws ib phau ntawd uas nws sau thaum nws mus rau Antartica. Nws ya nyoj hoom mus rau Chile. Ces nws caij ib lub nkoj mus rau Palmer Station. Thaum mus rau qhov ntawd, lub nkoj tau nres thiaj li cia tau cov ntses hiav txwv loj (whales) hla dhau lawm.

Lub chaws sob no kawg. Feem ntau mas, huab cua kuj txaus ntshai kawg. Txhua leej txhua tus ua zoo ua raws li kevcai ceeb faj.

Dewey tau siv sij hawm mus taug kev ncig xyuas ub no thiab. Nws tau mus xyuas tej koog pov txwv thiab tej chaws sob qub. Nyob rau ntawm ib qhov chaws sob qub, nws ntsia ib pab noog ntses uas tsuas nyob pem saum nabkuab thiab hauv hiavtxwv txias txias xwb (penguin). Nws pom ib cov ntses hiavtxwv loj hu ua orca no nrhiav mov noj.

Nyob Antartica mas lub hnub yeej tsis poob li. Lub hnub ua rau sawvdaws tsis paub pw. Thaum nws pw tsis tau, tus sau ntawd sau ntawv. Nws noj krill, ua yog ib yam nroj nyob hauv hiavtxwv, nrog cov neeg uas nrog nws sob ntawm lub chaws sob ntawd thiab.

Muaj ib tag kis txov txov, tus sau ntawv nce mus rau saum ib lub roob nab kuab. Lub hnub ntawm lub caij ntuj sov ntawd tau rau lub roob nab kuab ntawd thawg pleb. Nws yuav luag poob hauv. Tiam sis, nws rov mus tau txog rau pem qhov chaws sob lawm. Tus sau ntawd muaj ntau zaj nco txog.

Moonwalk Student Edition pages 612–623

Week at a Glance	Customize instruction every day for your English Language Learners.				
	Day 1	**Day 2**	**Day 3**	**Day 4**	**Day 5**
Teacher's Edition	Use the ELL Notes that appear throughout each day of the lesson to support instruction and reading.				
ELL Poster 25	• Assess Prior Knowledge • Develop Concepts and Vocabulary	• Preteach Tested Vocabulary	• Tell the Story	• Picture This	• Monitor Progress
ELL Teaching Guide	• Picture It! Lesson, pp. 169–170 • Multilingual Summaries, pp. 173–175	• ELL Reader Lesson, pp. 260–261	• Vocabulary Activities and Word Cards, pp. 171–172 • Multilingual Summaries, pp. 173–175		
ELL Readers	• Reread *Antarctica*	• Teach *Moons of Our Solar System*	• Reread *Moons of Our Solar System* and other texts to build fluency		
ELL and Transition Handbook	Use the following as needed to support this week's instruction and to conduct alternative assessments: • Phonics Transition Lessons • Grammar Transition Lessons • Assessment				

Picture It! Comprehension Lesson

Draw Conclusions

Use this lesson to supplement or replace the skill lesson on pages 608–609 of the Teacher's Edition.

Teach

Distribute copies of the Picture It! blackline master on page 170.

- Have students look at and describe the picture.Then read the paragraph aloud.
- Ask: *How do people live on Mars?* (very differently from people on Earth)
- Share the Skill Points (at right) with students.
- Have students find details that support their conclusion about life on Mars.

Skill Points

✓ The small pieces of information in a piece of writing are called **facts** and **details.**

✓ When you put those facts and details together, you can make a judgment or **draw a conclusion** about the text.

Practice

Read aloud the directions on page 170. Have students complete the graphic organizer. Have them keep their organizers for later reteaching.

Answers for page 170: *Conclusion:* Possible response: The lives of people on Mars are very different from those of people on Earth. *Supporting Details:* Children drink their breakfast, wear space suits, and take a space mobile to school. Schools have oxygen stations, flying vehicles, robots, and numbers instead of names.

Name ______________________________

Draw Conclusions

Look at the picture. **Read** the paragraph.

- What conclusion can you make about how people live on Mars? **Write** your conclusion in the box below.
- What details help you make that conclusion? **Write** the details in the boxes below.

A New Day on Mars

Jena and Jed were drinking their breakfasts in their Mars home. Mom was rushing about the kitchen. "I cleaned your space suits," she said. "And I put an extra battery in. I know you want to have plenty of energy today." Four new students were joining their class. Jena and Jed couldn't wait to show them how to use the school's oxygen station and the flying machines. They wanted to introduce the students to the school's robots too. "Beep!" The space mobile was waiting. Jena and Jed threw on their helmets and ran outside. They were sure the new students were going to like Mars School X-241.

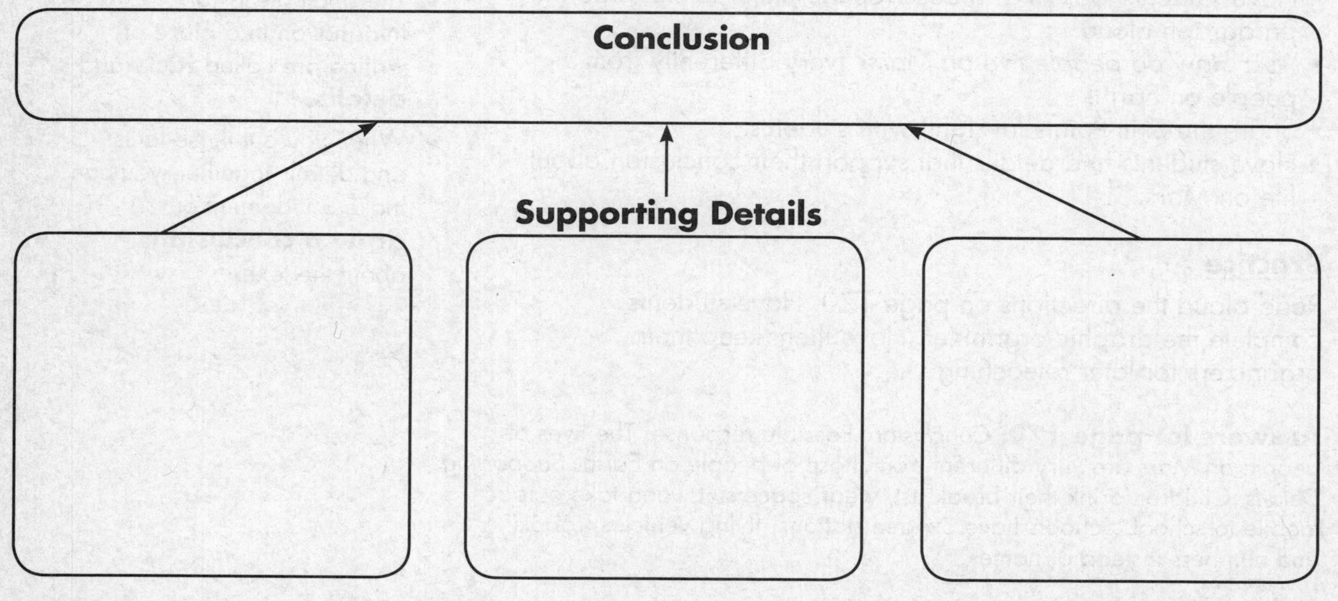

Vocabulary Activities and Word Cards

Copy the Word Cards on page 172 as needed for the following activities.
Use the blank cards for additional words that you want to teach.
Also see suggestions for teaching vocabulary in the ELL and Transition Handbook.

Definition Concentration	Find Your Partner	Past and Present Tense
• Create one set of Word Cards and eight blank cards for every pair of students. • Have pairs of students work together to write definitions for each word on the blank cards. Remind students that a definition tells what a word means. • Have students place the Word Cards and definition cards face down in rows on a table. • Instruct students to take turns turning over two cards and looking for a matched pair. A matched pair is a Word Card and its definition card. When a student finds a matched pair, the student keeps the cards. • To determine the winner, check which student has the most cards at the end of the game.	• Give one Word Card to each student, making sure that each student in the class has the same card as one other student. • Ask students to write definitions in their own words on the backs of their Word Cards. • Ask half of the students to place their cards on their desks word side up and half of the students to place their cards definition side up. • Have each student whose card has a definition facing up stand, one at a time, and read the definition to the class. • Have all students with word-side-up cards examine their cards to see if they match the definition. If a card matches, have that student stand up. Then have the two standing students exchange cards to see whether their cards match. • Continue the game until all students whose cards show definitions have read them to the class.	• Reproduce one set of Word Cards for each student. • Have students place all of the Word Cards facing up on the desk or table in front of them. • Remind them what a verb is. Then have them put all of the verbs in a pile. • Remind them how to identify a past tense verb. Then have them pull all of the past tense verbs out of the pile. • Have one student read each word and another student try to explain what it means. • Continue the exercise until all students have had the opportunity to participate.

loomed	**staggered**
summoning	**taunted**
trench	**trudged**
rille	**runt**

Multilingual Summaries

English

Moonwalk

Gerry and Vern Kandel visit the moon with their father. Vern always calls Gerry "Runt." Their father goes to work, and tells the boys to stay inside the shelter. But Vern wants to go for a moonwalk.

Vern dares Gerry to jump over rilles. Gerry jumps over a very big one, but Vern does not. Vern falls into the rille and hurts his leg. His moonsuit loses power. Gerry helps Vern to climb out of the rille and walk back to the shelter. They must get back before sunrise. Without power, Vern's moonsuit will get too hot, and he may run out of air.

Gerry takes Vern all the way back. Vern thanks him for saving his life. Vern promises never to call Gerry "Runt" again.

Spanish

Paseo lunar

Gerry y Vern Kandel visitan la Luna con su papá. Vern siempre llama a Gerry "Pequeño". Su papá se va a trabajar y le dice a los niños que se queden dentro del refugio. Pero Vern quiere dar un paseo lunar.

Vern desafía a Gerry a saltar sobre los *rilles* (valles lunares). Gerry salta uno muy grande, pero Vern no lo hace. Vern se cae dentro de un *rille* y se hace daño en la pierna. Su traje espacial pierde poder. Gerry ayuda a Vern a salir del *rille* y a regresar al refugio. Ellos tienen que llegar antes del amanecer. Sin poder, el traje lunar de Vern se calentará demasiado y puede quedarse sin aire.

Gerry lleva a Vern todo el camino de vuelta. Vern le da las gracias por salvarle la vida. Vern le promete que nunca más lo volverá a llamar "Pequeño".

Multilingual Summaries

Chinese

月球漫步

格裏、弗恩和他們的爸爸一起來到月球。弗恩常把格裏叫做“矮子”。爸爸去上班時，囑咐他們不要走出生活站，可是弗恩非常想出去做月球漫步。

弗恩慫恿格裏跳月球溝。格裏一下跳過很寬的溝，但弗恩沒跳過。他掉進溝裏，摔傷了腳，而且月球服也弄壞了，失去了電力。格裏把弗恩拉出深溝，扶著他往回走。他們必須在太陽升起前趕回生活站，不然弄壞了的月球服會很燙，而且弗恩的氧氣也會用完。

一路上全靠格裏的幫助，他們安全返回。弗恩非常感謝格裏救了他，發誓以後再也不叫他“矮子”。

Vietnamese

Đi Trên Mặt Trăng

Gerry và Vern Kandel đến mặt trăng với ba của họ. Vern lúc nào cũng gọi Gerry là “Runt” (thằng nhóc tì). Ba của họ đi làm, và dặn các cậu con trai ở trong khu trú ẩn. Nhưng Vern muốn được đi trên mặt trăng.

Vern thách thức Gerry nhảy qua các rãnh trên mặt trăng. Gerry nhảy qua một rãnh rất lớn, nhưng Vern không nhảy qua được. Vern bị rơi vào rãnh này và bị thương ở chân. Bộ đồ để mặc trên mặt trăng của nó bị mất năng lượng. Gerry giúp Vern leo ra khỏi cái rãnh và đi trở về khu trú ẩn. Họ phải trở về trước bình minh. Không có năng lượng bộ đồ mặt trăng của Vern sẽ trở nên rất nóng, và nó có thể bị hết khí để thở.

Gerry đưa Vern trở về. Vern cám ơn cậu bé đã cứu sống nó. Vern hứa không bao giờ gọi Gerry là “Runt” nữa.

Multilingual Summaries

Korean

달 산책

게리와 번 캔들은 아버지와 함께 달을 방문한다. 번은 게리를 항상 "꼬마" 라고 부른다. 아버지는 일을 하러 나가며 두 아들에게 숙소 안에 남아 있으라고 하지만 번은 달을 산책하고 싶어한다.

번이 게리보고 골짜기를 뛰어 넘어 보라고 하자 게리는 굉장히 큰 골짜기를 뛰어 넘는다. 하지만 번은 하지 않는다. 번은 골짜기로 떨어져서 다리를 다치게 된다. 그러자 그의 우주복이 동력을 잃어버리고 게리는 번이 골짜기 밖으로 나오도록 도운 후 숙소로 걸어 돌아간다. 그들은 해가 지기 전까지 돌아가야만 하지만 동력이 떨어진 번의 우주복은 너무 뜨거워져서 산소가 바닥 날지도 모른다.

게리는 번을 데리고 숙소까지 내내 간다. 번은 게리에게 자신의 생명을 구해 준 데 대해 고마워하고 게리를 다시는 "꼬마" 라고 부르지 않겠다며 약속한다.

Hmong

Nchim Lub Hli

Gerry thiab Vern Kandel nkawd mus xyuas lub hli nrog nkawd txiv. Vern yeej muab Gerry hu ua "Runt" tas mus li. Nkawd txiv mus ua hauj lwm, thiab hais rau ob tug tub tias kom nkawd nyob twj ywm hauv tsev. Tiam si Vern xav mus ncig lub hli.

Vern npav seb Gerry dhia puas dhau tej hav sauv. Gerry dhia dhau ib lub hav loj kawg, tiam sis Vern dhia tsis tau dhau. Vern poob rau hauv ib lub hav thiab ua raug nws txais ceg mob. Lub cev khaub ncaws hli poob hwj chim tag lawm. Gerry pab Vern nce tawm ntawm lub hav thiab rov qab mus tsev. Nkawd yuav tsum rov mus txog tsev ua ntej hnub tuaj. Vim Vern ces khaub ncaws tsis muaj xuj cim lawm nws yuav sov heev tuaj, thiab nws yuav tsis tau pab lawm los kuj muaj thiab.

Gerry coj Vern rov qab mus txog duab tsev. Vern ua nws tsaug uas nws tau cawm nws txog siab. Vern cog lus tias nws yuav tsis muab Gerry hu ua "Runt" tsiv lawm.

My Brother Martin Student Edition pages 642–654

Week at a Glance	Customize instruction every day for your English Language Learners.				
	Day 1	**Day 2**	**Day 3**	**Day 4**	**Day 5**
Teacher's Edition	Use the ELL Notes that appear throughout each day of the lesson to support instruction and reading.				
ELL Poster 26	• Assess Prior Knowledge • Develop Concepts and Vocabulary	• Preteach Tested Vocabulary	• Comic Strips	• Ten Questions	• Monitor Progress
ELL Teaching Guide	• Picture It! Lesson, pp. 176–177 • Multilingual Summaries, pp. 180–182	• ELL Reader Lesson, pp. 262–263	• Vocabulary Activities and Word Cards, pp. 178–179 • Multilingual Summaries, pp. 180–182		
ELL Readers	• Reread *Moons of Our Solar System*	• Teach *Ralph Bunche*	• Reread *Ralph Bunche* and other texts to build fluency		
ELL and Transition Handbook	Use the following as needed to support this week's instruction and to conduct alternative assessments: • Phonics Transition Lessons • Grammar Transition Lessons • Assessment				

Picture It! Comprehension Lesson

Cause and Effect

Use this lesson to supplement or replace the skill lesson on pages 638–639 of the Teacher's Edition.

Teach

Distribute copies of the Picture It! blackline master on page 177.

- Have students tell you what they see in the picture. Then read the paragraph aloud.
- Ask: *What caused schools to be unequal in the South?* (laws that forced African American and white children to go to different schools)
- Share the Skill Points (at right) with students.

Practice

Read aloud the directions on page 177. Have students underline the cause-and-effect clue words. Then ask them to fill in the causes and effects. Have students keep their organizers for later reteaching.

Skill Points

✓ The **effect** is the event that happens. The **cause** is what makes it happen.

✓ Clue words such as *so, therefore, because,* and *as a result* can show causes and effects.

Answers for page 177: *Cause-and-effect clue words:* so, because; *Cause:* She wasn't allowed to go to the school closer to her home. *Effect:* Separate schools for people of different skin colors are illegal.

Name ______________________________

Look at the picture. **Read** the paragraph.

- **Underline** the cause-and-effect clue words in the paragraph.
- **Write** the cause for the effect shown.
- **Write** the effect for the cause shown.

Fighting for Equal Schools

Linda Brown grew up in Topeka, Kansas, during the 1950s. At that time, white children and African American children could not go to the same school in many states. The school closest to Linda's home was for white children only, so she could not go to it. Because of the law, she had to walk a mile to get to school every morning. Linda's father thought the law separating children by skin color was unfair. He went to court to force the white school to accept his daughter. He won his case. Because of what he did, separate schools for people of different skin colors are not legal in the United States.

Cause		Effect
	→	Linda Brown had to walk a mile every morning to get to school.
Linda's father went to court to win the right for African American children to attend all schools.	→	

Vocabulary Activities and Word Cards

Copy the Word Cards on page 179 as needed for the following activities.
Use the blank card for an additional word that you want to teach.
Also see suggestions for teaching vocabulary in the ELL and Transition Handbook.

Cloze Sentences	Riddle Game	Skits
• Give each student a set of Word Cards and two pieces of paper. • Have students write one sentence using each vocabulary word. • On a second sheet of paper, have students rewrite each sentence, replacing the vocabulary word with a line. • Divide the class into pairs. Have each pair exchange the papers with their cloze sentences and try to fill in the missing vocabulary words. Have partners check one another's work.	• Divide the students into pairs, and give each pair a set of Word Cards. • Have students place the set of Word Cards face down in a pile. • Ask one partner to choose a card and make up a riddle about the word. Provide examples, such as: *These people never knew me, even though they are related to me;* or, *This person stands up and speaks to the people in a church.* Then have students tell their riddles to their partners. • Have the partner try to guess the word. Then have students switch roles. • Continue the activity until students have created riddles for every vocabulary word.	• Have students form small groups, and give each group a set of Word Cards. • Ask each group to write a short skit that uses all of the vocabulary words. Encourage students to be creative, making their skits interesting, exciting, funny, or silly. Allow them to improvise props and costumes from items in the classroom. • Invite each group to perform its skit for the class.

ancestors

avoided

generations

minister

numerous

pulpit

shielding

Multilingual Summaries

English

My Brother Martin

Christine was the sister of Martin Luther King, Jr., and their brother Alfred Daniel. The family called the boys M. L. and A. D.

They lived in a town with unfair laws. The laws kept black people separate from white people.

M. L. and A. D. played with the white boys across the street. One day, the boys across the street said that they could not play together anymore because M. L. and A. D. were black. The children did not understand. Their mother explained that many white people did not understand that everyone is the same. M. L. wanted to change this.

His father showed him how to stand up for what is right. Later, M. L. gave speeches and organized marches. The speeches and marches helped end the unfair laws. He dreamed a dream that changed the world.

Spanish

Mi hermano Martin

Martin Luther King, Jr., y Alfred Daniel eran los hermanos de Christine. La familia los llamaba M. L. y A. D.

Vivían en un pueblo que tenía leyes muy injustas. La ley mantenía separadas a las personas de raza negra y de raza blanca.

M. L. y A. D. jugaban con los niños blancos que vivían en la calle del frente. Un día los niños dijeron que no podrían jugar más con M. L. y A. D. porque ellos eran negros. Los niños no comprendían por qué las cosas eran así. Su madre les explicó que muchas de las personas blancas no entendían que todas las personas son iguales. M. L. quería que esto cambiara.

Su padre le enseñó cómo luchar por lo que es correcto. Más tarde, M. L. dio discursos y organizó marchas. Los discursos y las marchas ayudaron a terminar con las leyes injustas. Él tenía un sueño que cambió al mundo.

Multilingual Summaries

Chinese

我的兄弟—馬丁

克麗斯汀是小馬丁・路德・金恩的姐妹，他們還有一個兄弟叫做艾弗雷德・丹尼爾。家裡的人都叫他們 M.L. 和 A.D.。

他們住的小鎮法律很不公平，因為法律規定黑人不能接近白人。

馬丁和艾弗雷德時常和對街的白人男孩一起玩。有一天，那些對街男孩說他們不可以一起玩，因為馬丁和艾弗雷德是黑人。兄弟倆不明白為什麼黑人不能跟白人玩，他們的母親說，那是因為有很多白人不懂得其實每一個人都是平等的。馬丁不喜歡這樣，他想要改變這種不平等的情況。

馬丁的父親教他怎樣為正確的事挺身而出，據理力爭。長大以後，馬丁經常演講，而且還號召大家上街遊行，抗議不公平的法律。馬丁的演講和遊行終於讓不公平的法律廢除了，他追求公平的夢想改變了這個世界。

Vietnamese

Anh Martin của Tôi

Christine là em của Martin Luther King, Jr. và người anh khác là Alfred Daniel. Gia đình gọi hai người con trai là M.L. và A.D.

Họ sống trong một thành phố có những luật lệ bất công. Các luật lệ này tách rời người da đen với người da trắng.

M.L. và A.D. từng chơi chung với những đứa con trai da trắng ở bên kia đường. Một ngày kia, những đứa con trai bên kia đường nói là họ không thể chơi chung với nhau được nữa vì M.L. và A.D. là người da đen. Hai cậu bé không hiểu. Mẹ của họ giải thích rằng nhiều người da trắng không hiểu là mọi người đều như nhau. M.L. muốn thay đổi điều này.

Ba của ông chỉ cho ông cách tranh đấu cho những điều đúng. Sau này, M.L. đi diễn thuyết và tổ chức những cuộc tuần hành. Các bài diễn văn và những cuộc tuần hành giúp chấm dứt các luật lệ bất công. Ông đã mơ một giấc mơ làm thay đổi thế giới.

Multilingual Summaries

Korean

우리 형 마틴

크리스틴과 마틴 루터 킹 주니어 그리고 알프레드 다니엘은 남매이며, 그들 가족은 두 형제를 M.L과 A.D로 불렀다.

그들이 사는 마을의 법은 공평하지 않았고 백인과 흑인을 차별했다.

M.L과 A.D는 길 건너편의 백인 아이들과 놀고 있었는데 어느 날 길 건너편의 아이들이 M.L과 A.D가 흑인이라서 더 이상 같이 놀 수 없다고 말했다. 아이들은 이것을 이해하지 못했고 그들의 어머니는 아이들에게 많은 백인들은 모두가 평등하다는 것을 이해하지 못한다고 설명해주었다. M.L은 이것을 바꾸고 싶었다.

M.L의 아버지는 그에게 옳은 것을 옹호하는 방법을 보여주었다. 훗날 M.L은 연설을 하고 행진을 주도했다. 연설과 행진은 불평등한 법을 폐지하는 데 도움이 되었다. 그는 세상을 바꾸는 꿈을 꾸었던 것이다.

Hmong

Kuv Nus Martin

Christine tau yog Martin Luther King, Jr. tus muam thiab lawv tus nus Alfred Daniel tus muam. Tsev neeg hu nkawd hu ua M.L. thiab A.D.

Lawv nyob hauv ib lub zos uas tsis muaj txoj cai ncaaj ncees. Txoj cai hais kom cov neeg dub tsis txhob poo nrog cov neeg dawb.

M.L. thiab A.D. ua siv nrog cov me nyuam dawb nyob ze lawv. Muaj ib hnub, cov me nyuam dawb nyob ze lawv hais tias lawv ua siv tsis tau nrog lawv lawm vim M.L. thiab A.D. yog neeg dub. Cov me nyuam tsis to taub. Nkawd niam piav hais tias muaj ntau cov neeg dawb tsis to taub hais tias sawv daws yeej zoo ib yam. M.L. xav muaj qhov no pauv.

Nws txiv tau qhia nws kom sawv khov kho rau tej yam yog. Tom qab ntawd, M.L. tau hais ntau zaj lus thiab tau coj ntau txoj kev sawv mus kev. Tej lus thiab tej kev mus kev pab kom muab tej cai tsis ncaj ncees tso pov tseg. Nws ua ib zaj npau suav uas tau hloov lub ntiaj teb.

Jim Thorpe's Bright Path

Student Edition pages 664–679

Week at a Glance	Customize instruction every day for your English Language Learners.				
	Day 1	**Day 2**	**Day 3**	**Day 4**	**Day 5**
Teacher's Edition	Use the ELL Notes that appear throughout each day of the lesson to support instruction and reading.				
ELL Poster 27	• Assess Prior Knowledge • Develop Concepts and Vocabulary	• Preteach Tested Vocabulary	• Interview with Maria	• Your Abilities, Dreams, and Goals	• Monitor Progress
ELL Teaching Guide	• Picture It! Lesson, pp. 183–184 • Multilingual Summaries, pp. 187–189	• ELL Reader Lesson, pp. 264–265	• Vocabulary Activities and Word Cards, pp. 185–186 • Multilingual Summaries, pp. 187–189		
ELL Readers	• Reread *Ralph Bunche*	• Teach *The Carlisle Indian School*	• Reread *The Carlisle Indian School* and other texts to build fluency		
ELL and Transition Handbook	Use the following as needed to support this week's instruction and to conduct alternative assessments: • Phonics Transition Lessons • Grammar Transition Lessons • Assessment				

Picture It! Comprehension Lesson

Fact and Opinion

Use this lesson to supplement or replace the skill lesson on pages 660–661 of the Teacher's Edition.

Teach

Distribute copies of the Picture It! blackline master on page 184.

- Have students look at the picture and describe what is happening. Then read the paragraph aloud.
- Ask: *Which sentence shows an opinion in the paragraph?*
- Share the Skill Points (at right) with students.
- Have students find support for the opinions.

Practice

Read aloud the directions on page 184. Have students answer the questions at the bottom of the page. Have them save their work for later reteaching.

Answers for page 184: *Facts:* (Any two sentences from the paragraph other than the last sentence.) *Way to check if facts are correct:* Look in an encyclopedia or on the Internet. *Opinion:* Runners who win marathons are the best athletes in the world! *Is opinion well supported?* no

Skill Points

✓ Sentences that are **facts** can be shown to be true. Sentences that are **opinions** are beliefs or judgments. They cannot be proven true or false.

✓ Decide if opinions are well supported by using the text and what you already know. Ask: *Is the opinion well supported?*

Name ______________________________

Fact and Opinion

Look at the picture. **Read** the paragraph.

- What statements show facts? **Write** two sentences that are facts in the spaces below.
- How would you check to see if each fact is correct? **Write** your answers in the spaces below.
- Which sentence shows an opinion? **Write** It below.
- Is the opinion well supported? **Write** yes or no.

Ancient Runners

Thousands of years ago the Greeks invented many different sports. We still play some of them today. One of these sports is the marathon, a very long running race. Greek runners would race from Athens to Olympia. The distance was about 26 miles (42 kilometers). Today, marathons are still 26 miles long. Runners who win marathons are the best athletes in the world!

1. Fact: ______________________________

____

Way to check if fact is correct:

____

2. Fact: ______________________________

____

Way to check if fact is correct:

____

3. Opinion: ______________________________

____

Is the opinion well supported? ______________________________

Vocabulary Activities and Word Cards

Copy the Word Cards on page 186 as needed for the following activities.
Use the blank cards for additional words that you want to teach.
Also see suggestions for teaching vocabulary in the ELL and Transition Handbook.

True or False?	Find Your Partner	Tell a Story
• Make one set of Word Cards. • Ask a student to select a card. • Make up a sentence using the vocabulary word and ask the student if the sentence is true or false. For example: *A dormitory is where classes are held.* (false) • Ask the rest of the group whether they agree with the student's answer. • Repeat the exercise until all students have had a chance to choose a card.	• Give one Word Card to each student, making sure that each student in the class has the same card as one other student. • Ask students to write definitions in their own words on the backs of their Word Cards. • Ask half of the students to place their cards on their desks word side up and half of the students to place their cards definition side up. • Have each student whose card has a definition facing up stand, one at a time, and read the definition to the class. • Have all students with word-side-up cards examine their cards to see if they match the definition. If a card matches, have that student stand up. Then have the two standing students exchange cards to see whether their cards match. • Continue the game until all students whose cards show definitions have read them to the class.	• Distribute one set of Word Cards to each student. • Gather the students in a circle and explain that you will be telling a story. • Begin the story with a sentence that uses a vocabulary word. • Have the student to your right continue the story, adding a sentence that uses any of the other vocabulary words. • Have each student continue the story, adding a sentence that uses a vocabulary word. • Allow students to help one another think of sentences that continue the story. • Encourage students to be creative and to try to make the story exciting.

boarding school

dormitory

endurance

manual

reservation

society

Multilingual Summaries

English

Jim Thorpe's Bright Path

Jim Thorpe and his twin brother Charlie were born on an Indian reservation in 1887. Jim and Charlie played outdoors. Jim was always a faster runner than Charlie.

When the twins were six years old, their father sent them to boarding school. Jim hated being inside all day. Charlie encouraged Jim to keep studying. In their third year at school, Charlie got sick and died.

Jim did not want to go back to school. His father said he had to. Jim ran away. His father sent him to another school. At his new school, Jim was on the track team. He learned to play football. Later, he went to an Indian college. He was the best athlete on the track team, and he played football. Charlie had been right. Continuing his education helped Jim Thorpe find his path in life.

Spanish

El futuro brillante de Jim Thorpe

Jim Thorpe y su hermano gemelo Charlie nacieron en una reserva indígena en 1887. Jim y Charlie jugaban al aire libre. Jim siempre corría más rápido que su hermano.

Cuando los hermanos tenían seis años, sus padres los enviaron a un internado. A Jim no le gustaba estar en el interior de la escuela todo el día. Charlie lo animaba para que siguiera estudiando. Al tercer año de estar en la escuela, Charlie se enfermó y murió.

Jim no quería regresar a la escuela. Su padre le dijo que tenía que ir. Jim se escapó. Su padre lo envió a otra escuela. En la nueva escuela, Jim participó en el equipo de atletismo. También aprendió a jugar fútbol americano. Más tarde fue a una universidad indígena. Él era el mejor atleta del equipo de atletismo y también jugó fútbol americano. Charlie había tenido razón. Continuar con su educación había ayudado a Jim a encontrar su camino en la vida.

Multilingual Summaries

Chinese

吉姆・索普的光明之路

1887 年，吉姆・索普和他的雙胞胎兄弟查理在印第安保護區出生。吉姆和查理經常在戶外玩，每次他們比賽跑步，吉姆總是跑得比查理快。

6 歲那一年，這對雙胞胎的父親把他們送到寄宿學校唸書。吉姆不喜歡整天都待在教室裡，不過查理一直鼓勵他要好好唸書。在寄宿學校唸書的第三年，查理生病然後就死掉了。

吉姆不想再回到學校了，但是他父親說他一定得回去上學。吉姆逃跑不去學校，於是他父親又把他送到另一所學校去。在新學校裡，吉姆參加了田徑隊，還學會踢足球。之後他進了印地安大學，他是學校田徑隊裡最優秀的運動員，他也會踢足球。查理是對的，吉姆・索普因為繼續唸書，所以才能找到他人生的方向和道路。

Vietnamese

Con Đường Tươi Sáng của Jim Thorpe

Jim Thorpe và người anh sinh đôi của mình là Charlie sanh ra trong một khu của người Mỹ Da Đỏ vào năm 1887. Jim và Charlie chơi ở ngoài trời. Jim lúc nào cũng chạy nhanh hơn Charlie.

Khi hai anh em sinh đôi này được sáu tuổi, ba của họ đưa họ đi học trường nội trú. Jim ghét phải ngồi trong lớp cả ngày. Charlie khuyến khích Jim cứ tiếp tục học. Vào năm học thứ ba, Charlie ngã bệnh và qua đời.

Jim không muốn trở lại trường. Ba của cậu bảo cậu phải đi. Jim bỏ trốn. Ba của cậu đưa cậu đi học một trường khác. Ở trường mới, Jim được vào đội điền kinh. Cậu học chơi đá bóng bầu dục. Sau đó cậu đi học ở trường đại học của người Mỹ Da Đỏ. Cậu là vận động viên giỏi nhất trong đội điền kinh, và cậu cũng chơi đá bóng bầu dục. Charlie nói đúng. Tiếp tục việc giáo dục của mình đã giúp Jim Thorpe tìm được đường đi cho mình trong đời sống.

Multilingual Summaries

Korean

짐 토프의 밝은 미래

짐 토프와 그의 쌍둥이 형제 찰리는 1887년 인디언 보호구역에서 태어났다. 짐과 찰리는 집 밖에서 놀았고 짐은 늘 찰리보다 빨리 뛰었다.

쌍둥이 형제가 여섯 살이 되었을 때 아버지는 그들을 기숙 학교에 보냈다. 짐은 온종일 학교 안에만 있는 것이 싫었지만 찰리는 짐에게 계속 공부하도록 격려했다. 그들이 삼학년이 되었을 때 찰리는 병이 들어 죽고 말았다.

짐은 학교로 돌아가고 싶지 않았지만 아버지는 그래야만 한다고 말했다. 짐은 도망쳤고 다른 학교로 보내졌다. 새 학교에서 짐은 육상 팀에 가입했고 풋볼을 배웠다. 나중에 그는 인디언 대학에 들어갔고 육상팀의 최고 선수가 되었으며 풋볼도 했다. 찰리가 옳았다. 교육을 계속 받은 덕분에 짐 토프는 인생에서 자신의 길을 찾을 수 있었던 것이다.

Hmong

Jim Thorpe' Txoj Kev Kaj

Jim Thorpe' thiab nws tus kwv ntxaib Charlie tau yug nyob hauv cov neeg Qhab ib thaj chaw hauv xyoo 1887. Jim thiab Charlie ua siv nraum zoov. Jim yeej ib txwm dhia nrawm dua Charlie.

Thaum ob tug ntxaib tau muaj rau xyoo, nkawd txiv xa nkawd mus kawm ntawv deb. Jim tsis nyiam nyob hauv tsev ib hnub. Charlie txhawb kom Jim rau siab kawm ntawv. Thaum xyoo peb ntawm nkawd txoj kev kawm ntawv, Charlie tau muaj mob thiab taut as sim neej.

Jim tsis xav rov qab mus kawm ntawv. Nws txiv tau hais tias nws yuav tsum mus. Jim tau khiav tawm ntawm nws lub tsev mus. Nws txiv xa nws mus rau lwm lub tsev kawm ntawv. Nyob hauv nws lub tsev kawm ntawv tshiab, Jim tau nrog ib pab tub ntxhais sib xeem khiav. Nws kawm ua siv football. Tom qab ntawd, nws mus kawm ntawv hauv ib lub tsev kawm ntawv qib siab Qhab. Nws yog tus khiav nrawm tshaj hauv lawv pab, thiab nws ua siv football. Charlie yeej hais yog lawm. Txoj kev rau siab kawm ntawv pab tau Jim Thorpe' nrhiav tau nws txoj hau kev hauv lub neej no.

How Tía Lola Came to Stay

Student Edition pages 690–705

Week at a Glance	Customize instruction every day for your English Language Learners.				
	Day 1	**Day 2**	**Day 3**	**Day 4**	**Day 5**
Teacher's Edition	Use the ELL Notes that appear throughout each day of the lesson to support instruction and reading.				
ELL Poster 28	• Assess Prior Knowledge • Develop Concepts and Vocabulary	• Preteach Tested Vocabulary	• One Person's Perspective	• Our Mural	• Monitor Progress
ELL Teaching Guide	• Picture It! Lesson, pp. 190–191 • Multilingual Summaries, pp. 194–196	• ELL Reader Lesson, pp. 266–267	• Vocabulary Activities and Word Cards, pp. 192–193 • Multilingual Summaries, pp. 194–196		
ELL Readers	• Reread *The Carlisle Indian School*	• Teach *From Thailand to California*	• Reread *From Thailand to California* and other texts to build fluency		
ELL and Transition Handbook	Use the following as needed to support this week's instruction and to conduct alternative assessments: • Phonics Transition Lessons • Grammar Transition Lessons • Assessment				

Picture It! Comprehension Lesson

Character and Theme

Use this lesson to supplement or replace the skill lesson on pages 686–687 of the Teacher's Edition.

Teach

Distribute copies of the Picture It! blackline master on page 191.

- Have students look at and describe the pictures. Then read the story aloud.
- Ask: *Who is the main character?* (Mei)
- Share the Skill Points (at right) with students.
- Have students discuss Mei's goal, the plot events, and the theme of the story.

Practice

Read aloud the directions on page 191. Ask students to fill in the chart. Have them keep their organizers for later reteaching.

Answers for page 191: *Character*: Mei; *Goal*: to join the baseball team; *Plot Events*: Mei decides to try out for the team. She asks Jared for help. She practices every day. She becomes the best pitcher on the field. *Theme*: Possible response: Hard work pays off.

Skill Points

✓ **Characters** are people in a story. What they say and do helps us know what they are like.

✓ The **theme** is the meaning of the story. Sometimes the author says what the theme of the story is. Often the reader has to think about the story to find the theme.

Name ______________________________

Look at the picture. **Read** the story.

- Who is the main character? What is her goal? **Write** your ideas in the chart.
- What are the plot events in the story? **List** them in the chart.
- What is the theme of the story? **Write** your answer in the chart.

Mei's Hard Work

Mei wanted to try out for the baseball team. She hadn't played before, but she loved watching games on TV. Tryouts were in a week.

Mei asked her friend Jared to help her throw and catch. Jared was surprised to see how fast Mei could throw.

Mei practiced every day after school. By tryouts, she was the best pitcher on the field. Mei joined the team and became a great player.

Character	
Goal	
Plot Events	
Theme	

Vocabulary Activities and Word Cards

Copy the Word Cards on page 193 as needed for the following activities.
Use the blank card for an additional word that you want to teach.
Also see suggestions for teaching vocabulary in the ELL and Transition Handbook.

Definition Concentration	Context Game	Home Language Clues
• Create one set of Word Cards and seven blank cards for every pair of students. • Have pairs of students work together to write definitions for each word on the blank cards. Remind students that a definition tells what a word means. • Have students place the Word Cards and definition cards face down in rows on a table. • Instruct students to take turns turning over two cards and looking for a matched pair. A matched pair is a Word Card and its definition card. When a student finds a matched pair, the student keeps the cards. • To determine the winner, check which student has the most cards at the end of the game.	• Give a set of Word Cards to each student. • Have each student write a context sentence for each word on the back of each card. Remind students that context sentences are sentences that show the meaning of the word. Instruct students not to include the vocabulary word in the context sentence but to leave a blank where the word belongs. • Have students form pairs and exchange their cards with the context sides up. • Have students take turns looking at their partner's context sentence and guessing the vocabulary word. Have them discard each card into a correct or incorrect pile, depending on their guess. • To determine the winner, check which student has the most cards in the correct pile at the end of the game.	• Pair students who have writing proficiency in the same home language, and give each student a set of Word Cards. • Have students work together to write translations of the vocabulary words in their home language on the back of each card. (See the Multilingual Lesson Vocabulary beginning on page 272 for suggested translations.) • Have partners lay out the cards with the home language sides facing up. • Invite students to generate synonyms for each word in their home language. Then ask them to name the English vocabulary word with the same meaning. They can flip the cards over to check their answers.

affords

colonel

glint

lurking

palettes

quaint

resemblance

Multilingual Summaries

English

How Tía Lola Came to Stay

Miguel and Juanita have moved to Vermont with Mami, their mother. Mami's aunt, Tía Lola, comes to visit. She tells stories. Some nights they all explore the old house they live in.

Miguel wants his baseball team to practice in the field behind the house. Their landlord agrees. They name Tía Lola as the team manager.

One day Tía Lola paints the house purple. Mami is worried that the landlord will make them leave. He tells them to repaint the house or leave in three weeks.

Tía Lola has a plan. She makes uniforms for the baseball team. She also makes a flag with the team's name. The team is named for the landlord. When he sees the flag, he smiles and plays ball with the team.

Spanish

Cómo tía Lola llega para quedarse

Miguel y Juanita se han mudado para Vermont con Mami. La tía de Mami, tía Lola, llega de visita. Ella cuenta cuentos. Algunas noches todos exploran la vieja casa donde viven.

Miguel quiere que su equipo de béisbol practique en el campo detrás de la casa. El dueño de la casa les da permiso. Ellos nombran a la tía Lola como representante del equipo.

Un día, tía Lola pinta la casa de morado. Mami está preocupada de que el dueño los vaya a echar de la casa. Él les dice que tienen que volver a pintar la casa o abandonarla en tres semanas.

Tía Lola tiene un plan. Hace uniformes para el equipo de béisbol. También hace una bandera con el nombre el equipo. El equipo lleva el nombre del dueño de la casa. Cuando él ve la bandera, sonríe y juega pelota con el equipo.

Multilingual Summaries

Chinese

蒂亞・洛拉的妙計

馬吉爾和嘉妮塔跟著媽咪搬到佛蒙特，媽咪是他們的母親。媽咪的姑母蒂亞・洛拉來探望他們。蒂亞・洛拉會講故事給他們聽，有時晚上大家還會在自己居住的舊房子裡探險。

馬吉爾想帶他的棒球隊到房子後面的空地練習，房東同意了。於是球隊就請蒂亞・洛拉來當棒球隊領隊。

有一天，蒂亞・洛拉突然把房子漆成紫色。媽咪擔心房東會生氣，把他們趕出去。結果房東叫他們把房子漆回原來的顏色，否則三個禮拜以後就得搬家。

蒂亞・洛拉想到一個好辦法。她幫棒球隊隊員做制服，又做了一面旗子上面有棒球隊的隊名，這個隊名是用房東名字取的。當房東看到這面旗子的時候，他笑了，後來還和大家一起打棒球。

Vietnamese

Làm Thế Nào mà Tia Lola Đã Đến Ở

Miguel và Juanita dọn đến Vermont với Mami, mẹ của chúng. Cô của Mami, Tia Lola, đến thăm. Bà kể chuyện. Có nhiều đêm họ đi thám hiểm căn nhà cổ xưa là nơi họ đang sống.

Miguel muốn đội bóng chày của cậu tập dợt ở sân phía sau nhà. Chủ nhà đồng ý. Chúng gọi Tia Lola là người quản lý đội.

Ngày kia Tia Lola sơn ngôi nhà màu tím. Mami lo sợ là chủ nhà sẽ bắt họ dọn đi. Ông ấy bảo họ phải sơn lại ngôi nhà bằng không thì phải dọn ra trong 3 tuần lễ.

Tia Lola có một kế. Bà may các bộ đồng phục cho đội bóng chày. Bà cũng may một lá cờ có tên của đội. Đội mang tên ông chủ nhà. Khi ông ấy thấy lá cờ, ông mỉm cười và đi chơi bóng với đội.

Multilingual Summaries

Korean

티아 롤라가 머무는 법

미구엘과 주아니타는 그들의 어머니인 마미와 함께 버몬트로 이사한다. 어머니의 고모인 티아 롤라 가 놀러 와서 이야기를 들려준다. 밤이 되면 그들은 지금 살고 있는 낡은 집을 탐사하기도 했다.

미구엘은 그의 야구팀이 집 뒤뜰에서 연습하길 바라는데 집주인도 이를 허락한다. 그들은 곧 티아 롤라를 팀의 관리인으로 임명한다.

어느 날 티아 롤라는 집을 자주색으로 칠한다. 마미는 집주인이 그들을 내보내지 않을까 걱정한다. 집주인은 그들에게 집을 새로 칠하거나 아니면 3주 내로 집에서 나가라고 말한다.

티아 롤라에겐 계획이 있다. 그녀는 야구 팀의 유니폼과 팀의 이름을 새긴 깃발을 만들고 집주인의 이름을 따서 팀의 이름을 짓는다. 집주인은 깃발을 보고 미소를 짓더니 이들과 함께 야구를 한다.

Hmong

Ua Li Cas Tía Lola tau Los Nyob

Miguel thiab Juanita tau tsiv mus nyob hauv Vermont nrog Mami, nkawd niam. Mami tus viv ncaus, Tía Lola, tuaj saib lawv. Nws qhia dab neeg. Tej hmo lawv sawv daws mus ncig lub tsev qub uas nyob hauv.

Miguel xav kom nws pab ntaus pob xyaum hauv thaj chaw nyob ntawm lawv qaum tsev. Lawv tus tswv tsev kam lawv xyaum. Lawv hais kom Tía Lola ua tus coj lawv pab ntau pob.

Muaj ib hnub Tía Lola tau muab lub tsev thas xim paj yeeb. Mami tau txhawj nyob tsam tus tswv tsev hais kom lawv tawm tsev. Nws hais kom lawv rov qab thas lub tsev los sis tawm tsev ntawm peb lub lim tiam tom ntej.

Tía Lola muaj ib lub tswv yim. Nws tau ua kom pab ntau pob muaj ib cev khaub ncaw zoo li yam. Nws kuj ua ib tug chij uas muaj pab ntau pob lub npe. Pab ntau pob lub npe hu ua tus tswv tsev. Thaum nws pom tus chij, nws luag thiab ua siv nrog pab ntau pob.

To Fly

Student Edition pages 716–731

Week at a Glance	Customize instruction every day for your English Language Learners.				
	Day 1	**Day 2**	**Day 3**	**Day 4**	**Day 5**
Teacher's Edition	Use the ELL Notes that appear throughout each day of the lesson to support instruction and reading.				
ELL Poster 29	• Assess Prior Knowledge • Develop Concepts and Vocabulary	• Preteach Tested Vocabulary	• Charades	• A World Without Airplanes	• Monitor Progress
ELL Teaching Guide	• Picture It! Lesson, pp. 197–198 • Multilingual Summaries, pp. 201–203	• ELL Reader Lesson, pp. 268–269	• Vocabulary Activities and Word Cards, pp. 199–200 • Multilingual Summaries, pp. 201–203		
ELL Readers	• Reread *From Thailand to California*	• Teach *Thank You, Sir Isaac Newton!*	• Reread *Thank You, Sir Isaac Newton!* and other texts to build fluency		
ELL and Transition Handbook	Use the following as needed to support this week's instruction and to conduct alternative assessments: • Phonics Transition Lessons • Grammar Transition Lessons • Assessment				

Picture It! Comprehension Lesson

Generalize

Use this lesson to supplement or replace the skill lesson on pages 712–713 of the Teacher's Edition.

Teach

Distribute copies of the Picture It! blackline master on page 198.

- Have students look at the pictures and name the objects in the pictures. Then read the paragraph aloud.
- Ask: *What generalization does the author make in this paragraph?* (All inventions are made using earlier inventions.)
- Share the Skill Points (at right) with students.
- Have students find support for the generalization.

Practice

Read aloud the directions on page 198. Have students complete the graphic organizer. Have them keep their organizers for later reteaching.

Answers for page 198: *Generalization:* All inventions are made using earlier inventions. *Support:* Automobile inventors used what they knew about carriage, motor, and bicycle tires. Computer keyboard inventors used what they knew about typewriters and computers. Freezer inventors used what they knew about refrigerators.

Skill Points

✓ A **generalization** is a special kind of conclusion. It is a sentence that applies to many examples that are the same in some way.

✓ Generalizations are good, or **valid,** if they have many details to support them. Generalizations are bad, or **faulty,** if they do not have many details to support them.

Name ______________________________

Look at the picture. **Read** the paragraph.

- What generalization does the author make in this paragraph? **Write** the generalization in the box below.
- What details support the generalization? **Write** them in the boxes below.
- Is the generalization valid or faulty? **Discuss** your opinion with the class.

Inventions Make More Inventions

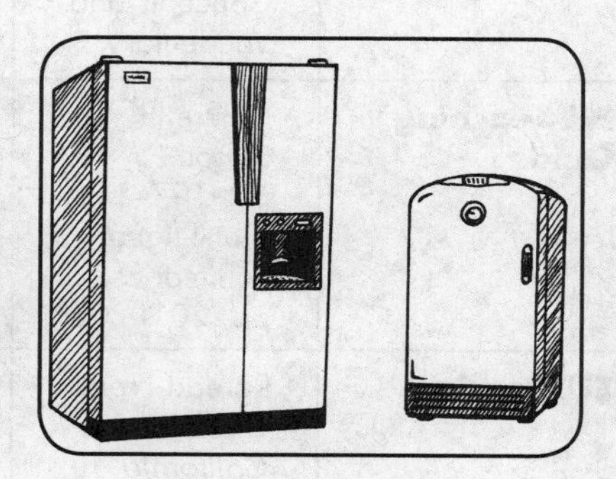

All inventions are made using earlier inventions. The man who invented the automobile used what he knew about horse-drawn carriages, motors, and bicycle tires. The people who invented the computer keyboard used what they knew about typewriters and computers. The people who invented the freezer used what they knew about refrigerators. None of these inventions would have been possible without the inventions that came before them.

Generalization

Support

Vocabulary Activities and Word Cards

Copy the Word Cards on page 200 as needed for the following activities.
Use the blank card for an additional word that you want to teach.
Also see suggestions for teaching vocabulary in the ELL and Transition Handbook.

Write a Story	Picture This	True or False?
• Divide the class into small story-writing groups, and give each group a set of Word Cards. • Within each group, distribute the Word Cards so that each student has at least one card. • Have students select one member of the group to record the story, another to make sure that each student contributes at least one sentence to the story, and a third to read the story to the class. • Have each group brainstorm ideas for the story. Tell the students that the story can be silly or serious but that it must include all of the vocabulary words. Then have each student come up with a sentence for the story using the Word Card or Cards he or she received. • Give students ten minutes to write their story. Then have one member of each group read the story to the class.	• Select the vocabulary words that you think can be clearly illustrated, and draw pictures illustrating the words on the back of one set of Word Cards. • Have one student select a card and describe the scene the illustration depicts. • Ask the rest of the class to guess which vocabulary word the illustration depicts.	• Make one set of Word Cards. • Ask a student to select a card. • Make up a sentence using the vocabulary word, and ask the student if the sentence is true or false. For example: *The rudder helps to steer the plane.* (true) • Ask the rest of the group whether they agree with the student's answer. • Repeat the exercise until all students have had a chance to choose a card.

cradle

drag

flex

glider

hangars

rudder

stalled

Multilingual Summaries

English

To Fly: The Story of the Wright Brothers

Orville and Wilbur Wright dreamed of flying. They wanted to make a flying machine. When he was young, Orville made and sold kites. He built the best kites in Dayton, Ohio.

During high school, Orville opened a printing shop. Wilbur worked with him. Later they started fixing bicycles. They opened a bicycle shop together with the printing shop.

The brothers read about men trying to fly. They got more information about flying. They built gliders and tested them. Then they built a motor and propellers for another airplane. They called that one the Flyer.

In December of 1903, the Wrights tried their Flyer. The airplane did not fly at first. But on December 17, it did fly! The Wright brothers made the very first flight in an engine-driven airplane.

Spanish

Volar: La historia de los hermanos Wright

Orville y Wilbur Wright soñaban con volar. Querían hacer una máquina voladora. Cuando era joven, Orville armaba y vendía cometas. Él hacía las mejores cometas de Dayton, Ohio.

Mientras estaba en la escuela secundaria, Orville abrió una imprenta. Wilbur trabajó con él. Después, comenzaron a arreglar bicicletas. Además de la imprenta, abrieron una tienda de bicicletas.

Los hermanos leían sobre hombres que trataban de volar. Consiguieron más información sobre vuelos. Construyeron planeadores y los probaron. Después, construyeron un motor y hélices para otro aeroplano. Lo llamaron Volador.

En diciembre de 1903, los Wright probaron su Volador. Al principio el aeroplano no voló. ¡Pero el 17 de diciembre sí voló! Los hermanos Wright hicieron el primer vuelo en un aeroplano de motor.

Multilingual Summaries

Chinese

想飛

奧維爾和韋伯・萊特一直夢想著能在天上飛。他們想要製造一台可以飛的機器。奧維爾年輕的時候，會做風箏而且還可以賣錢。他做的風箏是全俄亥俄州達頓市最好的。

唸中學的時候，奧維爾開了一家印刷店，韋伯也在店裡幫忙。後來他們又開始修理腳踏車。他們把印刷店和腳踏車店開在一起，共用一個店面。

兄弟倆讀了很多人嘗試飛行的故事，從故事裡，他們得到更多和飛行有關的資訊。他們造了一架滑翔機而且還進行了飛行測試。接著，他們又為另一架飛機製造馬達和螺旋槳。他們把飛機取名叫飛行者。

1903 年 12 月，萊特兄弟試飛他們的飛行者。剛開始飛機沒有飛起來。但是在 12 月 17 日試飛的時候，它竟然真的飛上天了！於是，萊特兄弟發明了世界上第一架引擎驅動飛機。

Vietnamese

Bay

Orville and Wilbur Wright mơ ước được bay. Họ muốn làm một máy để bay. Khi còn nhỏ, Orville làm diều bán. Ông ấy làm những con diều tốt nhất ở Dayton, Ohio.

Trong những năm trung học, Orville mở tiệm in. Wilbur làm việc với ông. Sau này họ bắt đầu sửa xe đạp. Họ mở một tiệm xe đạp cùng với tiệm in.

Hai anh em đọc sách về những người thử bay. Họ xây những chiếc máy lượn và thử bay chúng. Kế đến họ làm động cơ và các cánh quạt cho một chiếc máy bay khác. Họ gọi chiếc đó là "Flyer" (Người Bay).

Vào tháng Mười Hai năm 1903, hai anh em nhà họ Wright thử chiếc Flyer của họ. Thoạt đầu chiếc máy bay không bay. Nhưng vào ngày 17 tháng Mười Hai, chiếc này bay! Anh em nhà họ Wright đã bay chuyến bay đầu tiên trên một máy bay có động cơ.

Multilingual Summaries

Korean

비행

오빌과 윌버 라이트는 비행을 꿈 꾸었다. 형제는 날 수 있는 기계를 만들고 싶었다. 오빌은 어렸을 때 연을 만들어 팔았고 오하이오주의 데이턴에서 최고의 연을 만들었다.

고등학교 시절 오빌은 인쇄소를 차리고 윌버와 같이 일했다. 훗날 그들은 자전거 정비 일을 시작했고 인쇄소와 함께 자전거 가게도 차렸다.

라이트 형제는 비행을 시도하려는 사람에 대한 기사를 읽었고 비행에 대해 더 많은 정보를 얻었다. 글라이더를 만들어 테스트도 해보다가 이들은 다른 비행기의 모터와 프로펠러를 만들었다. 그리고 그것을 플라이어라고 불렀다.

1903년 12월 라이트 형제는 플라이어로 시험 비행을 하지만 처음에는 날지 못했다. 그렇지만 12월 17일 플라이어가 드디어 날게 된다. 라이트 형제가 바로 엔진으로 작동하는 최초의 비행기를 만든 것이다.

Hmong

Ya

Orville thiab Wilbur Wright ua npau suav ya. Nkawd xav ua kom tau ib lub dav hlau uas txawj ya. Thaum nws tseem yaus, Orville tau ua cov vuaj thiab muab lawv muag. Nws ua tau cov vauj uas zoo tshaj nyob rau hauv Dayton, Ohio.

Thaum nyob hauv high school, Orville qhib ib lub khw luam ntawv. Wilbur ua hauj lwm rau nws. Tom qab ntawd nkawd pib kho luv thim. Nkawd qhib ib lub khw luv thim nrog nkawd lub khw luam ntawv.

Ob tug kwv tij nyeem txog cov txiv neej uas tau sim ya. Nkawd kawm tau ntau yam txog txoj kev ya. Nkawd ua tau ib cov gliders thiab muab lawv sim. Ces nkawd ua tau ib lub cav thiab cov kiv cua rau ib lub dav hlau. Nkawd hu lub dav hlau ntawd hu ua lub Ya.

Hauv lub 12 Hlis Ntuj ntawm lub xyoo 1903, tug ob Wrights tau sim ya nkawd lub Ya. Xub thawj lub dav hlau tsis ya. Tiam sis nyob hauv lub 12 Hlis Ntuj Hnub Tim 17, nws tau ya. Ob tug kwv tij Wrights tau yog thawj thawj tug uas tau ya dav hlau uas muaj cav.

The Man Who Went to the Far Side of the Moon

Student Edition pages 742–755

Week at a Glance	Customize instruction every day for your English Language Learners.				
	Day 1	**Day 2**	**Day 3**	**Day 4**	**Day 5**
Teacher's Edition	Use the ELL Notes that appear throughout each day of the lesson to support instruction and reading.				
ELL Poster 30	• Assess Prior Knowledge • Develop Concepts and Vocabulary	• Preteach Tested Vocabulary	• Act It Out	• Our Dreams	• Monitor Progress
ELL Teaching Guide	• Picture It! Lesson, pp. 204–205 • Multilingual Summaries, pp. 208–210	• ELL Reader Lesson, pp. 270–271	• Vocabulary Activities and Word Cards, pp. 206–207 • Multilingual Summaries, pp. 208–210		
ELL Readers	• Reread *Thank You, Sir Isaac Newton!*	• Teach *Welcome to Space Camp*	• Reread *Welcome to Space Camp* and other texts to build fluency		
ELL and Transition Handbook	Use the following as needed to support this week's instruction and to conduct alternative assessments: • Phonics Transition Lessons • Grammar Transition Lessons • Assessment				

Picture It! Comprehension Lesson

Graphic Sources

Use this lesson to supplement or replace the skill lesson on pages 738–739 of the Teacher's Edition.

Teach

Distribute copies of the Picture It! blackline master on page 205.

- Have students look and describe the diagram. Then read the paragraph aloud.
- Ask: *What does the diagram show?* (phases or shapes of the Moon)
- Share the Skill Points (at right) with students.
- Have students tell which drawings show which phases of the Moon.

Practice

Read aloud the directions on page 205. Have students write the names for the phases of the Moon on the correct lines. Have students keep their work for later reteaching.

Answers for page 205: 1. New Moon. **2.** Half Moon or Quarter Moon **3.** Full Moon **4.** Half Moon or Quarter Moon

Skill Points

✓ **Graphic sources** show information in a visual way. Maps, charts, tables, diagrams, and pictures are some examples of graphic sources.

✓ You can look at graphic sources before you read to help you see what the text is about.

✓ Do not skip graphic sources. Look at them as you read to help understand the text.

Name ______________________________

Look at the picture. **Read** the paragraph.

- **Use** the information in the paragraph to add labels to the picture.

Phases of the Moon

Every few nights, the shape of the Moon seems to change. One night, the Moon cannot be seen. This is called a New Moon. Then the moon looks like a crescent that gets bigger, until half a circle is seen. This is called a Half Moon or Quarter Moon. A week later, a full circle, or Full Moon, is seen. This circle gets smaller, and a week later only half a circle is seen. After another week, it is a New Moon again. The Moon revolves around the Earth, and the Earth revolves around the Sun. We see different Moon shapes depending on where the Sun, Moon, and Earth are in relation to each other.

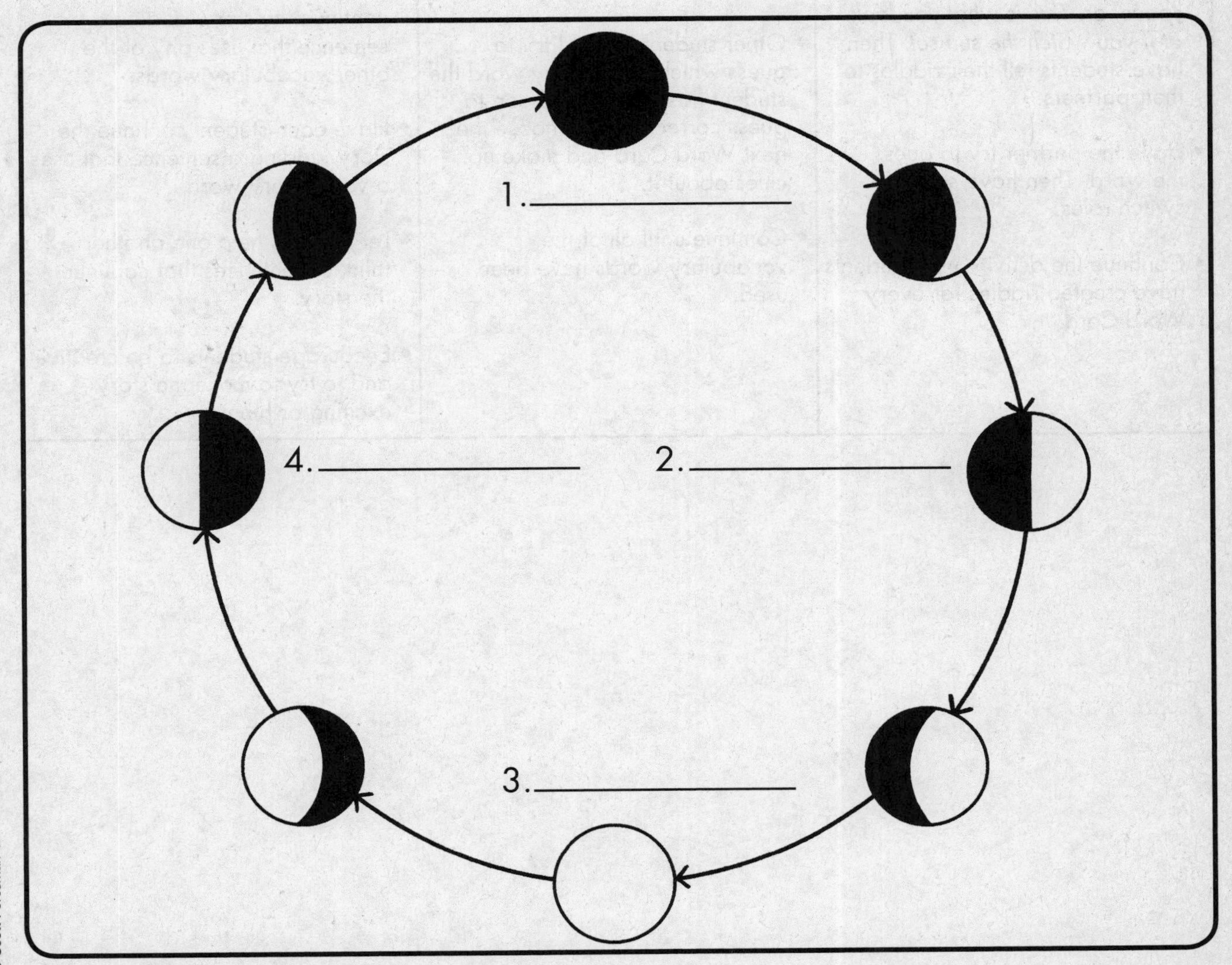

Vocabulary Activities and Word Cards

Copy the Word Cards on page 207 as needed for the following activities.
Use the blank card for an additional word that you want to teach.
Also see suggestions for teaching vocabulary in the ELL and Transition Handbook.

Riddle Game	Poster Clues	Tell a Story
• Divide the students into pairs, and give each pair a set of Word Cards. • Have students place the set of Word Cards face down in a pile. • Ask one partner to choose a card and make up a riddle about the word. Provide examples, such as: *These people get to go into outer space;* or, *This is what you look at if you watch the sun set.* Then have students tell their riddles to their partners. • Have the partner try to guess the word. Then have students switch roles. • Continue the activity until students have created riddles for every Word Card.	• Distribute sets of Word Cards to students. Then, from your own set of Word Cards, have one student pick a card without letting the others see it. • The student stands at the ELL Poster, points to the relevant area on it, and uses the information on the Poster to give hints about the vocabulary word. • Other students should try to guess which vocabulary word the student has. The first person to guess correctly may choose the next Word Card and make up clues about it. • Continue until all of the vocabulary words have been used.	• Distribute one set of Word Cards to each student. • Gather the students in a circle and explain that the group will be telling a story together. • Begin the story with a sentence that uses a vocabulary word. • Have the student to your right continue the story, adding a sentence that uses any of the other vocabulary words. • Have each student continue the story, adding a sentence that uses a vocabulary word. • Let students help one another think of sentences that continue the story. • Encourage students to be creative and to try to make the story exciting or funny.

astronauts	**capsule**
hatch	**horizon**
lunar	**module**
quarantine	

Multilingual Summaries

English

The Man Who Went to the Far Side of the Moon

Michael Collins, Neil Armstrong, and Buzz Aldrin are astronauts. They fly the Apollo 11 mission to the moon. Neil and Buzz land the lunar module on the moon. While Neil and Buzz do experiments on the moon, Michael is alone.

Michael flies the command module around the moon for almost thirty hours. When the command module is on the far side of the moon, the radio cannot reach the Earth. Michael has a lot of work to do. While orbiting the moon, Michael eats meals from special packages.

The three men land back on Earth. Doctors don't know if they may have caught any germs on the moon. They have to stay in a special trailer for seventeen days.

Michael decides not to travel anymore. This trip was special, but he doesn't want to go back.

Spanish

El hombre que fue al lado oscuro de la Luna

Michael Collins, Neil Armstrong y Buzz Aldrin son astronautas. Ellos van a la Luna en la misión del Apollo 11. Neil y Buzz alunizan el módulo lunar. Mientras Neil y Buzz hacen experimentos en la Luna, Michael está solo.

Durante casi treinta horas, Michael dirige el módulo de mando alrededor de la Luna. Cuando el módulo de mando está en el lado oscuro de la Luna, la señal de radio no puede llegar a la Tierra. Michael tiene mucho trabajo que hacer. Mientras está en la órbita de la Luna, Michael come comidas de paquetes especiales.

Los tres hombres regresan a la Tierra. Los médicos no saben si los astronautas han traído algún germen de la Luna. Ellos tienen que estar en una cámara especial durante diecisiete días.

Michael decide no viajar más. Ese viaje fue especial, pero él no quiere regresar.

Multilingual Summaries

Chinese

到過月球另一端的人

麥克・科林斯、尼爾・阿姆斯壯和巴茲・歐德林是太空人。他們搭乘太空穿梭機阿波羅 11 號到月球上要完成任務。尼爾和巴茲開著登月小艇在月球上登陸，然後忙著在上面做實驗，麥克自己一人，沒和他們一起。

麥克駕著指揮艙繞月球飛了快要 30 個小時。當飛到月球另一端的時候，他的無線電突然沒辦法和地球聯絡了。麥克還有很多工作要做，所以他又駕著指揮艙沿著月球軌道飛回去，途中，麥克要是肚子餓，就從特製的包包裡拿東西出來吃。

三個人完成任務，返回地球。醫生幫他們檢查身體，看看他們有沒有在月球上感染細菌。三個人都必須在一輛特製的拖車上待 17 天。

麥克決定以後不再去外太空了。這次繞月球飛的經驗雖然很特別，但是他一點都不想再去一次。

Vietnamese

Người Đã Đi Đến Phía Bên Kia Mặt Trăng

Michael Collins, Neil Armstrong, và Buzz Aldrin là các phi hành gia vũ trụ. Họ bay chuyến bay Apollo 11 lên mặt trăng. Neil và Buzz đáp khoang hạ xuống mặt trăng. Khi Neil và Buzz làm các thí nghiệm trên mặt trăng, Michael chỉ có một mình.

Michael bay khoang chỉ huy vòng quanh mặt trăng gần đến ba mươi tiếng đồng hồ. Khi khoang chỉ huy qua phía bên kia của mặt trăng, sóng rađiô không thể truyền đến Trái Đất. Michael có nhiều việc phải làm. Trong khi bay quanh quỹ đạo mặt trăng, Michael ăn những bữa ăn từ các gói đặc biệt.

Ba người trở về Trái Đất. Các bác sĩ không biết các phi hành gia vũ trụ có thể nhiễm các vi trùng trên mặt trăng hay không. Họ phải ở trong một nhà đặc biệt đến mười bảy ngày.

Michael quyết định không du hành nữa. Chuyến đi này đặc biệt, nhưng ông ấy không muốn đi nữa.

Multilingual Summaries

Korean

달의 저편으로 간 사나이

우주 비행사인 마이클 콜린스, 닐 암스트롱, 그리고 버즈 올드린은 아폴로 11호를 타고 달에 간다. 닐과 버즈는 달에 달 착륙선을 착륙시킨다. 닐과 부즈가 달에서 실험하는 동안 마이클은 홀로 있다.

마이클은 사령선을 타고 거의 30시간 동안 달 주위를 돈다. 사령선이 달의 저 건너편에 있는 동안 지구와의 무선 수신은 할 수 없다. 마이클은 할 일이 많다. 달의 궤도를 도는 동안 마이클은 특수 제작된 주머니에 담긴 음식을 먹는다.

세 사람이 지구로 돌아온다. 의사들은 그들이 달에서 어떤 병균에 감염되었을지도 모른다고 생각한다. 그리하여 그들은 17일 동안 특수 트레일러에서 지내게 된다.

마이클은 더 이상 우주 여행을 하지 않기로 결정한다. 이번 여행은 특별했지만 그는 우주로 돌아가고 싶지 않다.

Hmong

Tus Txiv Neej Uas Tau Mus Sab Deb Ntawm Lub Hli

Michael Collins, Neil Armstrong, thiab Buzz Aldrin yog cov neeg mus saum qaum ntuj. Lawv tau ya lub Apollo 11 mus saum lub hli. Neil thiab Buzz tsaws lub dav hlau mus saum qaum ntuj rau saum lub hli. Thaum Neil thiab Buzz ua ntau yam kev soj ntsuas saum lub hli, Michael nyob ib leeg.

Michael tsav lub dav hlau loj ncig lub hli siv li peb caug teev. Thaum lub dav hlau loj nyob sab deb ntawm lub hli, lub xov tooj cua txais tsis tau lus los hauv ntiaj teb los. Michael muaj ntau txoj hauj lwm ua. Thaum nws tseem ncig lub hli, Michael noj mov uas nyob hauv tej hnab.

Peb tug txiv neej tsaws rov lost saws rau hauv lub ntiaj teb. Cov kws tshuaj tsis paub xyuas lawv puas yuav kis tau tej kab mob nyob saum lub hli. Lawv tau nyob hauv ib qhov chaw tau kaum xyav hnub.

Michael txiav txim tsis rov qab mus dua lawm. Txoj kev mus saum lub hli yeej tseem ceeb, tiam sis nws tsis xav rov qab mus saum lub hli.

ELL Reader Lessons and Study Guides

Bears in Danger

by Joanna Chen

ELL Reader 4.1.1 Expository Nonfiction

INTRODUCE THE BOOK

Activate Prior Knowledge/Build Background Read the title, and discuss the difference between saying *dangerous bears* and *bears in danger.* Tell students that this book is about bears in Florida, and point out Florida on a map.

Preview/Use Text Features Preview the reader by talking about the photographs together, naming the labeled items, and reading the captions. Point out the *Did You Know?* box on page 2, the bar graph on page 3, and the *Extend Language* feature on page 4.

Preteach Vocabulary Review the tested vocabulary word that appears in this book: **positive**. Introduce these key words from the book: **danger** (p. 1), **habitat** (p. 2), and **survive** (p. 7). Discuss these words and add them to a Word Wall.

READ THE BOOK

Choose among these options for reading to support students at all English proficiency levels.

Read Aloud Read the book aloud as students follow along. Pause to verify comprehension and to explain unfamiliar concepts.

Monitored Reading Have students silently read a few pages at a time. Use the following questions to support comprehension:

- **Page 2** What is the habitat of the Florida black bear? (heavily wooded land)
- **Pages 3–4** What are human/bear conflicts? (times when people have seen bears in the woods or on roads, or when bears have come to places where people are)
- **Pages 5–8** Why is the number of human/bear conflicts in Florida increasing? (People are building homes and roads in bear habitats.)

Reread Have students reread the book with a partner, in small groups, or independently. Have students complete the Study Guide on page 213.

RESPOND

Answers to the Reader's Inside Back Cover:

Talk About It

1. People see a bear in the woods; bears look for food near areas where people live; bears cross a road as cars pass. (Main Idea and Details)

2. Possible response: Some programs teach children about the Florida black bear or organize family festivals about the bears. (Generalize)

Write About It

3. Students should explain that human/bear conflicts have greatly increased because humans are moving into areas where bears live. (Draw Conclusions)

Support writers at various English proficiency levels.

Beginning Display a sentence frame, such as *Human/bear conflicts have increased because* ___. Have students dictate an ending.

Intermediate Provide the same sentence frame, but have students copy it and write their own endings.

Advanced Have students write two or three sentences about human/bear conflicts.

Extend Language *Rapidly* means quickly; *constantly* means without stopping; *carefully* means with care, with caution. Invite students to give other examples of words ending in *-ly*.

Answers to page 213:

1. People are worried because there are many more human/bear conflicts than there were in the past.

2. 1,340

3. Possible response: People see a bear while hiking in the woods.

4. The number has dropped from 12,000 bears to about 1,500–3,000.

5. Roads divide the land bears need. Roads bring in vehicles that may hit bears.

Family Link Read aloud the Family Link activity on page 213 before sending copies of the Study Guide home with students. Later, have students share what family members say about bears.

Name ______________________________

Bears in Danger

- **Read** *Bears in Danger* again.
- Use the information in the book to **answer** the questions.

pages 2–3

1. Why are people worried about Florida black bears?

____

____

2. Look at the graph. How many human/bear conflicts happened in 2002?

____

page 4

3. Give one example of a human/bear conflict.

____

____

page 5

4. How has the number of Florida black bears changed from the 1900s until today?

____

____

pages 6–8

5. Why are roads bad for black bears? Give two reasons.

____

____

____

Family Link

Has anyone in your family seen a bear? Ask family members to share what they know about bears.

Talking to Lewis and Clark

by Henry Lee

ELL Reader 4.1.2 Expository Nonfiction

INTRODUCE THE BOOK

Activate Prior Knowledge/Build Background Read the title, and explain the photograph on the title page. Explain that Lewis and Clark were American explorers. They were among the very first European Americans to see much of the Western United States. Ask students to share what they know about sign languages.

Preview/Use Text Features Preview the reader by talking about the illustrations together, naming the labeled items, and reading the captions. Point out the map on pages 2–3.

Preteach Vocabulary Review the tested vocabulary words that appear in this book: **migrated** and **yearned**. Introduce these key words from the book: **nations** (p. 3) and **sign language** (p. 4). Discuss these words and add them to a Word Wall.

READ THE BOOK

Choose among these options for reading to support students at all English proficiency levels.

Read Aloud Read the book aloud as students follow along. Pause to verify comprehension and to explain unfamiliar concepts.

Monitored Reading Have students read aloud a few pages at a time. Use the following questions to support comprehension:

- **Pages 2–3** Who were Lewis and Clark? (men hired by President Jefferson to explore the Louisiana Territory)
- **Pages 4–5** Why did the different nations of Native Americans on the Great Plains use sign language to communicate? (Each nation spoke a different language.)
- **Pages 6–8** How many languages were Lewis and Clark's words translated into so the Salish chief could understand them? (five)

Reread Have students reread the book with a partner, in small groups, or independently. Have them complete the Study Guide on page 215.

RESPOND

Answers to the Reader's Inside Back Cover:

Talk About It

1. They did not speak their languages. (Drawing Conclusions)

2. use sign language; learn a common language, such as English; or use interpreters

Write About It

3. Possible responses: Lewis and Clark are men with white skin. They don't speak any of our languages, but they have many people with them who help them speak with us. They seem peaceful.

Support writers at various English proficiency levels.

Beginning Let students draw and label pictures that show Lewis and Clark from a Native American's perspective. Have them write or dictate sentences about their pictures.

Intermediate Have students brainstorm a list of words they can use when writing about Lewis and Clark.

Advanced Have students also write about what Native Americans might have thought were the reasons why Lewis and Clark were exploring their land.

Extend Language The past tense of *write* is *wrote*. Invite students to share other past tense verbs they find in the text.

Answers to page 215:

1. France

2. only English

3. through Plains Sign Language

4. through their interpreter, George Drouillard

5. a Shoshone princess who served as an interpreter for Lewis and Clark

Family Link Read aloud the Family Link activity on page 215 before sending copies of the Study Guide home with students. Later, have students share what family members say about sign languages.

Name ______________________________

Talking to Lewis and Clark

- **Read** *Talking to Lewis and Clark* again.
- Use the information in the book to **answer** the questions below.

Pages	Question	Answer
2	**1.** Which country sold the Louisiana Territory to the United States?	
3	**2.** What languages did Meriwether Lewis and William Clark speak?	
4	**3.** How did the Native American tribes living in the Great Plains communicate with one another?	
5	**4.** How did Lewis and Clark communicate with the tribes that lived in the Great Plains?	
6–7	**5.** Who was Sacajawea?	

Family Link

Does anyone in your family know a sign language? Ask family members to share what they know.

Our Trip Out East

by Luz Nuncio Schick

ELL Reader 4.1.3 Autobiography

INTRODUCE THE BOOK

Activate Prior Knowledge/Build Background Read the title, and discuss what *trip* and *out East* mean. Tell students that this is a story about a family that takes a long trip in a car.

Preview/Use Text Features Preview the reader by talking about the photographs together and reading the captions. Point out the map on page 6 and the *Extend Language* feature on page 8.

Preteach Vocabulary Review the tested vocabulary words that appear in this book: **amazed** and **homeland**. Introduce these key words from the book: **photographs** (p. 2) and **station wagon** (p. 5). Discuss these words and add them to a Word Wall.

READ THE BOOK

Choose among these options for reading to support students at all English proficiency levels.

Read Aloud Read the book aloud as students follow along. Pause to verify comprehension and to explain unfamiliar concepts.

Monitored Reading Have students silently read a few pages at a time. Use the following questions to support comprehension:

- **Pages 2–4** Where was the family living when they took the trip east? (Chicago) Who is Abuelita? (the grandmother)
- **Pages 5–7** Why did the family drive to New Jersey? (The father got a job there.) How did the family travel to New Jersey? (in their station wagon)
- **Pages 8–10** Where did the family live in Flemington? (in a farmhouse) What did they see in New York? (skyscrapers)
- **Pages 11–12** Why did the family move back to Chicago? (Papi's job ended.) What was the happiest trip the family ever took? (the trip out East)

Reread Have students reread the book with a partner, in small groups, or independently. Have them complete the Study Guide on page 217.

RESPOND

Answers to the Reader's Inside Back Cover:

Talk About It

1. because she missed her very much (Cause and Effect)

2. The whole family was together; Abuelita was with them. (Cause and Effect)

Write About It

3. Answers will vary. Descriptions can be about Flemington, New York City, or Chicago. (Sequence)

Support writers at various English proficiency levels.

Beginning Let students draw and label a picture that shows what the family does in a particular place. Have them write or dictate a sentence about the picture.

Intermediate Have students brainstorm a list of places described in the story before they begin their writing.

Advanced Have students include as many details as they can.

Extend Language *Click* is the English word for the sound a camera makes. Invite students to share home-language words for *click* and *hissed.*

Answers to page 217:

Answers should include the following information: *Chicago:* Abuelita arrives from Mexico. The family begins its trip in the station wagon. *Flemington:* The family rents a farmhouse. The girls explore the farmlands. The family spends a day in New York City. *Chicago:* The family returns to Chicago. Abuelita returns to Mexico. The family later takes more trips.

Family Link Read aloud the Family Link activity on page 217 before sending copies of the Study Guide home with students. Later, have students share their family members' stories about trips in the United States.

Name ______________________________

Our Trip Out East

- **Read** *Our Trip Out East* again.
- Use information in the book to **fill in** the sequence organizer. **Describe** all of the events that happened in each place, in the order in which they happened.

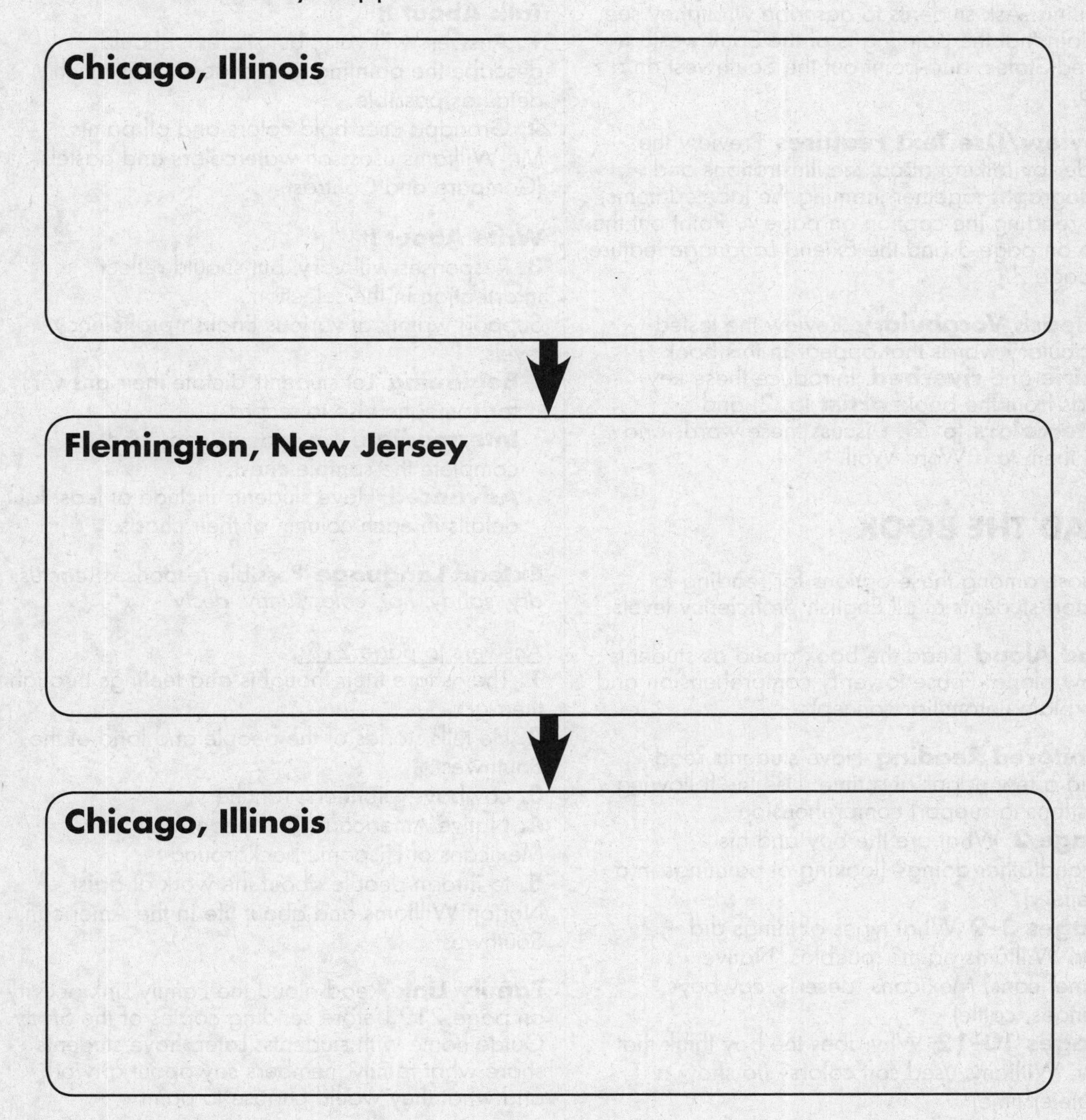

Family Link

Has anyone in your family taken a long trip in the United States? Where did they go? What did they see? Ask family members to describe a trip they took.

Painting the Southwest

by Ladislao Gutierrez

ELL Reader 4.1.4 Realistic Fiction

INTRODUCE THE BOOK

Activate Prior Knowledge/Build Background Read the title, and discuss the painting. Ask students to describe what they see. Explain that the painting is of the Southwestern United States, and point out the Southwest on a map.

Preview/Use Text Features Preview the reader by talking about the illustrations and photographs together, naming the labeled items, and reading the caption on page 4. Point out the map on page 3 and the *Extend Language* feature on page 7.

Preteach Vocabulary Review the tested vocabulary words that appear in this book: **prairie** and **riverbed**. Introduce these key words from the book: **artist** (p. 2) and **watercolors** (p. 2). Discuss these words and add them to a Word Wall.

READ THE BOOK

Choose among these options for reading to support students at all English proficiency levels.

Read Aloud Read the book aloud as students follow along. Pause to verify comprehension and to explain unfamiliar concepts.

Monitored Reading Have students read aloud a few pages at a time. Use the following questions to support comprehension:

- **Page 2** What are the boy and his grandfather doing? (looking at paintings in a gallery)
- **Pages 3–9** What types of things did Mr. Williams paint? (pueblos, Native Americans, Mexicans, deserts, cowboys, ranges, cattle)
- **Pages 10–12** Why does the boy think that Mr. Williams used soft colors? (to show a quieter time)

Reread Have students reread the book with a partner, in small groups, or independently. Have them complete the Study Guide on page 219.

RESPOND

Answers to the Reader's Inside Back Cover:

Talk About It

1. Answers will vary, but students should describe the painting they choose in as much detail as possible.
2. Grandpa uses bold colors and oil paints. Mr. Williams uses soft watercolors and pastels. (Compare and Contrast)

Write About It

3. Responses will vary, but should reflect information in the selection.
Support writers at various English proficiency levels.

Beginning Let students dictate their answers for someone else to record.
Intermediate Let students copy and complete the sample chart.
Advanced Have students include at least four details in each column of their charts.

Extend Language Possible responses: *cactus, dry, sandy, hot, cold, sunny, dusty*

Answers to page 219:
1. They share their thoughts and feelings through their art.
2. He tells stories of the people and land of the Southwest.
3. cowboys, pioneers, ranchers
4. Native Americans, European Americans, Mexicans of Hispanic background
5. to inform people about the work of artist Norton Williams and about life in the American Southwest

Family Link Read aloud the Family Link activity on page 219 before sending copies of the Study Guide home with students. Later, have students share what family members say about artwork and what they would choose to paint.

Name ______________________________

Painting the Southwest

- **Read** *Painting the Southwest* again.
- Use the information in the book to **answer** the questions below.

pages 2–4

1. How do artists "talk" to people?

____

____

2. What stories does Williams tell through his paintings?

____

____

pages 5–9

3. What types of people did Williams paint?

____

____

4. Which people have lived in the Southwest?

____

____

pages 10–12

5. What were the author's purposes in writing this book?

____

____

Family Link

Does anyone in your family paint or draw? If they were to paint people or places, what would they paint?

For Purple Mountain Majesties

by Al Cantu

ELL Reader 4.1.5 Expository Nonfiction

INTRODUCE THE BOOK

Activate Prior Knowledge/Build Background Read the title, and discuss its meaning and origin. If possible, sing or play "America the Beautiful" for the class. Ask volunteers to describe mountains they have seen, in the United States or elsewhere.

Preview/Use Text Features Preview the reader by talking about the photographs together, naming the labeled items, and reading the captions. Point out the *Extend Language* feature and the map on page 3.

Preteach Vocabulary Review the tested vocabulary words that appear in this book: **wilderness**, **impressive**, and **slope**. Introduce these key words from the book: **mountains** (p. 3) and **peaks** (p. 4). Discuss these words and add them to a Word Wall.

READ THE BOOK

Choose among these options for reading to support students at all English proficiency levels.

Read Aloud Read the book aloud as students follow along. Pause to verify comprehension and to explain unfamiliar concepts.

Monitored Reading Have students silently read a few pages at a time. Use the following questions to support comprehension:

- **Pages 2–3** What is "America the Beautiful"? (a song) What is a mountain range? (a row of mountains)
- **Pages 4–5** What are two mountain ranges in Alaska? (the Brooks and the Alaska)
- **Pages 6–7** Which mountain ranges are on the West Coast of North America? (the Coastal Range and the Cascades)
- **Page 8** Which mountain range runs from northwest to southeast California? (the Sierra Nevada)

Reread Have students reread the book with a partner, in small groups, or independently. Have them complete the Study Guide on page 221.

RESPOND

Answers to the Reader's Inside Back Cover:

Talk About It

1. The far western United States has many mountain ranges. (Main Idea and Details)

2. Answers will vary, but students should describe one of following mountain ranges: Brooks, Alaska, Coastal, Cascades, Sierra Nevada. (Main Idea and Details)

Write About It

3. Alaska: tallest peak in United States, Mount McKinley/Denali; Brooks: Northern Alaska, covered with ice and snow; Coastal: from Alaska to northern California, not tall; Cascades: from southern Canada to northern California, peaks covered with snow, Mount Rainier; Sierra Nevada: northwest to southeast of California; Mount Whitney; Yosemite, Kings Canyon, and Sequoia National Parks (Main Idea and Details)

Support writers at various English proficiency levels.

Beginning Pair students with more-proficient speakers to complete their charts.

Intermediate Have students look through the book to find details they can use in their writing.

Advanced Have students help less-proficient speakers complete their charts.

Extend Language Words may include *Majesties, peak, valley,* and *string.*

Answers to page 221:

Possible facts:

The Coastal Range mountains are not tall.

Mt. McKinley is the tallest peak in North America.

The Sierra Nevada runs through most of the length of California.

Mountains in the Brooks range are covered with ice and snow most of the year.

Opinions will vary.

Family Link Read aloud the Family Link activity on page 221 before sending copies of the Study Guide home with students. Later, have students share what family members say about mountain ranges they have seen.

Name ______________________________

For Purple Mountain Majesties

- **Read** *For Purple Mountain Majesties* again.
- Use the information in the book. **Write** facts and opinions in the chart. The first row has been done for you.
- In the fact column, **write** four more facts from the book. In the opinion column, **write** four opinions of your own based on information in the book.

Fact	**Opinion**
Katharine Lee Bates wrote the song "America the Beautiful."	Her song is the most beautiful song ever written.
1.	
2.	
3.	
4.	

Family Link

Has anyone in your family ever been to the mountain ranges described in this book? Ask family members to share what they know about mountain ranges they have seen.

Girls Playing Basketball

by Yvonne Johnson

ELL Reader 4.2.1 Drama

INTRODUCE THE BOOK

Activate Prior Knowledge/Build Background Read the title, and discuss the picture. Ask students to guess the year. Ask volunteers to describe the difference between the girls in the photograph and girls playing basketball today.

Preview/Use Text Features Preview the reader by talking about the photographs together, naming the labeled items, and reading the captions. Point out the diagrams on pages 7 and 11, the *Extend Language* feature on page 3, and the time line on page 12.

Preteach Vocabulary Review the tested vocabulary words that appear in this book: **jersey** and **swat**. Introduce these key words from the book: **physical education** (p. 4) and **rough** (p. 6). Discuss these words and add them to a Word Wall.

READ THE BOOK

Choose among these options for reading to support students at all English proficiency levels.

Read Aloud Read the book aloud as students follow along. Pause to verify comprehension and to explain unfamiliar concepts.

Monitored Reading Assign roles, and have students read their roles aloud. Use the following questions to support comprehension:

- **Pages 2–5** Who invented basketball? (Dr. James Naismith)
- **Pages 6–9** What did Clara Gregory Baer call the game she invented? (*basquette*) How were the rules of her game different from the rules invented by Senda Abbott? (Her game had more divisions on the court, and girls could not talk or yell during the game.)
- **Pages 10–11** How does girls' basketball differ from boys' basketball today? (The ball is smaller.)

Reread Have students reread the book with a partner, in small groups, or independently. Have them complete the Study Guide on page 223.

RESPOND

Answers to the Reader's Inside Back Cover:

Talk About It

1. to make basketball less rough for girls (Cause and Effect)

2. First, girls wore long skirts, blouses, hats, and gloves. Then, they wore long bloomers. In the 1920s, they began wearing short bloomers with long stockings underneath. Today, they wear jerseys and shorts, like boys. (Sequence)

Write About It

3. Answers will vary.

Support writers at various English proficiency levels.

Beginning Have students draw and label a picture that shows a sport and one of its rules. Have them write or dictate a sentence about the picture.

Intermediate Have students use the diagram and paragraph at the bottom of page 11 as a model for their own writing.

Advanced Have students write two paragraphs, one describing the sport and one describing the rules.

Extend Language *Dribble* means to bounce the ball while moving. *Pass* means to throw the ball to another player. *Shoot* means to try to throw the ball into the basket.

Answers to page 223:

Cause box 1: Boys' basketball seemed too rough for girls.

Effect box 2: Clara Gregory Baer had girls wear bloomers.

Effect box 3: The rules of the game today are very similar for boys and girls; dress is identical.

Family Link Read aloud the Family Link activity on page 223 before sending copies of the Study Guide home with students. Later, have students share what family members say about girls playing sports.

Name ____

- **Read** *Girls Playing Basketball* again.
- Use the information in the book to **fill in** the cause-and-effect boxes below.

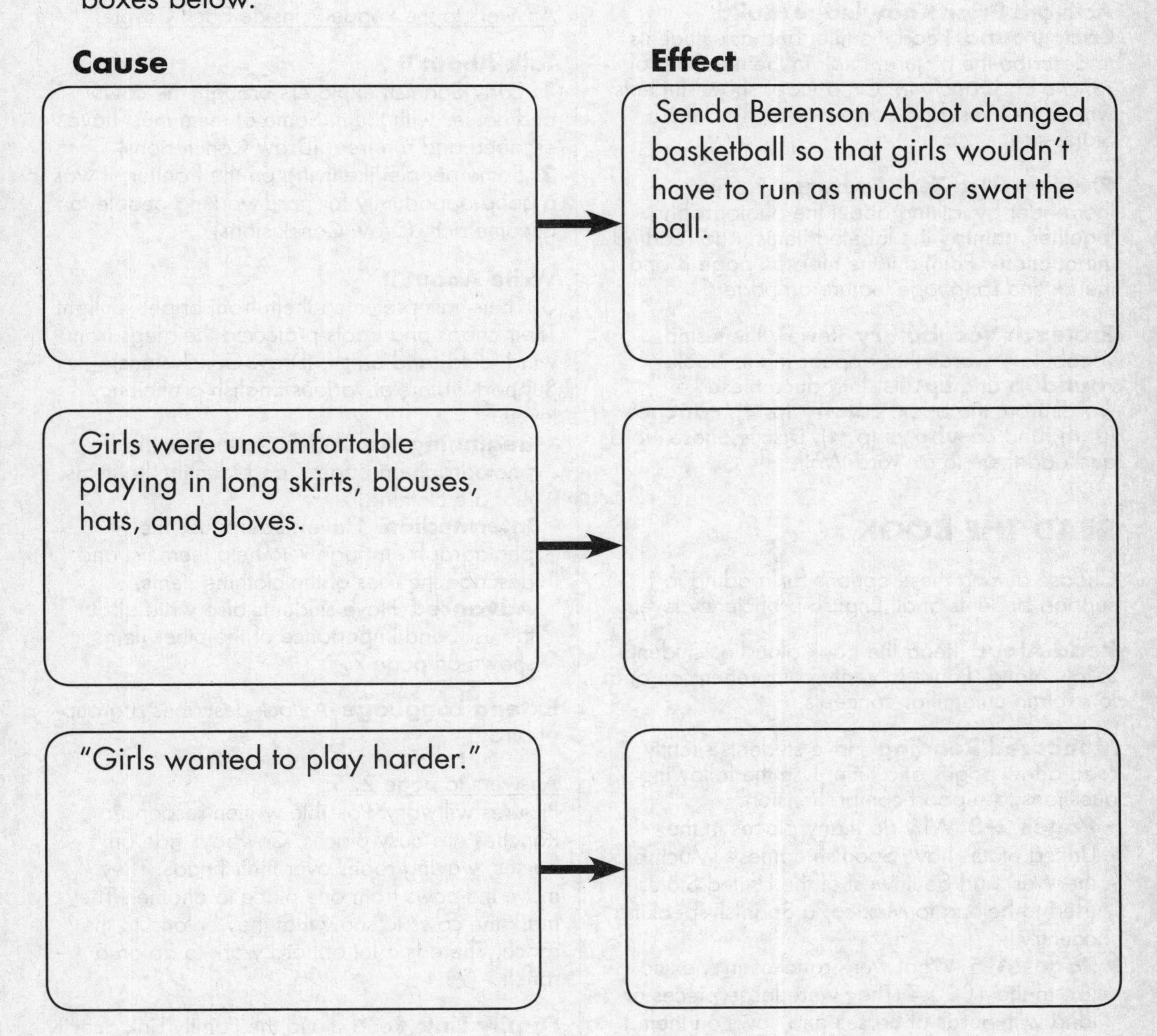

Family Link

Do any of the girls or women in your family play sports? What sports do they play? What do the people in your family think about girls playing basketball, softball, and other sports?

First, It Was a Rancho

by Luz Paredes

ELL Reader 4.2.2 Expository Nonfiction

INTRODUCE THE BOOK

Activate Prior Knowledge/Build Background Read the title, and ask students to describe the picture. Explain the meaning of *rancho* and *ranching*. On a map, show students where the West and Southwest of the United States are.

Preview/Use Text Features Preview the reader by talking about the photographs together, naming the labeled items, and reading the captions. Point out the map on page 3 and the *Extend Language* feature on page 6.

Preteach Vocabulary Review the tested vocabulary words that appear in this book: **roundup** and **spurs**. Introduce these key words from the book: **colony** (p. 4), **ranches** (p. 4), and **cowboys** (p. 4). Discuss these words and add them to a Word Wall.

READ THE BOOK

Choose among these options for reading to support students at all English proficiency levels.

Read Aloud Read the book aloud as students follow along. Pause to verify comprehension and to explain unfamiliar concepts.

Monitored Reading Have students silently read a few pages at a time. Use the following questions to support comprehension:

- **Pages 2–3** Why do many places in the United States have Spanish names? (Much of the West and Southwest of the United States used to belong to Mexico, a Spanish-speaking country.)
- **Pages 4–5** What were ranches in Mexico like in the 1800s? (They were large pieces of land with herds of horses and cows on them.)
- **Pages 6–8** How are cowboys and *vaqueros* similar? (They both herd cattle on horseback, brand animals to identify them, hold roundups, and wear spurs and similar clothing.)

Reread Have students reread the book with a partner, in small groups, or independently. Have them complete the Study Guide on page 225.

RESPOND

Answers to the Reader's Inside Back Cover:

Talk About It

1. Early Spanish explorers brought the cows and horses with them. Some of them must have escaped and run free. (Draw Conclusions)

2. Some people like living on the frontier; it was a good opportunity for hard-working people to become rich. (Draw Conclusions)

Write About It

3. Their hats protected them from bright sunlight. Their chaps and boots protected their legs from wind, cold, and brush. (Draw Conclusions)

Support writers at various English proficiency levels.

Beginning Ask students to look at the photograph on page 7 and identify the items that are clothing.

Intermediate Have students use the photograph on page 7 to help them list and describe the uses of the clothing items.

Advanced Have students also write about the uses and importance of the other items shown on page 7.

Extend Language A *flock* describes a group of birds.

Answers to page 225:

Pictures will vary. Possible written response: Ranches are busy places. Cowboys ride on horses, waving ropes over their heads. They move the cows from one place to another. They mark the cows to show that they belong to the ranch. There is a lot of hard work to do on a ranch.

Family Link Read aloud the Family Link activity on page 225 before sending copies of the Study Guide home with students. Later, have students share what family members say about life on a ranch.

Name ______________________________ **First, It Was a Rancho**

- **Read** *First, It Was a Rancho* again.
- Use the information in the book to **draw** a picture and **write** a description of a ranch.

____

____

____

____

Family Link

How would your family like to live on a cattle ranch? Ask them what they think life would be like there. Ask them what they think would be the best part and the worst part of living on a ranch.

Hello, Good-bye, and Other Customs

by Anthony James

ELL Reader 4.2.3 Expository Nonfiction

INTRODUCE THE BOOK

Activate Prior Knowledge/Build Background Read the title, and define the word *custom*. Then discuss different ways students know of greeting people. Ask volunteers to demonstrate different customs.

Preview/Use Text Features Preview the reader by paging through the book and talking about the photographs together. Point out the *Extend Language* feature on page 6.

Preteach Vocabulary Review the tested vocabulary words that appear in this book: **capable** and **awkward**. Introduce these key words from the book: **custom** (p. 1), **greet** (p. 2), and **bowing** (p. 4). Discuss these words and add them to a Word Wall.

READ THE BOOK

Choose among these options for reading to support students at all English proficiency levels.

Read Aloud Read the book aloud as students follow along. Pause to verify comprehension and to explain unfamiliar concepts.

Monitored Reading Have students silently read a few pages at a time. Use the following questions to support comprehension:

- **Pages 2–3** What are customs? (ways people do things such as greet or speak to people)
- **Pages 4–5** When do people in Japan bow? (to say *hello, good-bye, I'm sorry,* or *thank you*)
- **Pages 6–7** What do people in France do when they meet one another? (kiss on both cheeks) What do Arab men do when they meet other men? (shake hands)
- **Page 8** What are some of the things people have customs for? (dressing, eating, celebrating, working, giving and receiving gifts)

Reread Have students reread the book with a partner, in small groups, or independently. Have them complete the Study Guide on page 227.

RESPOND

Answers to the Reader's Inside Back Cover:

Talk About It

1. Possible response: It begins a conversation or relationship; it may be a person's first impression of someone. (Drawing Conclusions)

2. In many countries, people treat older people with respect.

Write About It

3. Possible response: *Japan:* bowing. *Both:* saying the words for *hello* and *good-bye. France:* kissing both cheeks. (Compare and Contrast) Support writers at various English proficiency levels.

Beginning Provide a copy of the Venn diagram for students to fill in.

Intermediate Let students copy and complete the sample Venn diagram.

Advanced Have students make a second Venn diagram and compare two more customs.

Extend Language *Waist* is the homophone of *waste*. Invite students to share other homophones they know.

Answers to page 227:

United States: shaking hands, hugging and kissing

Japan: bowing

France: kissing both cheeks

Arab countries: shaking hands, placing hand over heart; men shake hands only with men

India and Thailand: folding hands in prayer, bowing slightly

Philippines: younger people bring their forehead to touch the hand of older people.

Family Link Read aloud the Family Link activity on page 227 before sending copies of the Study Guide home with students. Later, have students share what family members say about their customs for saying *hello* and *good-bye*.

Name ________________________________

Hello, Good-bye, and Other Customs

- **Read** *Hello, Good-bye, and Other Customs* again.
- Use the information in the book to **fill in** the chart.

Country	Greeting Custom
United States	
Japan	
France	
Arab countries	
India and Thailand	
Philippines	

Family Link

Talk with people in your family about how they say *hello* and *good-bye.* Do they use the same custom for everyone they meet, or do they use different customs for different people? When they were your age, did people greet one another the same way they do today?

A Mill Girl's Day

by Camilla Black

ELL Reader 4.2.4 Historical Fiction

INTRODUCE THE BOOK

Activate Prior Knowledge/Build Background Read the title, and discuss the meaning of the word *mill*. Tell students that this story takes place in the early 1800s, when many children had to work.

Preview/Use Text Features Preview the reader by talking about the illustrations together, naming the labeled items, and reading the caption on page 3. Point out the diagram on page 9.

Preteach Vocabulary Review the tested vocabulary words that appear in this book: **immense** and **dismay**. Introduce these key words from the book: **mill** (p. 1), **deafening** (p. 4), and **threads** (p. 5). Discuss these words and add them to a Word Wall.

READ THE BOOK

Choose among these options for reading to support students at all English proficiency levels.

Read Aloud Read the book aloud as students follow along. Pause to verify comprehension and to explain unfamiliar concepts.

Monitored Reading Have students silently read a few pages at a time. Use the following questions to support comprehension:

- **Pages 2–3** Where does Molly work? (in a cotton mill in Lowell) Who works in the mill with her? (young women aged 15–30)
- **Pages 4–7** Where does Molly eat her meals? (at the boarding house) What does she plan to do with the money she earned this week? (buy a book, a hat, and a concert ticket, and send money to her family)
- **Pages 8–12** What do the mill girls do other than work? (eat, go to concerts and lectures, read, write letters, go to church, go shopping)

Reread Have students reread the book with a partner, in small groups, or independently. Have them complete the Study Guide on page 229.

RESPOND

Answers to the Reader's Inside Back Cover:

Talk About It

1. Working in the mills was hard because of the long hours, low pay, and unhealthy conditions. (Fact and Opinion)

2. Molly is a responsible girl; she will visit Eliza. (Draw Conclusions)

Write About It

3. Mill rules: Girls have to work two machines; take only short breaks; are paid only for what they produce. Exciting things in Lowell: concerts, lectures, reading, shopping (Fact and Opinion)

Support writers at various English proficiency levels.

Beginning Let students dictate their ideas for someone else to record.

Intermediate Let students copy and complete the sample chart.

Advanced Have students include at least three details in each column of their charts.

Extend Language A *school book* is a book for school. A *supermarket baker* bakes at a supermarket. Invite students to share other word combinations they know.

Answers to page 229:

Morning: Molly works on two machines next to her friend Eliza. She has breakfast at 7:00 A.M. and then returns to the mill. *Afternoon:* She has dinner at noon and then works all day. She also does the work of a friend who is ill. *Evening:* She finishes work, has supper, goes to a lecture, and goes home to bed.

Family Link Read aloud the Family Link activity on page 229 before sending copies of the Study Guide home with students. Later, have students share what their family members, friends, or neighbors said about working in a factory.

Name ________________________________

- **Read** *A Mill Girl's Day* again.
- Use the information in the book to **complete** the sequence organizer about Molly's day. The first circle has been started for you.

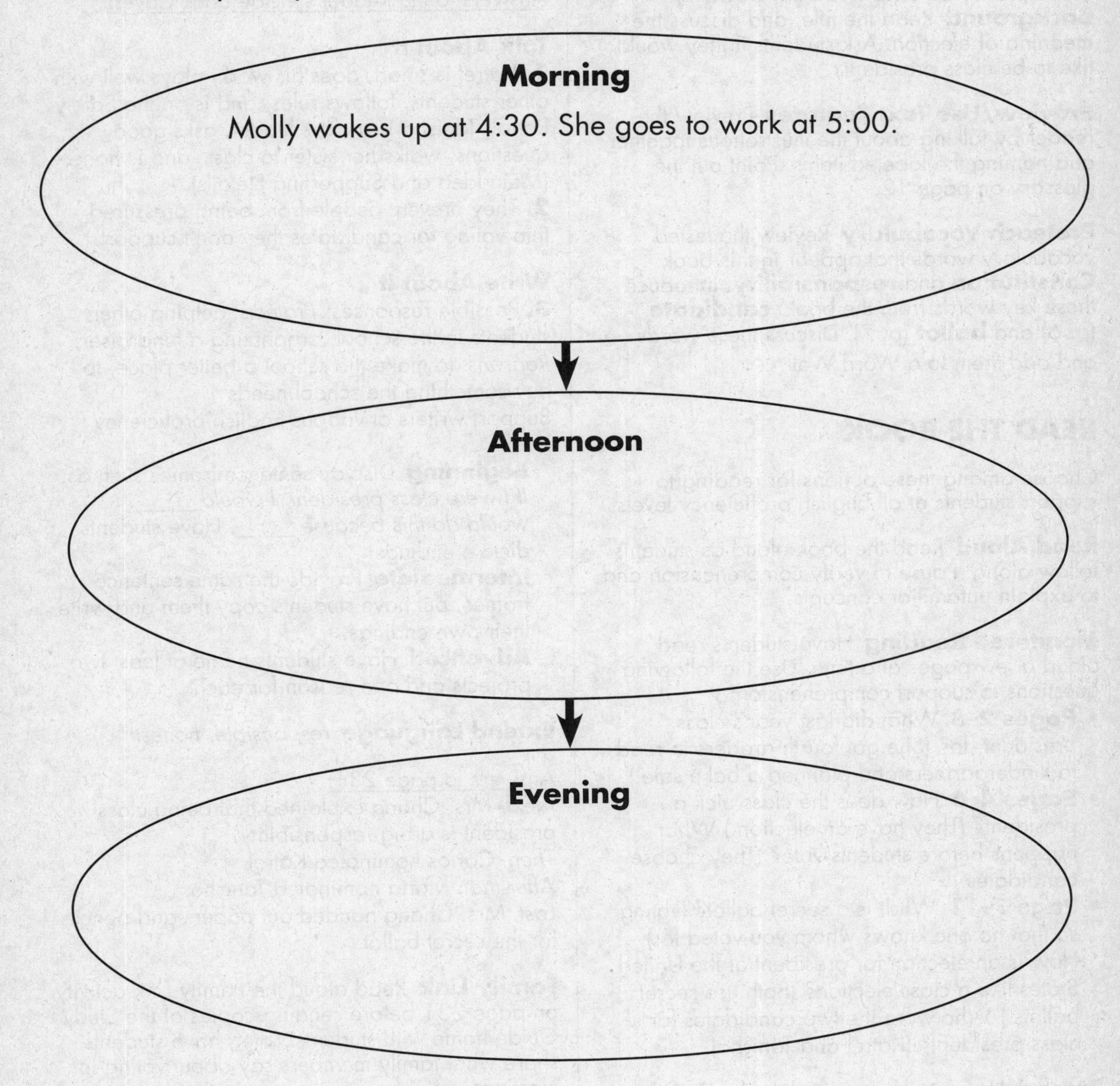

Family Link

Ask your friends, family, and neighbors if they have ever worked in a mill or factory. Ask them to share what they know about factory work.

The Fourth Grade Election

by Chandler Roberts

ELL Reader 4.2.5 Realistic Fiction

INTRODUCE THE BOOK

Activate Prior Knowledge/Build Background Read the title, and discuss the meaning of *election.* Ask students if they would like to be class president.

Preview/Use Text Features Preview the reader by talking about the illustrations together and naming the labeled items. Point out the glossary on page 12.

Preteach Vocabulary Review the tested vocabulary words that appear in this book: **Constitution** and **responsibility**. Introduce these key words from the book: **candidate** (p. 6) and **ballot** (p. 7). Discuss these words and add them to a Word Wall.

READ THE BOOK

Choose among these options for reading to support students at all English proficiency levels.

Read Aloud Read the book aloud as students follow along. Pause to verify comprehension and to explain unfamiliar concepts.

Monitored Reading Have students read aloud a few pages at a time. Use the following questions to support comprehension:

- **Pages 2–3** What did last year's class president do? (She got fourth graders to read to kindergartners and planned a bake sale.)
- **Pages 4–6** How does the class pick a president? (They have an election.) What happens before students vote? (They choose candidates.)
- **Page 7–11** What is a secret ballot? (voting so that no one knows whom you voted for) How is an election for president of the United States like a class election? (Both use secret ballots.) Who were the two candidates for class president? (Katrel and Tanisha)

Reread Have students reread the book with a partner, in small groups, or independently. Have them complete the Study Guide on page 231.

RESPOND

Answers to the Reader's Inside Back Cover:

Talk About It

1. Katrel is smart, does his work, plays well with other students, follows rules, and is on the Safety Patrol. Tanisha is a class leader, asks good questions, walks her sister to class, and is honest. (Main Idea and Supporting Details)

2. They prevent people from being pressured into voting for candidates they don't support.

Write About It

3. Possible responses: *Projects:* helping other students in the school, organizing a fundraiser; *Reasons:* to make the school a better place, to buy something the school needs

Support writers at various English proficiency levels.

Beginning Display sentence frames such as: *If I were class president, I would* _____. *I would do this because* _____. Have students dictate endings.

Intermediate Provide the same sentence frames, but have students copy them and write their own endings.

Advanced Have students name at least two projects and one reason for each.

Extend Language *responsible, honest*

Answers to page 231:

Next, Mrs. Chang explained that being class president is a big responsibility.

Then, Carlos nominated Katrel.

After that, Marta nominated Tanisha.

Last, Mrs. Chang handed out papers and pencils for the secret ballot.

Family Link Read aloud the Family Link activity on page 231 before sending copies of the Study Guide home with students. Later, have students share what family members say about voting in elections.

Name ______________________

The Fourth Grade Election

- **Read** *The Fourth Grade Election* again.
- Use the information in the book to **complete** the sequence organizer shown below. The first box is filled in for you.

First, Mrs. Chang announced that today the students would elect a class president.

↓

Next,

↓

Then,

↓

After that,

↓

Last,

Family Link

Has anyone in your family voted in an election? Ask family members to share their experiences voting. Ask them if they used a voting machine like the one shown in the book.

Leaves

by Emily Robertson

ELL Reader 4.3.1 Poetry

INTRODUCE THE BOOK

Activate Prior Knowledge/Build Background Read the title, and help the class make a web of what they know about leaves. Post the web on the wall.

Preview/Use Text Features Preview the reader by talking about the photographs together, naming the labeled items, and reading the captions. Point out the diagram on page 3 and the *Extend Language* feature on page 5.

Preteach Vocabulary Review the tested vocabulary words that appear in this book: **frost** and **fascinated**. Introduce these key words from the book: **photosynthesis** (p. 3) and **buds** (p. 6). Discuss these words and add them to a Word Wall.

READ THE BOOK

Choose among these options for reading to support students at all English proficiency levels.

Read Aloud Read the book aloud as students follow along. Pause to verify comprehension and to explain unfamiliar concepts.

Monitored Reading Have students read aloud a few pages at a time. Use the following questions to support comprehension:

- **Pages 2–4** What is photosynthesis? (the process in which leaves use sunlight to make food for trees)
- **Pages 5–8** What happens to leaves during the cold months? (They stop producing chlorophyll, change color, and fall from trees.) How do dead leaves help plants grow? (When they decay, they turn into humus.) What happens to the days in the spring? (They get longer.)

Reread Have students reread the book with a partner, in small groups, or independently. Have them complete the Study Guide on page 233.

RESPOND

Answers to the Reader's Inside Back Cover:

Talk About It

1. They are making chlorophyll; the green color blocks the natural color of the leaves. (Cause and Effect)

2. There is less light, which stops the process of photosynthesis. (Cause and Effect)

Write About It

3. *Spring:* Leaves open and begin making food. *Summer:* Leaves continue making food. *Fall:* Because of shorter days, leaves make less food, change color, and begin to fall. *Winter:* Leaves have fallen; the tree and its new leaves are sleeping. (Sequence)

Support writers at various English proficiency levels.

Beginning Let students dictate the details in their time lines for someone else to record.

Intermediate Have students look through the book to find details they can use in their time lines.

Advanced Have students include at least two details for each season in their time lines.

Extend Language Possible responses: winter: *snowy, cold;* fall/autumn: *cool, windy;* spring: *rainy, warm;* summer: *hot, sunny;* Invite students to draw pictures that represent a season and the adjectives they chose. Invite them to share their pictures with the class.

Answers to page 233:

1. gold, red, orange, or purple

2. spring and summer

3. There is not enough light.

4. They change into bright colors, then eventually become brown; their stems grow brittle.

5. They sprout into leaves and flowers.

Family Link Read aloud the Family Link activity on page 233 before sending copies of the Study Guide home with students. Later, have students talk about which seasons their families like best.

Name ______________________________

- **Read** *Leaves* again.
- Use the information in the book to **answer** the questions below.

pages 2–3

1. During the fall, what color are leaves like the one shown on page 3?

____

____

pages 4–5

2. During which time of the year does photosynthesis take place?

____

____

3. Why does photosynthesis stop in the fall?

____

____

pages 6–7

4. What happens to the leaves in the fall?

____

____

5. What do buds do in the spring?

____

____

Family Link

Talk to your family about the different seasons of the year. Which season do they like best? What color are the trees at that time of year?

Friendly Giants: California Gray Whales

by Sanjay Patel

ELL Reader 4.3.2 Expository Nonfiction

INTRODUCE THE BOOK

Activate Prior Knowledge/Build Background Read the title, and ask the class to brainstorm what they know about whales. Tell students that this book is about whales in the Pacific Ocean. Point out the Pacific Ocean, Alaska, California, and Mexico on a map.

Preview/Use Text Features Preview the reader by talking about the photographs and illustrations together, naming the labeled items, and reading the captions. Point out the diagram on page 5, the map on page 7, and the *Extend Language* feature on page 8.

Preteach Vocabulary Review the tested vocabulary words that appear in this book: **massive** and **lagoon**. Introduce these key words from the book: **calf** (p. 3), **ton** (p. 4), and **migration** (p. 7). Discuss these words and add them to a Word Wall.

READ THE BOOK

Choose among these options for reading to support students at all English proficiency levels.

Read Aloud Read the book aloud as students follow along. Pause to verify comprehension and to explain unfamiliar concepts.

Monitored Reading Have students silently read a few pages at a time. Use the following questions to support comprehension:

- **Pages 2–3** Why do gray whales come to Baja California? (to mate and have calves)
- **Pages 4–5** How long and heavy are adult gray whales? (35–50 feet long; 40,000–80,000 pounds)
- **Pages 6–8** Why do calves stay with their mothers? (to drink milk and learn to swim)

Reread Have students reread the book with a partner, in small groups, or independently. Have them complete the Study Guide on page 235.

RESPOND

Answers to the Reader's Inside Back Cover:

Talk About It

1. They are safe and warm, have lots of food, and are salty, which helps calves float as they learn to swim. (Main Idea and Details)

2. Blubber is a thick layer of fat. The thick layer keeps whales warm. (Cause and Effect)

Write About It

3. Whales feel rubbery; a person might feel scared, amazed, or funny touching a whale. Support writers at various English proficiency levels.

Beginning Display a sentence frame such as *A person might feel ____ touching a whale.* Have students dictate the missing word.

Intermediate Provide the same sentence frame, but have students copy it and write in the missing word.

Advanced Have students include at least one detail about what it is like touching a whale and two details about how a person might feel doing so.

Extend Language *Calves.* Mention other words that end in *-f,* and show how to change their endings in the plural *(leaf, shelf, wolf).*

Answers to page 235:

Possible responses:

p. 4: What do gray whales eat? tiny creatures that live near the bottom of the ocean

p. 6: How often do whales give birth, and how do the calves survive? They have one calf every two years. The calves nurse for seven months. They stay with their mothers in the lagoons for up to three months while they learn to swim.

p. 7: What is the migration route of the California gray whale? from Alaska to Baja, California, a distance of 14,000 miles round trip

Family Link Read aloud the Family Link activity on page 235 before sending copies of the Study Guide home with students. Later, have students share what family members say about whales.

Name ______________________________

Friendly Giants: California Gray Whales

- **Read** *Friendly Giants: California Gray Whales* again.
- **Read** each heading in the chart below. Then, **rewrite** each as a question. The first question is written for you.
- Next, **answer** each question using information from the book. The first answer is written for you.

Pages	Heading	Heading as Question	Answer
2–3	"The Friendlies"	Why are gray whales called "the friendlies?"	because they come right up to boats
4	Feeding		
6	Calves		
7	Migration		

Family Link

Has anyone in your family ever seen or touched a whale? Ask family members to share what they know and what they would like to know about whales.

Meet the Moon!

by Robert Decker

ELL Reader 4.3.3 Expository Nonfiction

INTRODUCE THE BOOK

Activate Prior Knowledge/Build Background Read the title, and ask volunteers to share what they know about the Moon.

Preview/Use Text Features Preview the reader by talking about the photographs and illustrations together, naming the labeled items, and reading the captions. Point out the diagram on page 6 and the *Extend Language* feature on page 7.

Preteach Vocabulary Review the tested vocabulary word that appears in this book: **brilliant**. Introduce these key words from the book: **expert** (p. 2), **scientists** (p. 3), and **eclipse** (p. 7). Discuss these words and add them to a Word Wall.

READ THE BOOK

Choose among these options for reading to support students at all English proficiency levels.

Read Aloud Read the book aloud as students follow along. Pause to verify comprehension and to explain unfamiliar concepts.

Monitored Reading Have students silently read a few pages at a time. Use the following questions to support comprehension:

- **Pages 2–3** What is the Moon's surface like? (It is covered with holes and smooth areas; it has mountains and valleys.) Where do some scientists think the Moon came from? (They think that 4–5 billion years ago it was part of the Earth.)
- **Pages 4–5** Why is there no life on the Moon? (because it has no air, water, or other gases that living things need)
- **Pages 6–8** How long does it take the Moon to go through all its phases? (29 days) What happens during a lunar eclipse? (The Moon seems to turn red or orange.) Who was the first man to walk on the moon? (Neil Armstrong)

Reread Have students reread the book with a partner, in small groups, or independently. Have them complete the Study Guide on page 237.

RESPOND

Answers to the Reader's Inside Back Cover:

Talk About It

1. Possible response: They see it in the sky almost every day. (Fact and Opinion)
2. Answers will vary.

Write About It

3. *Earth:* water, air, life; larger; *Both:* round, in space, receive light from the Sun, mountains, valleys, craters; *Moon:* no air, water, or life; smaller; orbits the Earth (Compare and Contrast)
Support writers at various English proficiency levels.

Beginning Provide a copy of the Venn diagram for students to fill in.
Intermediate Have students look through the book to find ideas they can use in their writing.
Advanced Have students include at least three points of comparison or contrast in each section of their Venn diagrams.

Extend Language *smaller, fuller, lighter, darker*

Answers to page 237:
Supporting Details: The Moon has no air, water, or life on it. A day on the Moon is about a month long. The Moon has one sixth the gravity of Earth.

Family Link Read aloud the Family Link activity on page 237 before sending copies of the Study Guide home with students. Later, ask students to share their families' experiences with eclipses.

Name ______________________________

- **Read** *Meet the Moon!* again.
- Use the information in the book. **Write** supporting details for the main idea shown below.

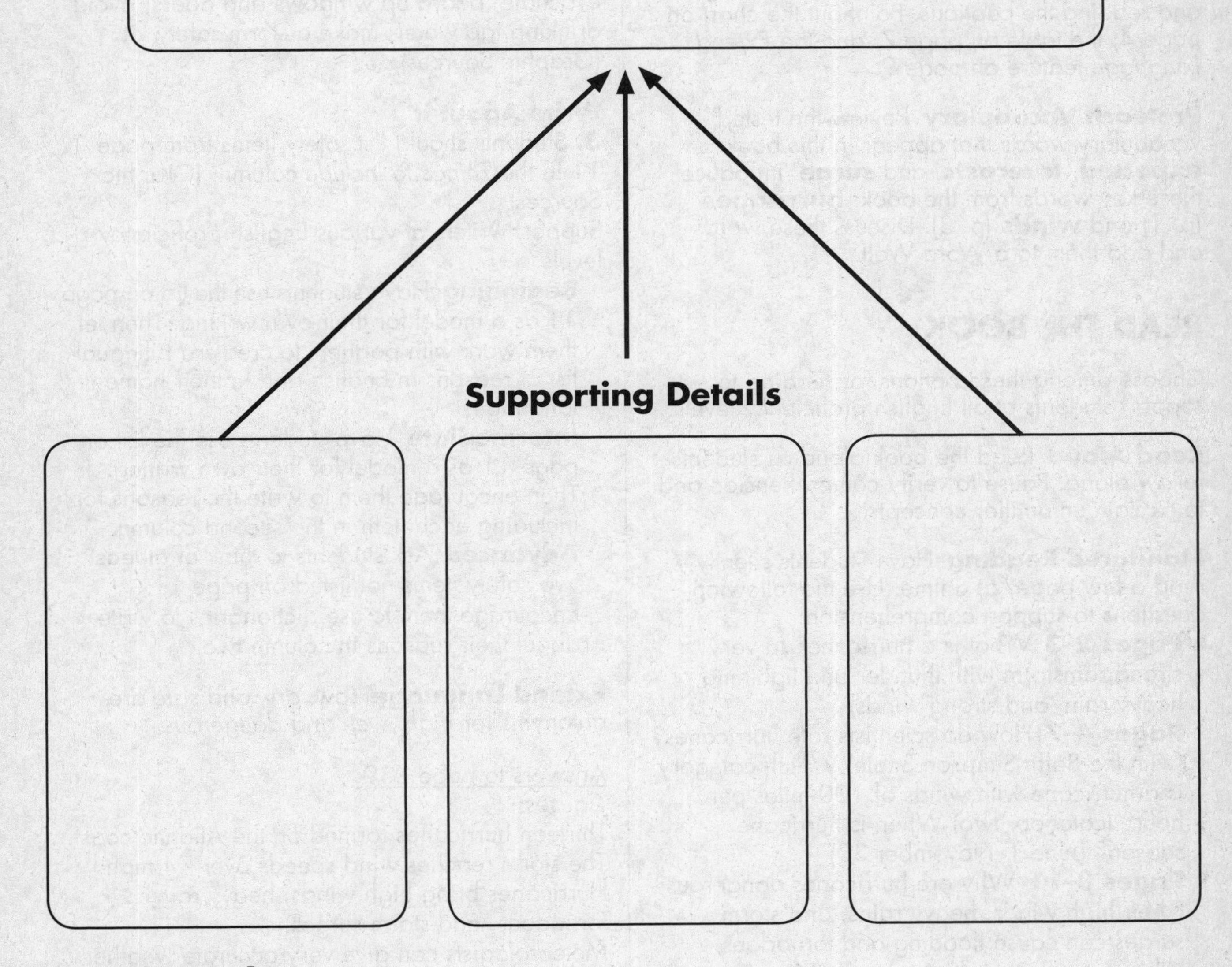

Family Link

Has anyone in your family ever seen a lunar or solar eclipse? Ask family members to share what they have seen.

Watch Out for Hurricanes!

by Rosemarie B. Ferrara — ELL Reader 4.3.4 Expository Nonfiction

INTRODUCE THE BOOK

Activate Prior Knowledge/Build Background Read the title, and tell students that hurricanes are very strong rainstorms. Ask volunteers to share experiences with hurricanes.

Preview/Use Text Features Preview the reader by talking about the photographs together and reading the captions. Point out the chart on page 4, the table on page 7, and the *Extend Language* feature on page 9.

Preteach Vocabulary Review the tested vocabulary words that appear in this book: **expected**, **forecasts**, and **surge**. Introduce these key words from the book: **hurricanes** (p. 1) and **winds** (p. 3). Discuss these words and add them to a Word Wall.

READ THE BOOK

Choose among these options for reading to support students at all English proficiency levels.

Read Aloud Read the book aloud as students follow along. Pause to verify comprehension and to explain unfamiliar concepts.

Monitored Reading Have students silently read a few pages at a time. Use the following questions to support comprehension:

- **Pages 2–3** What is a hurricane? (a very strong rainstorm with thunder and lightning, heavy rain, and strong winds)
- **Pages 4–7** How do scientists rate hurricanes? (with the Saffir-Simpson Scale) Which category is a hurricane with winds of 100 miles per hour? (category two) When is hurricane season? (June 1–November 30)
- **Pages 8–11** Why are hurricanes dangerous? (Their high winds, heavy rains, and storm surges can cause flooding and tornadoes, killing people and destroying buildings.)

Reread Have students reread the book with a partner, in small groups, or independently. Have them complete the Study Guide on page 239.

RESPOND

Answers to the Reader's Inside Back Cover:

Talk About It

1. Answers will vary.

2. Possible response: listen to a weather report; stay inside; know where to go if you must evacuate; board up windows and doors; avoid drinking tap water; make a storm safety kit (Graphic Sources)

Write About It

3. Students should list safety items from page 11 in the *Things to Include* column. (Graphic Sources)

Support writers at various English proficiency levels.

Beginning Have students use the list on page 11 as a model for their own writing. Then let them work with partners to create a bilingual list of reasons in English and in their home language.

Intermediate Have students use the list on page 11 as a model for their own writing. Then encourage them to write the reasons for including each item in the second column.

Advanced Ask students to think of at least two safety items not listed on page 11. Encourage them to use dictionaries to write about their reasons in column two.

Extend Language *Low, dry,* and *safe* are antonyms for *high, wet,* and *dangerous.*

Answers to page 239:

Causes:

Thirteen hurricanes formed on the Atlantic coast.

The storm reaches wind speeds over 74 mph.

Hurricanes bring high winds, heavy rain, tornadoes, and storm surges.

Meteorologists can give very accurate weather forecasts.

Family Link Read aloud the Family Link activity on page 239 before sending copies of the Study Guide home with students. Later, have students share what family members say about their experiences in storms.

Name ______________________________

Watch Out for Hurricanes!

- **Read** *Watch Out for Hurricanes!* again.
- Use the book to **find** the causes of the effects shown below. **Write** your answers in the correct box.

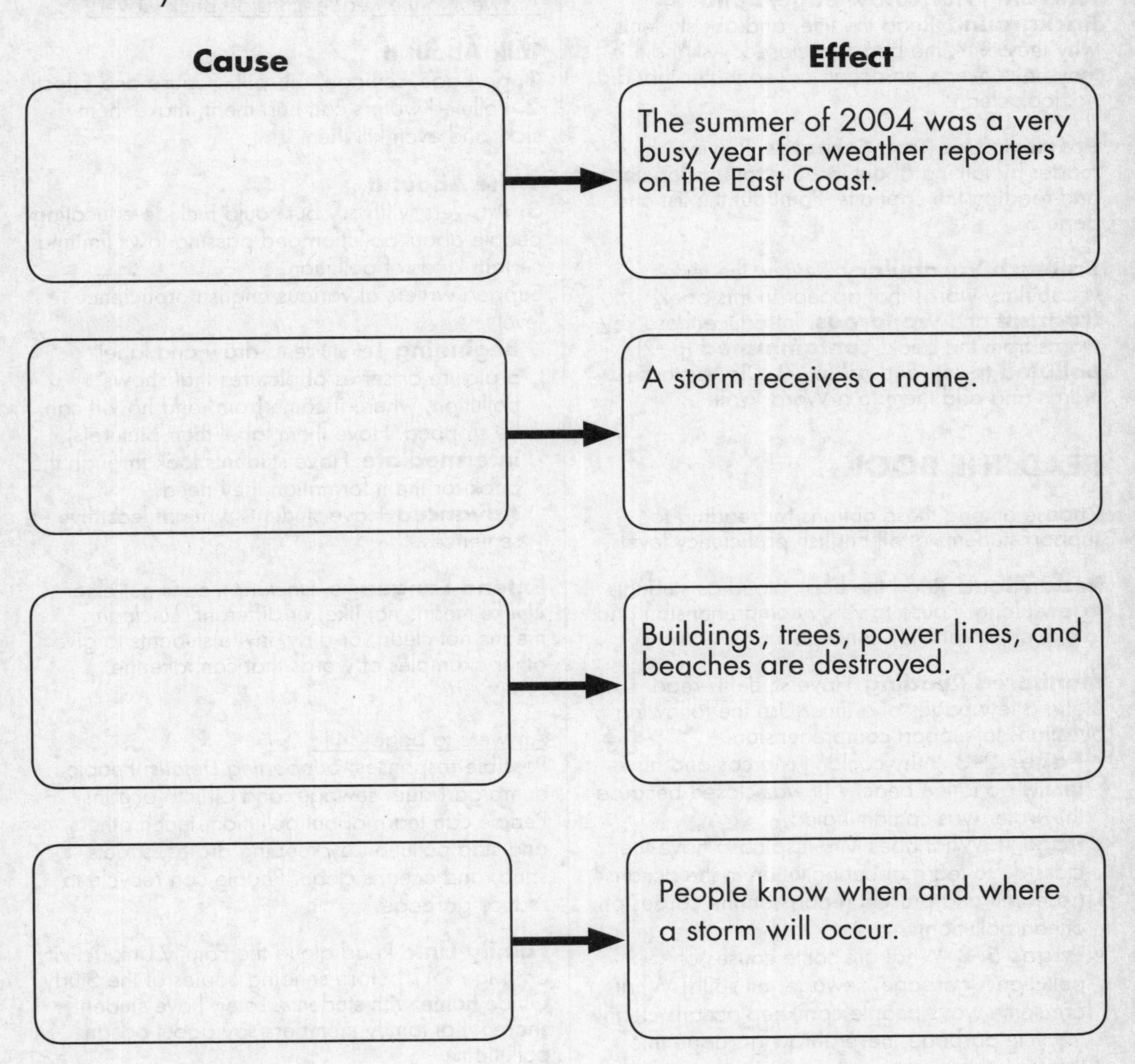

Cause	Effect
	The summer of 2004 was a very busy year for weather reporters on the East Coast.
	A storm receives a name.
	Buildings, trees, power lines, and beaches are destroyed.
	People know when and where a storm will occur.

Family Link

Has anyone in your family ever been in a bad storm or a hurricane? Ask family members to share their experiences with rain and wind storms.

No Swimming Today!

by José Fernando Colón

ELL Reader 4.3.5 Realistic Fiction

INTRODUCE THE BOOK

Activate Prior Knowledge/Build Background Read the title, and ask students why they think the beach is closed. Ask them if they have ever seen ocean or sea water that did not look clean.

Preview/Use Text Features Preview the reader by talking about the illustrations together and reading the captions. Point out the list on page 8.

Preteach Vocabulary Review the tested vocabulary words that appear in this book: **fragrant** and **wondrous**. Introduce these key words from the book: **contaminated** (p. 2), **polluted** (p. 4), and **oil** (p. 7). Discuss these words and add them to a Word Wall.

READ THE BOOK

Choose among these options for reading to support students at all English proficiency levels.

Read Aloud Read the book aloud as students follow along. Pause to verify comprehension and to explain unfamiliar concepts.

Monitored Reading Have students read aloud a few pages at a time. Use the following questions to support comprehension:

- **Pages 2–3** Why couldn't Marcos and his family go to the beach? (It was closed because the water was contaminated.)
- **Page 4** What does Mrs. Espinosa have the class do to learn about pollution in the oceans? (research and present reports on the causes of ocean pollution)
- **Pages 5–8** What are some causes of pollution? (garbage, sewage, oil spills) What are some ways people can keep oceans clean? (recycle garbage, never throw garbage into the sea, never pour oil or chemicals down the drain)

Reread Have students reread the book with a partner, in small groups, or independently. Have them complete the Study Guide on page 241.

RESPOND

Answers to the Reader's Inside Back Cover:

Talk About It

1. garbage, sewage, oil spills (Cause and Effect)
2. Polluted waters can hurt them, make them sick, and even kill them.

Write About It

3. Answers will vary but could include educating people about pollution and passing laws limiting certain kinds of pollution.
Support writers at various English proficiency levels.

Beginning Let students draw and label a picture or series of pictures that shows pollution, where it came from, and how it can be stopped. Have them label their picture(s).
Intermediate Have students look through the book for the information they need.
Advanced Have students write at least five sentences.

Extend Language *Unclear* means not clear. *Unlike* means not like, or different. *Unclean* means not clean, or dirty. Invite students to give other examples of words that can take the prefix *-un*.

Answers to page 241:
Possible responses: *Supporting Details*: People dump garbage, sewage, and oil into oceans. People can learn about pollution, teach others, and stop pollution by keeping drains, streets, sand, and oceans clean. People can recycle to reduce garbage.

Family Link Read aloud the Family Link activity on page 241 before sending copies of the Study Guide home with students. Later, have students share what family members say about ocean pollution.

Name ______________________ **No Swimming Today!**

- **Read** *No Swimming Today!* again.
- Use the book to **find** three details that support the main idea shown below.

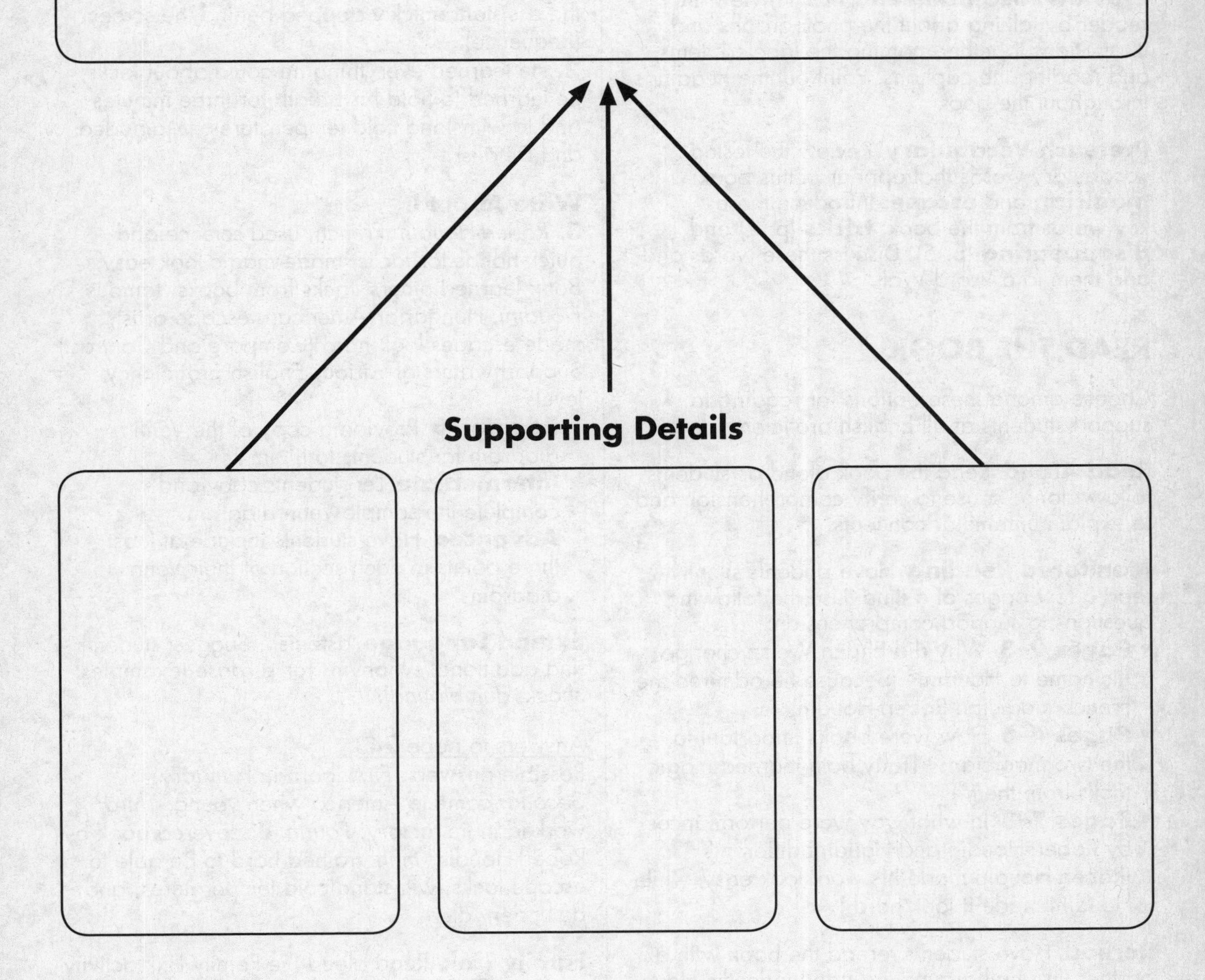

Family Link

Has anyone in your family seen a polluted or dirty ocean? Ask family members to share what they know about polluted water.

Two Master Magicians

by Alicia Morton

ELL Reader 4.4.1 Nonfiction

INTRODUCE THE BOOK

Activate Prior Knowledge/Build Background Read the title, and explain the meaning of *master magicians.* Ask students if they know any magic tricks or have seen a magician perform.

Preview/Use Text Features Preview the reader by talking about the photographs and illustrations together, naming the labeled items, and reading the captions. Point out the headings throughout the book.

Preteach Vocabulary Review the tested vocabulary words that appear in this book: **magician** and **escape**. Introduce these key words from the book: **tricks** (p. 2) and **disappearing** (p. 5). Discuss these words and add them to a Word Wall.

READ THE BOOK

Choose among these options for reading to support students at all English proficiency levels.

Read Aloud Read the book aloud as students follow along. Pause to verify comprehension and to explain unfamiliar concepts.

Monitored Reading Have students silently read a few pages at a time. Use the following questions to support comprehension:

- **Pages 2–3** Why did Ehrich Weisz change his name to Houdini? (because he admired the French magician Robert-Houdin)
- **Pages 4–6** How were books important to the two magicians? (They both learned magic tricks from them.)
- **Pages 7–8** In what way were performances by Robert-Houdin and Houdini different? (Robert-Houdin made his work look easy, while Houdini made it look hard.)

Reread Have students reread the book with a partner, in small groups, or independently. Have them complete the Study Guide on page 243.

RESPOND

Answers to the Reader's Inside Back Cover:

Talk About It

1. He had a small screen in front of a larger backdrop, both made of the same material. When he waved his cape in front of his assistant, the assistant quickly stepped behind the screen. (Sequence)

2. He learned everything he could about locks; he learned to hold his breath for three minutes and to withstand cold temperatures. (Main Idea and Details)

Write About It

3. *Robert-Houdin:* French, used science and quick hands for tricks, made magic look easy; *Both:* learned others' tricks from books, famous; *Houdini:* Hungarian-American, escape artist, made escapes look hard (Compare and Contrast)

Support writers at various English proficiency levels.

Beginning Provide a copy of the Venn diagram for students to fill in.

Intermediate Let students copy and complete the sample Venn diagram.

Advanced Have students include at least three points in each section of their Venn diagrams.

Extend Language astonish; Suggest students find additional synonyms for *surprise* (examples: *shock, dumbfound).*

Answers to page 243:

Possible answers: *First:* born in Hungary; *Second:* came to America when young; *Third:* worked in tie factory; *Fourth:* discovered book by Robert-Houdin; *Fifth:* trained hard to be able to escape locks, withstand cold temperatures, and be underwater

Family Link Read aloud the Family Link activity on page 243 before sending copies of the Study Guide home with students. Later, have students share what family members told them about magicians and magic tricks.

Name ______________________________

- **Read** *Two Master Magicians* again.
- Use the information in the book. **Write** five events in Harry Houdini's life in the order in which they occurred.

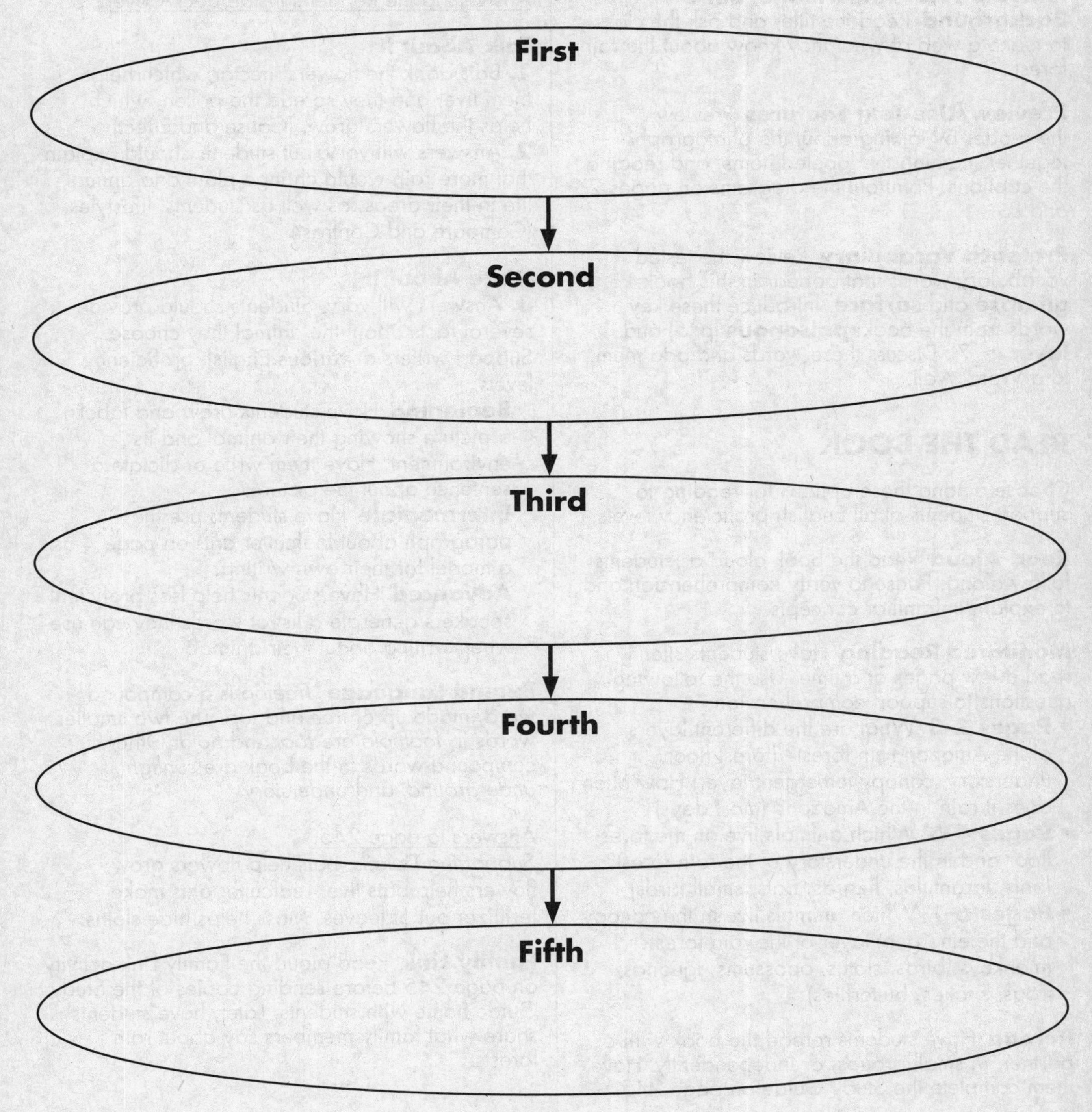

Family Link

Does anyone in your family know magic tricks? Ask family members to share what they know about magicians and magic tricks.

Life in the Amazon Rain Forest

by Ronald Scheibel

ELL Reader 4.4.2 Expository Nonfiction

INTRODUCE THE BOOK

Activate Prior Knowledge/Build Background Read the title, and ask the class to make a web of what they know about the rain forest.

Preview/Use Text Features Preview the reader by talking about the photographs together, naming the labeled items, and reading the captions. Point out the diagrams on pages 2 and 8.

Preteach Vocabulary Review the tested vocabulary words that appear in this book: **glimpse** and **surface**. Introduce these key words from the book: **poisonous** (p. 5) and **layer** (p. 7). Discuss these words and add them to a Word Wall.

READ THE BOOK

Choose among these options for reading to support students at all English proficiency levels.

Read Aloud Read the book aloud as students follow along. Pause to verify comprehension and to explain unfamiliar concepts.

Monitored Reading Have students silently read a few pages at a time. Use the following questions to support comprehension:

- **Pages 2–3** What are the different layers of the Amazon rain forest? (forest floor, understory, canopy, emergent layer) How often does it rain in the Amazon? (most days)
- **Pages 4–5** Which animals live on the forest floor and in the understory of the rain forest? (ants, tarantulas, lizards, bats, small birds)
- **Pages 6–7** Which animals live in the canopy and the emergent layer of the rain forest? (monkeys, birds, sloths, opossums, iguanas, frogs, snakes, butterflies)

Reread Have students reread the book with a partner, in small groups, or independently. Have them complete the Study Guide on page 245.

RESPOND

Answers to the Reader's Inside Back Cover:

Talk About It

1. Bats drink the flowers' nectar, which helps them live, and they spread the pollen, which helps the flowers grow. (Cause and Effect)

2. Answers will vary, but students should explain that more rain would change plant and animal life in their areas, as well as students' lifestyles. (Compare and Contrast)

Write About It

3. Answers will vary. Students should provide several facts about the animal they choose. Support writers at various English proficiency levels.

Beginning Have students draw and label a picture showing their animal and its environment. Have them write or dictate a sentence about the picture.

Intermediate Have students use the paragraph about leafcutter ants on page 4 as a model for their own writing.

Advanced Have students help less proficient speakers generate a list of words they can use when writing about their animal.

Extend Language *Treetop* is a compound word, made up of *tree* and *top*. The two smaller words in *foothold* are *foot* and *hold*. Other compound words in the book are *sunlight*, *underground*, and *understory*.

Answers to page 245:

Supporting Details: Bats help flowers grow; flowers help bats live. Leafcutter ants make fertilizer out of leaves. Moss helps hide sloths.

Family Link Read aloud the Family Link activity on page 245 before sending copies of the Study Guide home with students. Later, have students share what family members say about rain forests.

Name ___________________________

- **Read** *Life in the Amazon Rain Forest* again.
- Use the information in the book. **Write** details that support the generalization shown below.

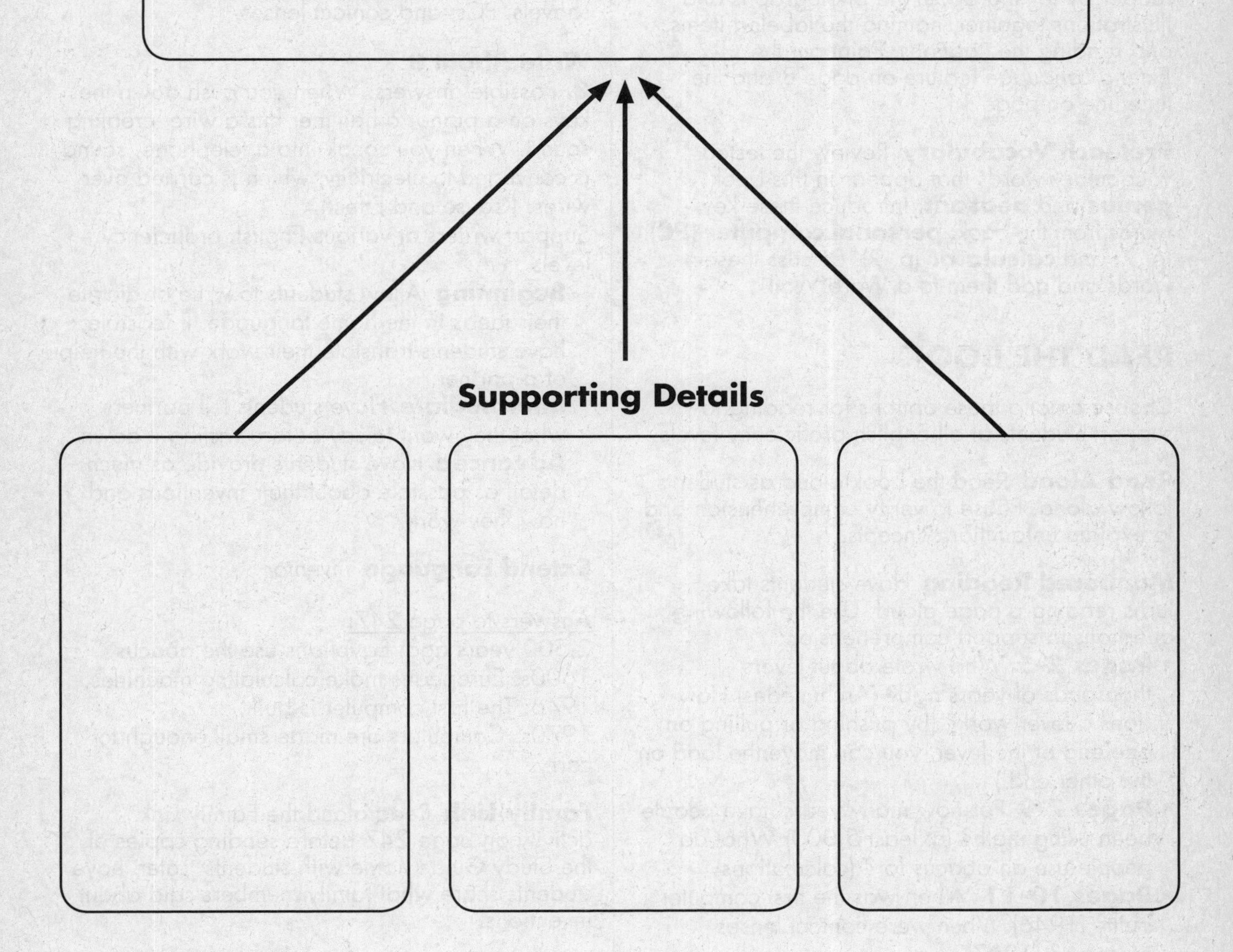

Family Link

Has anyone in your family ever been to a rain forest? Ask family members to share what they know about rain forests.

Inventions

by Hiro Takahashi

ELL Reader 4.4.3 Expository Nonfiction

INTRODUCE THE BOOK

Activate Prior Knowledge/Build Background Read the title, and explain the word *inventions.* Then ask the class to brainstorm a list of inventions used in the classroom.

Preview/Use Text Features Preview the reader by talking about the photographs and illustrations together, naming the labeled items, and reading the captions. Point out the *Extend Language* feature on page 8 and the time line on page 11.

Preteach Vocabulary Review the tested vocabulary words that appear in this book: **genius** and **peasant**. Introduce these key words from the book: **personal computer (PC)** (p. 7) and **calculator** (p. 9). Discuss these words and add them to a Word Wall.

READ THE BOOK

Choose among these options for reading to support students at all English proficiency levels.

Read Aloud Read the book aloud as students follow along. Pause to verify comprehension and to explain unfamiliar concepts.

Monitored Reading Have students take turns reading a page aloud. Use the following questions to support comprehension:

- **Pages 2–5** Who wrote about levers thousands of years ago? (Archimedes) How does a lever work? (By pushing or pulling on one end of the lever, you can move the load on the other end.)
- **Pages 7–9** For how many years have people been using math? (at least 5,000) What do people use an abacus for? (calculations)
- **Pages 10–11** When was the first computer built? (1946) When were contact lenses invented? (1887)

Reread Have students reread the book with a partner, in small groups, or independently. Have them complete the Study Guide on page 247.

RESPOND

Answers to the Reader's Inside Back Cover:

Talk About It
1. often from someone else's invention or from an idea from long ago (Cause and Effect)
2. Answers will vary but could include scissors, shovels, PCs, and contact lenses.

Write About It
3. Possible answers: When you push down the keys on a piano, a hammer hits a wire, creating sound. When you speak into a telephone, sound is converted to electricity, which is carried over wires. (Cause and Effect)
Support writers at various English proficiency levels.

Beginning Allow students to write or dictate their ideas in the home language. If feasible, have students translate their work with the help of a partner.
Intermediate Have students tell partners what they want to say before writing it down.
Advanced Have students provide as much detail as possible about their inventions and how they work.

Extend Language *inventor*

Answers to page 247:
2,500 years ago: Egyptians use the abacus.
1600s: Europeans make calculating machines.
1946: The first computer is built.
1970s: Computers are made small enough to carry.

Family Link Read aloud the Family Link activity on page 247 before sending copies of the Study Guide home with students. Later, have students share what family members said about inventions.

Name ______________________________

- **Read** *Inventions* again.
- Use the information in the book to **make** a time line of the invention of personal computers. The first entry has been done for you.

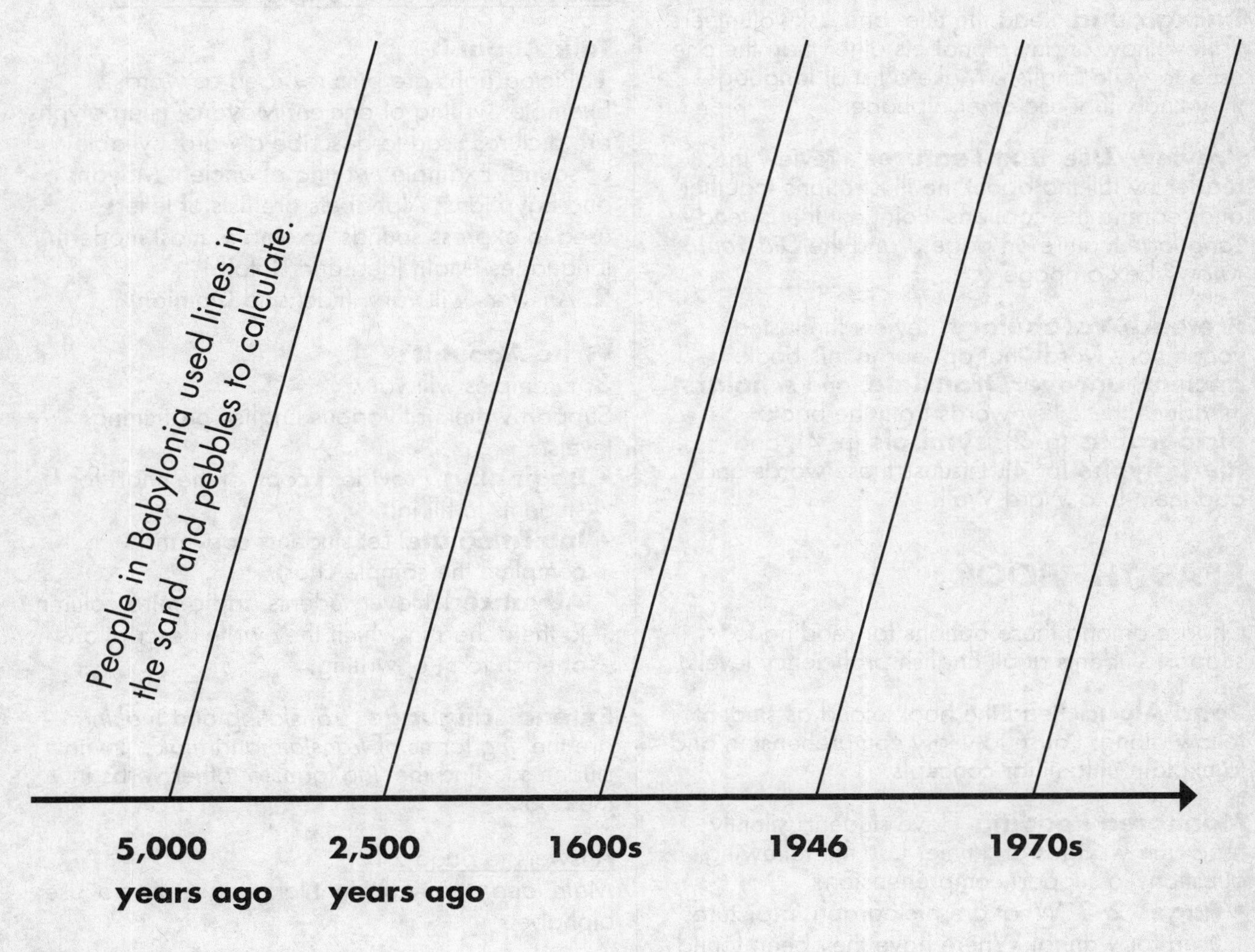

Family Link

What inventions do your family members like and use most? What inventions do they use today that had not been invented when they were your age?

Alphabets and Other Writing Systems

by S. Michele McFadden

ELL Reader 4.4.4 Expository Nonfiction

INTRODUCE THE BOOK

Activate Prior Knowledge/Build Background Read the title, and ask volunteers if they know of any alphabets other than the one used to write English. Make a list of languages they know that use other alphabets.

Preview/Use Text Features Preview the reader by talking about the illustrations together and reading the captions. Point out the *Extend Language* feature on page 3 and the *Did You Know?* box on page 6.

Preteach Vocabulary Review the tested vocabulary words that appear in this book: **ancient**, **uncover**, **translate**, and **scholars**. Introduce these key words from the book: **pictographs** (p. 2), **symbols** (p. 4), and **hieroglyphs** (p. 4). Discuss these words and add them to a Word Wall.

READ THE BOOK

Choose among these options for reading to support students at all English proficiency levels.

Read Aloud Read the book aloud as students follow along. Pause to verify comprehension and to explain unfamiliar concepts.

Monitored Reading Have students silently read a few pages at a time. Use the following questions to support comprehension:

- **Pages 2–3** What are pictographs? (pictures used for writing) Where have they been found? (in caves, pots, shells)
- **Pages 4–6** What do hieroglyphs stand for? (words, syllables, or sounds) Who was Jean-François Champollion? (the man who translated hieroglyphics) Which people used hieroglyphics? (the ancient Egyptians and the ancient Mayans)
- **Pages 7–8** How are most languages written today? (with alphabets)

Reread Have students reread the book with a partner, in small groups, or independently. Have them complete the Study Guide on page 249.

RESPOND

Answers to the Reader's Inside Back Cover:

Talk About It

1. Pictographs are pictures used as words. Example: writing of ancient Mayans; Hieroglyphs are pictures used to describe a word, syllable, or sound. Example: writing of ancient Mayans and Egyptians; Alphabets are lists of letters used to express sounds. Example: most modern languages (Main Idea and Details)

2. Answers will vary. (Fact and Opinion)

Write About It

3. Examples will vary.

Support writers at various English proficiency levels.

Beginning Provide a copy of the chart for students to fill in.

Intermediate Let students copy and complete the sample chart.

Advanced Have students add a third column to their chart in which they write descriptions of each form of writing.

Extend Language *Translating* and *making* are the *-ing* forms of *translate* and *make.* Invite students to find the *-ing* forms of other verbs in the book.

Answers to page 249:

Main Idea: Many ancient languages did not use alphabets.

Family Link Read aloud the Family Link activity on page 249 before sending copies of the Study Guide home with students. Later, have students discuss other alphabets their families are familiar with.

Name ______________________________

Alphabets and Other Writing Systems

- **Read** *Alphabets and Other Writing Systems* again.
- **Write** the main idea of the supporting details shown in the organizer below.

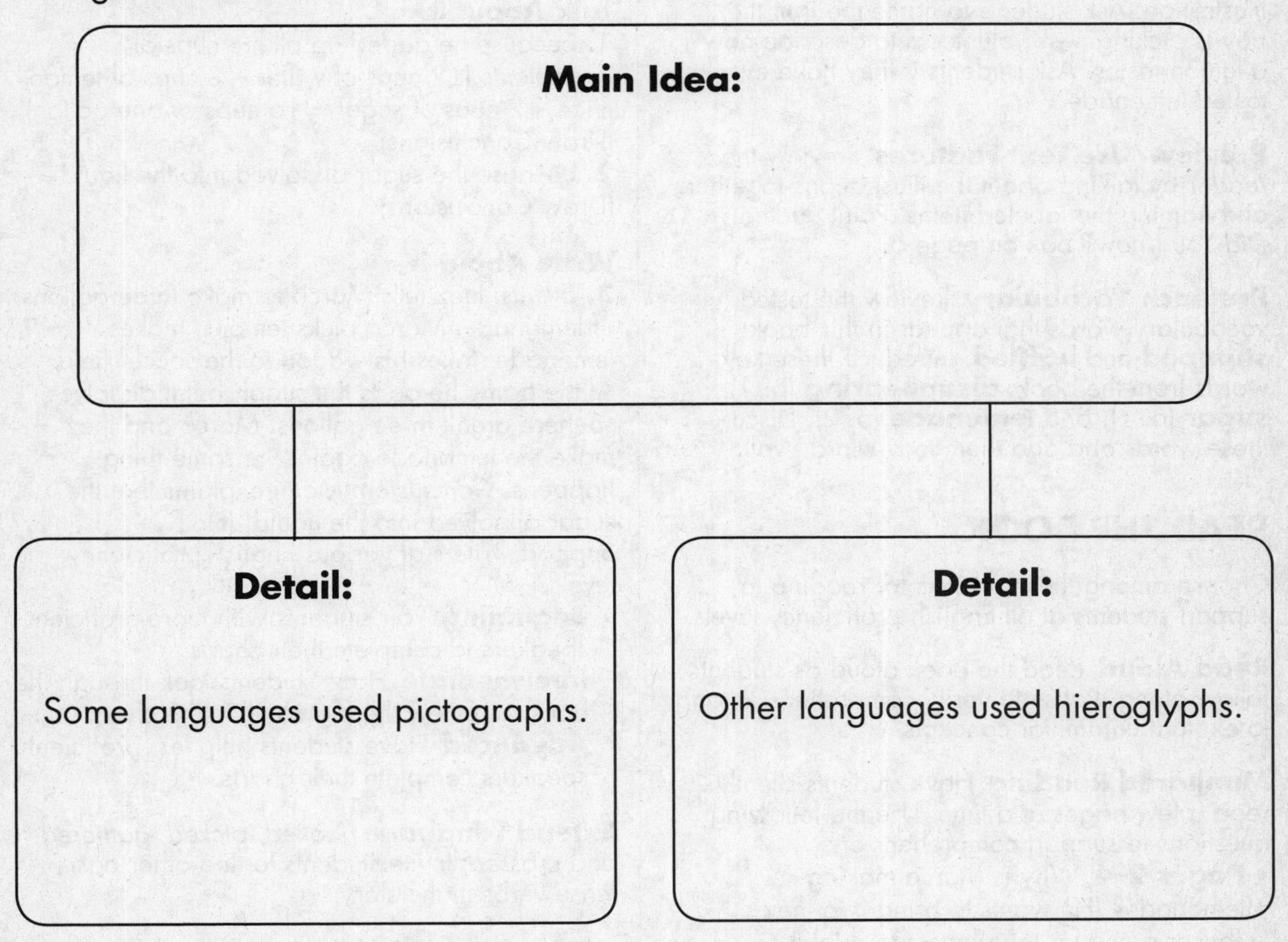

Family Link

Does anyone in your family know how to write in an alphabet other than English? Which one? How many letters are there in that alphabet? What do some of the letters look like?

The Case of the Disappearing Sugar

by Fritz Kedding

ELL Reader 4.4.5 Mystery Story

INTRODUCE THE BOOK

Activate Prior Knowledge/Build Background Read the title, and discuss the illustration. Ask students to name the fruit the boy is picking. Ask volunteers to describe how a lemon tastes. Ask students if they have ever tasted lemonade.

Preview/Use Text Features Preview the reader by talking about the illustrations together and naming the labeled items. Point out the *Did You Know?* box on page 6.

Preteach Vocabulary Review the tested vocabulary words that appear in this book: **stumped** and **baffled**. Introduce these key words from the book: **disappearing** (p. 1), **sugar** (p. 1), and **lemonade** (p. 2). Discuss these words and add them to a Word Wall.

READ THE BOOK

Choose among these options for reading to support students at all English proficiency levels.

Read Aloud Read the book aloud as students follow along. Pause to verify comprehension and to explain unfamiliar concepts.

Monitored Reading Have students silently read a few pages at a time. Use the following questions to support comprehension:

- **Pages 2–4** Why is Marco making lemonade? (He wants to bring it to Inéz's soccer game for the players to drink.)
- **Pages 5–7** How does Marco make the lemonade? (He mixes 12 cups of water, 2 cups of lemon juice, and 2 cups of sugar for each gallon of lemonade.)
- **Pages 8–12** What happened to the sugar? (It dissolved into the liquid.)

Reread Have students reread the book with a partner, in small groups, or independently. Have them complete the Study Guide on page 251.

RESPOND

Answers to the Reader's Inside Back Cover:

Talk About It

1. because he added up all the cups of ingredients (12 cups of water + 2 cups of lemon juice + 2 cups of sugar = 16 cups or one gallon) (Draw Conclusions)

2. because the sugar dissolved into the liquid (Draw Conclusions)

Write About It

3. *Events:* Inez tells Marco to make three gallons of lemonade. Marco picks lemons, makes lemonade, takes his wagon to the soccer field. At the game he adds the sugar, but it dissolves, so there aren't three gallons. Marco and Inez make the lemonade again; the same thing happens. *Conclusion:* Mami explains that the sugar dissolved into the liquid. (Plot)

Support writers at various English proficiency levels.

Beginning Pair students with more-proficient speakers to complete their charts.

Intermediate Have students look through the book to review the plot to fill in the chart.

Advanced Have students help less-proficient speakers complete their charts.

Extend Language *looked, picked, gathered,* and *crossed*; Invite students to find other past-tense verbs in the story.

Answers to page 251:

1. because he forgot to add sugar
2. He cut the lemons.
3. He was going to be late to the game.
4. because he did not make 3 full gallons of lemonade
5. It seemed to disappear.

Family Link Read aloud the Family Link activity on page 251 before sending copies of the Study Guide home with students. Later, have students share their families' recipes for fruit drinks and desserts.

Name ______________________

The Case of the Disappearing Sugar

- **Read** *The Case of the Disappearing Sugar* again.
- Use the information in the book to **answer** the questions below.

pages 2–3

1. Why didn't people like the lemonade Marco brought to the last soccer game?

____

____

pages 4–5

2. How did Marco's father help him?

____

____

pages 6–7

3. Why didn't Marco add the sugar to the lemonade at home?

____

____

pages 8–9

4. Why was Inez unhappy with her brother?

____

____

pages 10–12

5. What happened when Inez added the sugar to the water and lemon juice?

____

____

Family Link

Does anyone in your family make fruit drinks or desserts out of fruit? Ask your family to share their recipes with you.

The Treasure Fleet

by Natalie Cross

ELL Reader 4.5.1 Nonfiction

INTRODUCE THE BOOK

Activate Prior Knowledge/Build Background Read the title, and ask students to describe what they see in the picture. Explain that a treasure is something valuable, such as money, jewels, or gold. Explain that a fleet is a group of ships.

Preview/Use Text Features Preview the reader by talking about the illustrations and photographs together and reading the captions. Point out the maps on pages 3, 4, and 5.

Preteach Vocabulary Review the tested vocabulary words that appear in this book: **navigation** and **cargo**. Introduce these key words from the book: **treasure** (p. 1), **fleet** (p. 1), and **Chinese** (p. 3). Discuss these words and add them to a Word Wall.

READ THE BOOK

Choose among these options for reading to support students at all English proficiency levels.

Read Aloud Read the book aloud as students follow along. Pause to verify comprehension and to explain unfamiliar concepts.

Monitored Reading Have students silently read a few pages at a time. Use the following questions to support comprehension:

- **Pages 2–3** Why did Emperor Zhu Pi want his fleet to travel to other countries? (He wanted them to trade and to show how powerful China was.)
- **Pages 4–6** How many ships and men were part of the first Treasure Fleet voyage? (300 ships, 28,000 men) What kinds of treasures were on the ships? (silk, porcelain dishes and vases)
- **Pages 7–8** Why did the Treasure Fleet stop sailing? (The new emperor feared land attacks and wanted to use China's money to strengthen the army.)

Reread Have students reread the book with a partner, in small groups, or independently. Have them complete the Study Guide on page 253.

RESPOND

Answers to the Reader's Inside Back Cover:

Talk About It
1. The sailors brought rice, fresh water, fish, fruit, and tubs of soil to grow vegetables. They knew how to make fresh water from salty water. (Main Idea and Details)
2. Possible response: China was a great naval and trading power in the 1400s. (Author's Purpose)

Write About It
3. Answers will vary but should include descriptions of their duties or what they saw in port.
Support writers at various English proficiency levels.

Beginning Display a sentence frame such as *Dear Diary, Today we landed in India. We saw many* _____. Have students dictate endings.
Intermediate Provide the same sentence frame, but have students copy it and write their own endings.
Advanced Have students describe trading some of the goods from the Treasure Fleet for other goods.

Extend Language Possible responses: *sailboat, motorboat, battleship, aircraft carrier, yacht, canoe, kayak, rowboat, dinghy*

Answers to page 253:
1405: The first Treasure Fleet voyage begins.
1433: The Treasure Fleet makes its last voyage.
1500s: Countries of Europe rule the seas.

Family Link Read aloud the Family Link activity on page 253 before sending copies of the Study Guide home with students. Later, have students share what family members say about sailing.

Name ______________________________

The Treasure Fleet

- **Read** *The Treasure Fleet* again.
- Use the information in the book to **fill in** the time line. The first entry has been done for you.

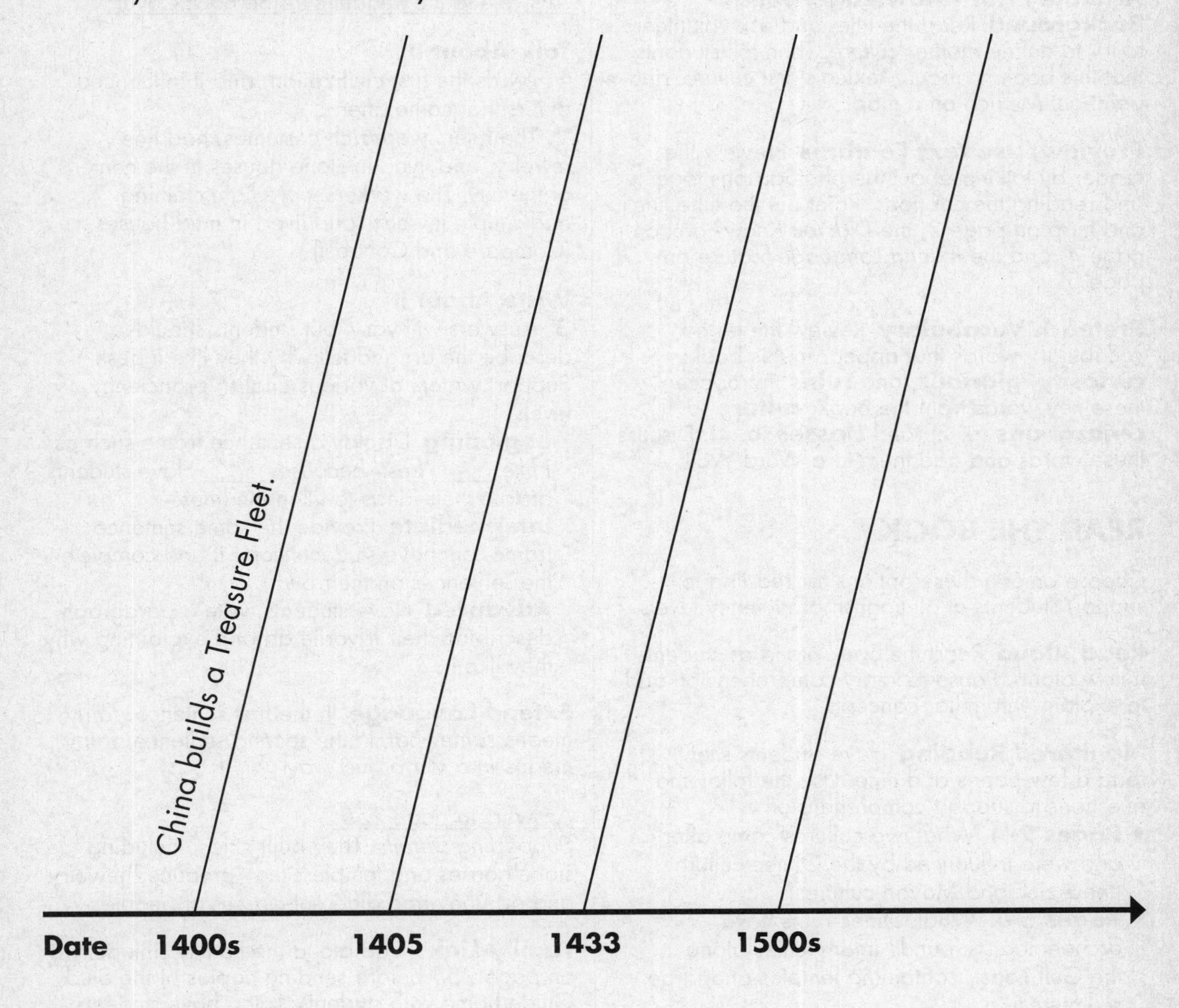

Family Link

Sailors who sailed on the Chinese ships had hard lives, but they got to visit many interesting places. Talk to the people in your family about the Treasure Fleet trips. Ask them if they would be willing to eat dried food and live on a ship for months at a time if they could travel all over the world.

Mexico's Mother Culture

by Eva Moreno

ELL Reader 4.5.2 Expository Nonfiction

INTRODUCE THE BOOK

Activate Prior Knowledge/Build Background Read the title, and ask volunteers to try to define *mother culture*. Then tell students that this book is about Mexico's first culture, and point out Mexico on a map.

Preview/Use Text Features Preview the reader by talking about the photographs together and reading the captions. Point out the time line and map on page 2, the *Did You Know?* box on page 4, and the *Extend Language* feature on page 5.

Preteach Vocabulary Review the tested vocabulary words that appear in this book: **curiosity**, **glorious**, and **ruins**. Introduce these key words from the book: **culture** (p. 1), **civilizations** (p. 2), and **classes** (p. 4). Discuss these words and add them to a Word Wall.

READ THE BOOK

Choose among these options for reading to support students at all English proficiency levels.

Read Aloud Read the book aloud as students follow along. Pause to verify comprehension and to explain unfamiliar concepts.

Monitored Reading Have students silently read a few pages at a time. Use the following questions to support comprehension:

- **Pages 2–4** What two cultures came after and were influenced by the Olmec culture? (the Aztec and Mayan cultures)
- **Pages 5–7** What Olmec ruins have archaeologists found? (many cities along the Gulf coast, containing temples and large sculptures)
- **Page 8** What happened to the Olmec civilization? Why did this happen? (About 2,400 years ago, the Olmecs abandoned their largest cities. No one knows why.)

Reread Have students reread the book with a partner, in small groups, or independently. Have them complete the Study Guide on page 255.

RESPOND

<u>Answers to the Reader's Inside Back Cover:</u>

Talk About It

1. It was the first civilization, and it influenced others that came after.

2. The rulers wore rich costumes, had fine jewelry, and lived in stone houses in the center of the city. The workers wore light clothing, had simple jewelry, and lived in mud houses. (Compare and Contrast)

Write About It

3. Answers will vary, but students should describe the art and tell why they like it best. Support writers at various English proficiency levels.

Beginning Display a sentence frame such as *I like _____ best, because _____*. Have students dictate their ideas to fill in the lines.

Intermediate Provide the same sentence frame, but have students copy it and complete the sentences on their own.

Advanced Have students write a paragraph describing their favorite art and explaining why they like it.

Extend Language In the first sentence, *fairly* means *somewhat*. In the second sentence, *fairly* means *in a fair or just way*.

<u>Answers to page 255:</u>

Supporting Details: They built cities, including stone houses and temples; they produced jewelry and art; they had different classes of people.

Family Link Read aloud the Family Link activity on page 255 before sending copies of the Study Guide home with students. Later, have students share what family members say about ancient civilizations.

Name ______________________________

Mexico's Mother Culture

- **Read** *Mexico's Mother Culture* again.
- **Find** details that support the conclusion shown below. **Write** them in the *Supporting Details* boxes.

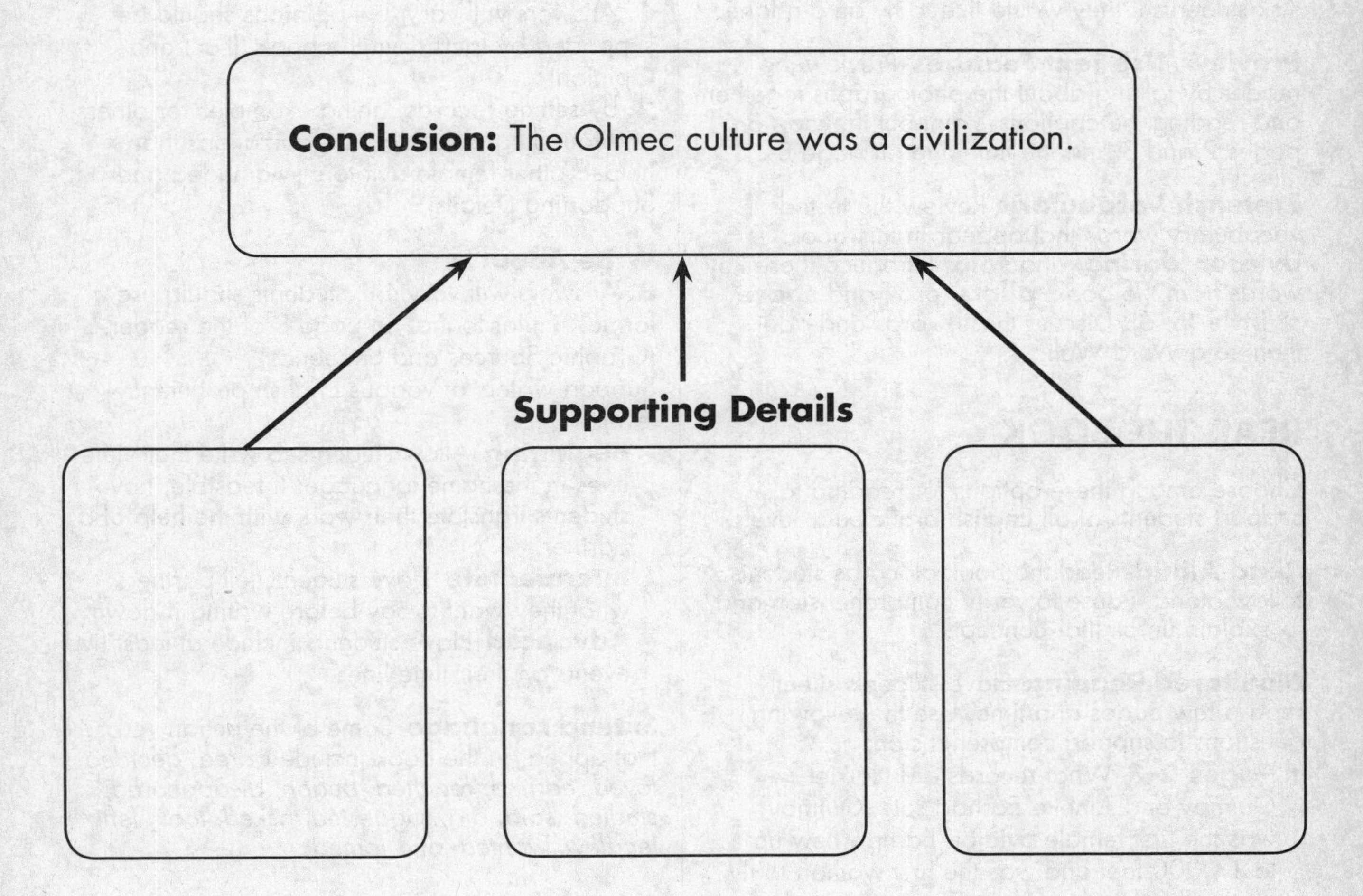

Family Link

Does anyone in your family know about ancient civilizations in their home countries? Ask family members to share what they know.

Women Who Dared to Fly

by Mei Hua Chen

ELL Reader 4.5.3 Expository Nonfiction

INTRODUCE THE BOOK

Activate Prior Knowledge/Build Background Read the title, and ask students to discuss what they think the book will be about. Ask students if they would like to fly an airplane.

Preview/Use Text Features Preview the reader by talking about the photographs together and reading the captions. Point out the map on pages 2 and 3 and the time line on page 8.

Preteach Vocabulary Review the tested vocabulary words that appear in this book: **aviator**, **daring**, and **solo**. Introduce these key words from the book: **pilots** (p. 2) and **space shuttle** (p. 6). Discuss these words and add them to a Word Wall.

READ THE BOOK

Choose among these options for reading to support students at all English proficiency levels.

Read Aloud Read the book aloud as students follow along. Pause to verify comprehension and to explain unfamiliar concepts.

Monitored Reading Have students silently read a few pages at a time. Use the following questions to support comprehension:

- **Pages 2–3** What records did Harriet Quimby and Amelia Earhart set? (Quimby was the first female aviator. Earhart flew up to 14,000 feet and was the first woman to fly across the Atlantic Ocean.)
- **Pages 4–5** Why were Katherine Cheung and Jackie Cochran famous? (Cheung was the first Asian American female aviator. Cochran led the Women's Airforce Service Pilots.)
- **Pages 6–7** What did Eileen Collins and Kalpana Chawla do? (They were both astronauts on space shuttles.)

Reread Have students reread the book with a partner, in small groups, or independently. Have them complete the Study Guide on page 257.

RESPOND

Answers to the Reader's Inside Back Cover:

Talk About It

1. Answers will vary, but opinions should be supported by facts from the book. (Fact and Opinion)

2. by setting records, being examples for others, and founding or leading organizations that helped other female aviators (Main Idea and Supporting Details)

Write About It

3. Answers will vary, but students should use a format similar to that on page 8 of the reader. (Graphic Sources and Sequence)

Support writers at various English proficiency levels.

Beginning Allow students to write their time lines in the home language. If feasible, have students translate their work with the help of a partner.

Intermediate Have students tell partners what they want to say before writing it down.

Advanced Have students include at least five events on their time lines.

Extend Language Some of the action verbs that appear in the book include *dared, decided, loved, earned, reached, began, disappeared, studied, said, did, suggested, asked, took, left, let, flew, wanted,* and *joined.*

Answers to page 257:

Possible Supporting Details: Quimby was the first woman to get a pilot's license, in 1911. Earhart flew across the Atlantic solo in 1932. Cheung was the first Asian American to earn a pilot's license, in 1932. Cochran was led the WASP during World War II. Recently, Collins and Chawla flew into space.

Family Link Read aloud the Family Link activity on page 257 before sending copies of the Study Guide home with students. Later, have students share what family members say about being a pilot or an astronaut.

Name ______________________________

Women Who Dared to Fly

- **Read** *Women Who Dared to Fly* again.
- **Find** supporting details for the main idea shown below. **Write** them in the boxes.

Main Idea: American women have been aviators for almost 100 years.

Detail:

Detail:

Detail:

Family Link

Would anyone in your family like to fly? Would they like to be astronauts? Ask people in your family if they think it would be exciting to be an aviator.

Antarctica: The Science Continent

by Nathaniel Mellard

ELL Reader 4.5.4 Nonfiction

INTRODUCE THE BOOK

Activate Prior Knowledge/Build Background Read the title, and show students where Antarctica is on a globe. Ask volunteers to tell you what they know about Antarctica. Ask them what they think it would be like to live there.

Preview/Use Text Features Preview the reader by talking about the photographs together, naming the labeled items, and reading the captions. Point out the map on page 2, the *Extend Language* feature on page 4, the *Did You Know?* box on page 9, and the list on page 11.

Preteach Vocabulary Review the tested vocabulary words that appear in this book: **continent** and **icebergs**. Introduce these key words from the book: **science** (p. 1), **explorers** (p. 3), and **treaty** (p. 10). Discuss these words and add them to a Word Wall.

READ THE BOOK

Choose among these options for reading to support students at all English proficiency levels.

Read Aloud Read the book aloud as students follow along. Pause to verify comprehension and to explain unfamiliar concepts.

Monitored Reading Have students silently read a few pages at a time. Use the following questions to support comprehension:

- **Pages 2–5** Why did explorers go to Antarctica? (to find out what was there; to see if people could live there)
- **Pages 6–8** What questions did scientists have about Antarctica? (How do animals survive there? How big are the icebergs? Will they melt? How will changes in Antarctica affect the world?)
- **Pages 9–12** How does the Antarctica Treaty protect the land and animals? (It keeps Antarctica clean of pollution and weapons, allows all scientists to study and share information, and prohibits killing animals or mining for minerals.)

Reread Have students reread the book with a partner, in small groups, or independently. Have them complete the Study Guide on page 259.

RESPOND

<u>Answers to the Reader's Inside Back Cover:</u>

Talk About It

1. Some explorers died; ice covers the land; the temperature is below freezing. (Main Idea and Supporting Details)

2. Answers will vary, but most students will think the treaty is good because it protects the land and animals and encourages different countries to cooperate.

Write About It

3. Answers will vary, but may include listening to others, respecting others, and not shouting in class. (Graphic Sources)

Support writers at various English proficiency levels.

Beginning Pair students with more-proficient speakers to complete their list of class rules.

Intermediate Have students use the treaty on page 11 or your own classroom's list of rules as a model for their own writing.

Advanced Have students help less-proficient speakers write their lists.

Extend Language *Unnecessary*. Invite students to think of other words that begin with the prefix *un-*.

<u>Answers to page 259:</u>

1. They didn't have enough clothing, food, or water for the cold.

2. They studied how people live in cold places and brought enough clothes, food, and water.

3. glaciers, rocks, volcanoes, climate, icebergs, wildlife

4. 4,000

5. They wanted to protect the land and animals.

Family Link Read aloud the Family Link activity on page 259 before sending copies of the Study Guide home with students. Later, have students share what family members say about Antarctica.

Study Guide

Name ______________________________

Antarctica: The Science Continent

- **Read** *Antarctica: The Science Continent* again.
- Use the information in the book to **answer** the questions.

pages 2–5

1. Why did some of the first explorers die in Antarctica?

____

____

2. How did other explorers learn to survive in Antarctica?

____

____

pages 6–8

3. What are some of the things scientists are interested in studying in Antarctica?

____

____

pages 9–12

4. About how many people come to Antarctica every year?

____

5. Why did many countries come together to write the Antarctica Treaty?

____

____

Family Link

Ask family members what they think it would be like to spend six months in Antarctica. What would be the most interesting part of living there? What would they miss most?

Moons of Our Solar System

by Mick Roszel

ELL Reader 4.5.5 Expository Nonfiction

INTRODUCE THE BOOK

Activate Prior Knowledge/Build Background Read the title, and explain that the solar system is the system of planets and other bodies that circle the sun. Ask students if they know the names of any of the planets in our solar system.

Preview/Use Text Features Preview the reader by talking about the photographs together, naming the labeled items, and reading the captions. Point out the diagrams on pages 2 and 4, the *Did You Know?* box on page 3, and the glossary on page 12.

Preteach Vocabulary Review the tested vocabulary word that appears in this book: **trench**. Introduce these key words from the book: **solar system** (p. 1), **moons** (p. 1), and **planet** (p. 2). Discuss these words and add them to a Word Wall.

READ THE BOOK

Choose among these options for reading to support students at all English proficiency levels.

Read Aloud Read the book aloud as students follow along. Pause to verify comprehension and to explain unfamiliar concepts.

Monitored Reading Have students read aloud a few pages at a time. Use the following questions to support comprehension:

- **Pages 2–4** Which planets in our solar system have at least one moon? (all but Mercury and Venus)
- **Pages 5–8** How many moons does Mars have? (2) What is the largest moon in our solar system? (Ganymede, one of Jupiter's moons)
- **Pages 9–12** Why is Titan interesting to scientists? (It has clouds and may even have weather.) What are some of the ways you can describe a moon? (diameter, shape, color, surface, craters, water, ice, atmosphere)

Reread Have students reread the book with a partner, in small groups, or independently. Have them complete the Study Guide on page 261.

RESPOND

Answers to the Reader's Inside Back Cover:

Talk About It

1. an object in space that circles a planet
2. the names of the planets, the path of their orbit, and the order from the Sun (Graphic Sources)

Write About It

3. Graph should reflect the following data: Jupiter: 61; Saturn: 33; Uranus: 26; Neptune: 13; Pluto: 1 (Graphic Sources)
Support writers at various English proficiency levels.

Beginning Provide a copy of the graph for students to fill in. Be sure it is large enough to fit up to 61 moons.
Intermediate Let students copy and complete the sample graph.
Advanced After students complete their graphs, have them write sentences that tell how many moons each planet has.

Extend Language The Earth's Moon and a soccer ball can be called spheres.

Answers to page 261:
Possible responses:
Detail: Each moon is a different size. Some are larger than a planet; some are smaller than a town.
Detail: Each moon has its own shape. Some are round; others are irregularly shaped.
Detail: Each moon has its own surface features. Some have craters, ice caps, water, or volcanoes.

Family Link Read aloud the Family Link activity on page 261 before sending copies of the Study Guide home with students. Later, have students share what family members say about which moon they would like to visit.

Name ______________________________

Moons of Our Solar System

- **Read** *Moons of Our Solar System* again.
- Use the information in the book to **write** details that support the conclusion shown below.

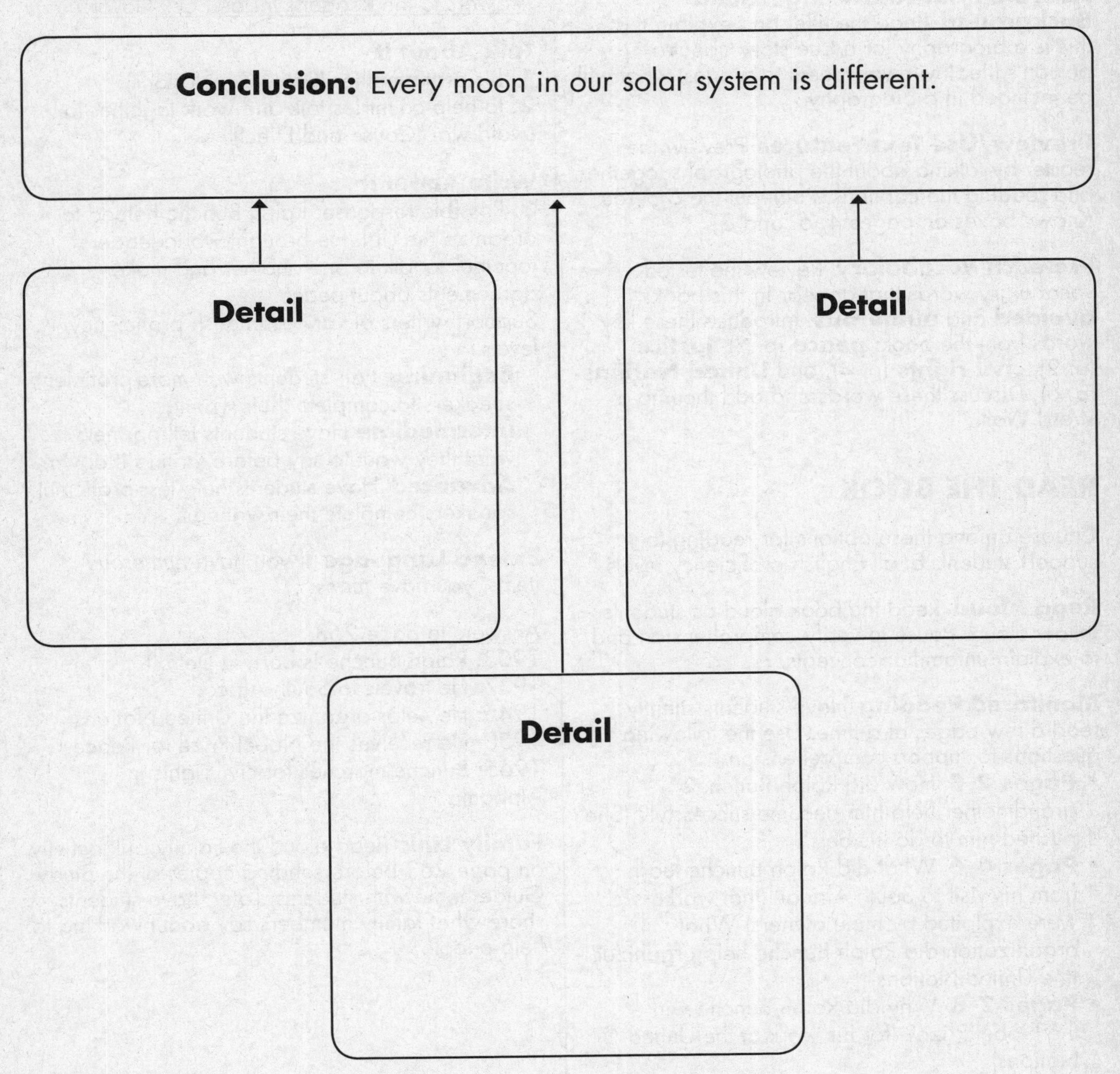

Family Link

Ask the people in your family if they would like to travel into space. Describe some of the different moons in our solar system to them, and ask them which one they would visit if they could.

Ralph Bunche: Quiet Hero

by Daniel Tracy

ELL Reader 4.6.1 Biography

INTRODUCE THE BOOK

Activate Prior Knowledge/Build Background Read the title, and explain that this is a biography, or a true story about a person's life. Invite volunteers to suggest what will be included in a biography.

Preview/Use Text Features Preview the reader by talking about the photographs together and reading the captions. Point out the *Did You Know?* boxes on pages 4, 6, and 8.

Preteach Vocabulary Review the tested vocabulary words that appear in this book: **avoided** and **numerous**. Introduce these key words from the book: **peace** (p. 2), **justice** (p. 2), **civil rights** (p. 4), and **United Nations** (p. 6). Discuss these words and add them to a Word Wall.

READ THE BOOK

Choose among these options for reading to support students at all English proficiency levels.

Read Aloud Read the book aloud as students follow along. Pause to verify comprehension and to explain unfamiliar concepts.

Monitored Reading Have students silently read a few pages at a time. Use the following questions to support comprehension:

- **Pages 2–3** How did Ralph Bunche's grandmother help him become successful? (She pushed him to do his best.)
- **Pages 4–6** What did Ralph Bunche learn from his visit to South Africa? (that workers were exploited by mine owners) What organization did Ralph Bunche help organize? (the United Nations)
- **Pages 7–8** Why did Ralph Bunche win the Nobel Prize? (for his work at the United Nations)

Reread Have students reread the book with a partner, in small groups, or independently. Have them complete the Study Guide on page 263.

RESPOND

Answers to the Reader's Inside Back Cover:

Talk About It

1. his grandmother (Draw Conclusions)

2. to help countries talk and work together to avoid war (Cause and Effect)

Write About It

3. Possible response: Ralph Bunche helped to organize the UN. He brought world leaders together to talk to one another and make agreements about peace.

Support writers at various English proficiency levels.

Beginning Pair students with more-proficient speakers to complete their writing.

Intermediate Have students tell partners what they want to say before writing it down.

Advanced Have students help less-proficient speakers complete their writing.

Extend Language If you have *numerous* items, you have *many.*

Answers to page 263:

1903: Ralph Bunche is born in Detroit.
1937: He travels to South Africa.
1945: He helps organize the United Nations.
1950: He receives the Nobel Prize for Peace.
1965: Bunche marches for civil rights in Alabama.

Family Link Read aloud the Family Link activity on page 263 before sending copies of the Study Guide home with students. Later, have students share what family members say about working to help people.

Name ________________________________

- **Read** *Ralph Bunche: Quiet Hero* again.
- Use the information in the book to fill in the time line below. **Write** one important event from Ralph Bunche's life for each year shown.

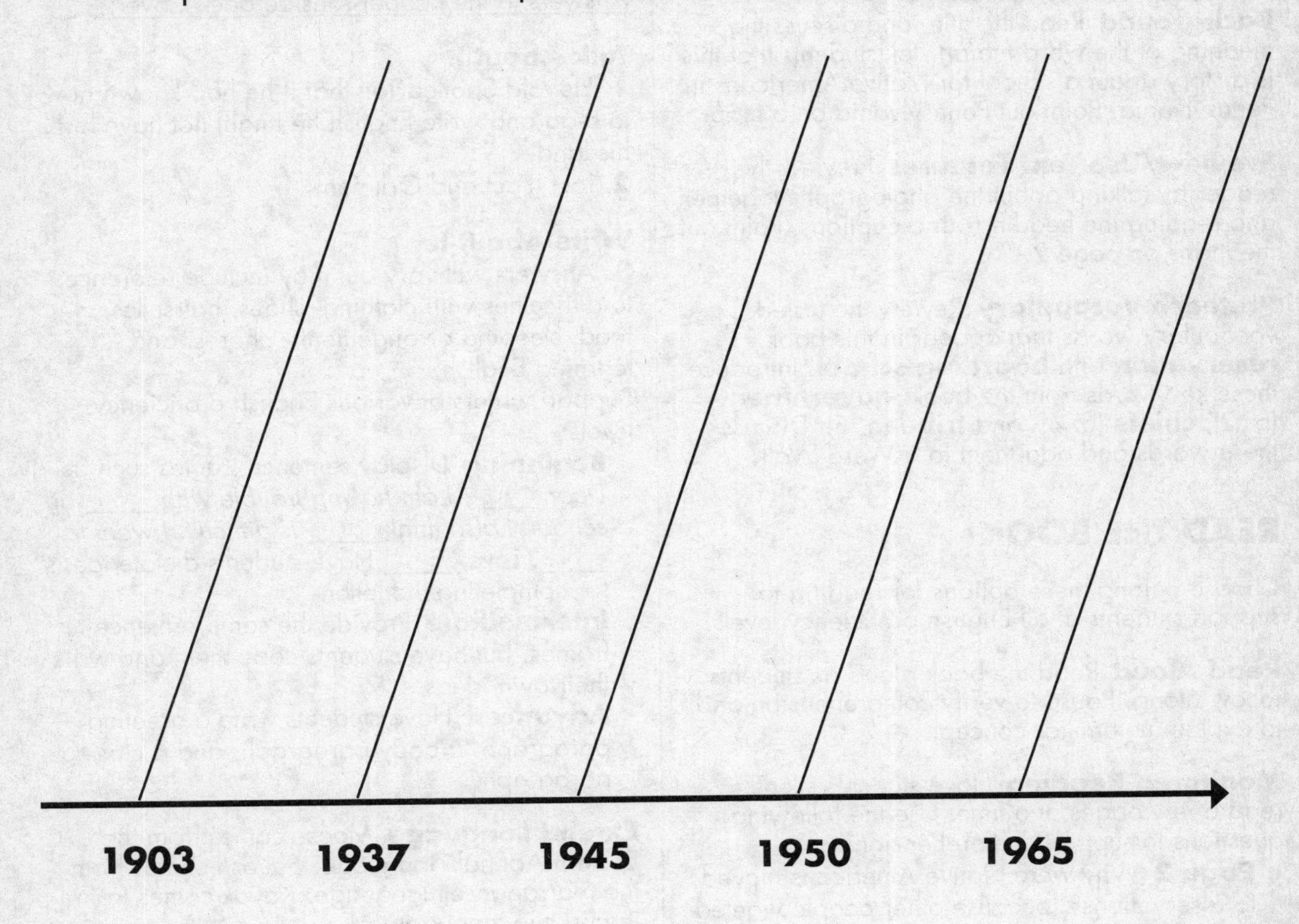

Family Link

Has anyone in your family ever worked to help people? Ask family members to share what they know about working to help people.

The Carlisle Indian School

by Amanda Turner

ELL Reader 4.6.2 Nonfiction

INTRODUCE THE BOOK

Activate Prior Knowledge/Build Background Read the title, and discuss the meaning of the word *Indian*. Tell students that this is a story about a school for Native Americans in Pennsylvania. Point out Pennsylvania on a map.

Preview/Use Text Features Preview the reader by talking about the photographs together and reading the headings and captions. Point out the maps on page 2.

Preteach Vocabulary Review the tested vocabulary words that appear in this book: **reservation** and **boarding school**. Introduce these key words from the book: **government** (p. 2), **chiefs** (p. 4), and **tribe** (p. 5). Discuss these words and add them to a Word Wall.

READ THE BOOK

Choose among these options for reading to support students at all English proficiency levels.

Read Aloud Read the book aloud as students follow along. Pause to verify comprehension and to explain unfamiliar concepts.

Monitored Reading Have students silently read a few pages at a time. Use the following questions to support comprehension:

- **Page 2** Why were Native Americans moved to reservations? (because other people wanted to live on their land)
- **Pages 3–5** Why were Native American children sent to boarding schools? (to make them act more like white people)
- **Pages 6–8** What were some things Native American children learned at the Carlisle School? (English; dressing like other Americans; how to clean, cook, grow crops, and build) What was life like for the children at Carlisle? (much like military life; lonely and difficult)

Reread Have students reread the book with a partner, in small groups, or independently. Have them complete the Study Guide on page 265.

RESPOND

Answers to the Reader's Inside Back Cover:

Talk About It

1. He told Spotted Tail that if he had known how to read and write English he might not have lost his land.

2. fact (Fact and Opinion)

Write About It

3. Answers will vary but may include references to difficulties with clothing, shoes, hairstyles, food, sleeping arrangements, chores, and learning English.

Support writers at various English proficiency levels.

Beginning Display sentence frames such as *Dear _____, I am having trouble with _____ at school. I also think _____ is difficult. I want to _____. Love, _____* Have students dictate ideas for completing the letter.

Intermediate Provide the same sentence frames, but have students copy them and write their own ideas.

Advanced Have students write a greeting paragraph, a body paragraph, and a closing paragraph.

Extend Language *Moose* comes from the Eastern Abenaki language. *Squash* comes from the Narragansett language. *Kayak* comes from the Eskimo language.

Answers to page 265:

F, F, O, O, O

Family Link Read aloud the Family Link activity on page 265 before sending copies of the Study Guide home with students. Later, have students share what their family members think about sending Native American children to boarding schools.

Name ______________________________

- **Read** *The Carlisle Indian School* again.
- Next to each sentence below, **write** *F* for *Fact* or *O* for *Opinion*.

1. By 1890, Native Americans in the West had lost most of their land. _____

2. Captain Richard Pratt wanted to send Native American children to boarding schools. _____

3. Spotted Tail should not have agreed to send the children away to school. _____

4. Sending Native American children to boarding school was a good idea. _____

5. Children should have fun at school, not scrub floors. _____

Family Link

Ask the people in your family what they think about forcing children to change the way they dress, the way they wear their hair, and the way they think. Ask them if they think sending Native American children to schools such as the Carlisle School was good or bad for the children.

From Thailand to California

by Somchit Dundee

ELL Reader 4.6.3 Realistic Fiction

INTRODUCE THE BOOK

Activate Prior Knowledge/Build Background Read the title, and explain that this is a story about a girl who moves from Thailand to California. Point out the places on a map.

Preview/Use Text Features Preview the reader by talking about the illustrations and photographs together, naming the labeled items, and reading the captions. Point out the maps on pages 2 and 5.

Preteach Vocabulary Review the tested vocabulary words that appear in this book: **glint** and **resemblance**. Introduce these key words from the book: **journal** (p. 3) and **deaf** (p. 8). Discuss these words and add them to a Word Wall.

READ THE BOOK

Choose among these options for reading to support students at all English proficiency levels.

Read Aloud Read the book aloud as students follow along. Pause to verify comprehension and to explain unfamiliar concepts.

Monitored Reading Have students silently read a few pages at a time. Use the following questions to support comprehension:

- **Pages 2–3** Why is Nongnoot moving to California? (to help take care of her cousin while her aunt and uncle work)
- **Pages 4–8** What does Nongnoot think of classes at her new school? (She thinks they are hard.) What is special about her friend Heather? (She is deaf and knows sign language.)
- **Pages 9–12** How does Nongnoot learn to write poetry? (She describes Heather's painting and her feelings about Koh Lanta.)

Reread Have students reread the book with a partner, in small groups, or independently. Have them complete the Study Guide on page 267.

RESPOND

<u>Answers to the Reader's Inside Back Cover:</u>

Talk About It

1. leaving her family, friends, and homeland (Draw Conclusions)

2. happy, because she has a friend and has discovered how to write poetry, which makes her feel closer to Koh Lanta (Draw Conclusions)

Write About It

3. *Koh Lanta:* people are friendly; people drive motorbikes and tuk-tuks; students go home for lunch, eat fresh food; people eat on floor; located on sea, nature all around. *San José:* people don't smile, are in hurry; people drive cars and trucks; students eat prepared foods in cafeteria; people eat at tables; not as much nature (Compare and Contrast)

Support writers at various English proficiency levels.

Beginning Provide a copy of the chart for students to fill in.

Intermediate Have students look through the book to find details they can use in their charts.

Advanced Have students include at least five points of comparison in their charts.

Extend Language *ball, call, tall, hall, mall, fall, wall; tack, sack, lack, Jack, pack, knack, rack, shack; my, bye, hi, lie, pie, sigh, spy, try, why, tie, die, shy; start, heart, dart, smart, art, tart, part; mother, other*

<u>Answers to page 267:</u>

1. Koh Lanta Yai, Thailand and San José, California

2. to remember Koh Lanta

3. Students eat prepared foods in a cafeteria in San José, but go home to eat fresh food in Thailand.

4. Japanese Friendship Garden; It is beautiful, with ponds trees, birds, fish, and shrines.

5. She feels closer to her village.

Family Link Read aloud the Family Link activity on page 267 before sending copies of the Study Guide home with students. Later, have students share what family members say about eating customs in their country of origin.

Name ______________________________

From Thailand to California

- **Read** *From Thailand to California* again.
- Use the information in the book to **answer** the questions.

pages 2–5

1. Where does the story take place?

____

2. Why does Nongnoot decide to keep a picture journal?

____

page 6

3. How is eating lunch at school in San José different from eating lunch in Koh Lanta?

____

____

pages 8–9

4. What is Heather's favorite place in San José? What is it like?

____

____

pages 10–12

5. How does Nongnoot feel when she writes poems about Koh Lanta?

____

Family Link

What foods do people eat in your or your family's home country? Are meal times there the same as in the United States? Do schoolchildren there eat in a cafeteria or go home for lunch? Ask family members to describe how their eating customs are different from those in the United States.

Thank You, Sir Isaac Newton!

by Aaron Showley

ELL Reader 4.6.4 Expository Nonfiction

INTRODUCE THE BOOK

Activate Prior Knowledge/Build Background Read the title, and explain that Isaac Newton was a scientist who lived about 300 years ago.

Preview/Use Text Features Preview the reader by talking about the photographs and illustrations together, naming the labeled items, and reading the captions. Point out the diagram on page 4 and the *Did You Know?* boxes on pages 4, 7, and 10.

Preteach Vocabulary Review the tested vocabulary words that appear in this book: **glider** and **drag**. Introduce these key words from the book: **motion** (p. 3) and **roller coaster** (p. 8). Discuss these words and add them to a Word Wall.

READ THE BOOK

Choose among these options for reading to support students at all English proficiency levels.

Read Aloud Read the book aloud as students follow along. Pause to verify comprehension and to explain unfamiliar concepts.

Monitored Reading Have students take turns reading a page aloud. Use the following questions to support comprehension:

- **Pages 2–3** What did Sir Isaac Newton discover? (the laws of motion)
- **Pages 4–5** What does Newton's First Law of Motion say? (Objects continue doing what they are doing unless a force acts on them.)
- **Pages 6–7** Why does water spill out of a cup if the person holding the cup is in a car that suddenly stops? (The water keeps moving, because the car has brakes to stop it but the water does not.)
- **Pages 8–11** How does a roller coaster work? (A motor brings the train to the top of a hill. Gravity pulls the train down the hill. As the train goes downhill, it gains momentum. Momentum moves the train on the tracks.)

Reread Have students reread the book with a partner, in small groups, or independently. Have them complete the Study Guide on page 269.

RESPOND

Answers to the Reader's Inside Back Cover:

Talk About It

1. Something that isn't moving won't move unless something moves it. Something that is moving won't stop moving unless something stops it. (Graphic Sources)

2. friction, gravity, something pulling from another direction like a person pulling on a dog's leash

Write About It

3. Definitions: *motion:* movement; *gravity:* force that pulls objects toward one another; *force:* power/energy; *friction:* rubbing of one object against another; *momentum:* motion that continues until an object is stopped (Graphic Sources)

Support writers at various English proficiency levels.

Beginning Allow students to write or dictate their definitions in the home language.

Intermediate Have students look through the book to find words they can use in their definitions.

Advanced Have students use dictionaries to help them define the words.

Extend Language *Motionless* means *without motion. Locomotion* means *the act of moving. Motion picture* means a *movie,* which is made of pictures that move.

Answers to page 269:

Possible responses: *Supporting Details:* A drink held in a car spills when the car suddenly stops. A soccer ball doesn't move unless someone kicks it or picks it up. To stop my bike, I press the brakes.

Family Link Read aloud the Family Link activity on page 269 before sending copies of the Study Guide home with students. Later, have students share what family members say about roller coasters.

Name ____________________________

- **Read** *Thank You, Sir Isaac Newton!* again.
- Use the information in the book and your experiences to **write** supporting details for the generalization.

Generalization: We see proof of Newton's First Law of Motion everywhere.

Supporting Details

Family Link

Has anyone in your family ridden a roller coaster? Ask family members to tell what kinds of roller coasters they have ridden or seen.

Welcome to Space Camp

by Mary Kate O'Day

ELL Reader 4.6.5 Nonfiction

INTRODUCE THE BOOK

Activate Prior Knowledge/Build Background Read the title, and ask students what they think space camp is. Ask them what they think people do at space camp.

Preview/Use Text Features Preview the reader by talking about the photographs together, naming the labeled items, and reading the captions. Point out the *Did You Know?* boxes on pages 3, 5, and 10, and the diagram on page 7.

Preteach Vocabulary Review the tested vocabulary words that appear in this book: **module**, **astronauts**, and **lunar**. Introduce these key words from the book: **camp** (p. 1), **spaceships** (p. 3), and **team** (p. 8). Discuss these words and add them to a Word Wall.

READ THE BOOK

Choose among these options for reading to support students at all English proficiency levels.

Read Aloud Read the book aloud as students follow along. Pause to verify comprehension and to explain unfamiliar concepts.

Monitored Reading Have students read aloud a few pages at a time. Use the following questions to support comprehension:

- **Pages 2–3** Why do spacecraft need powerful rockets? (to escape Earth's gravity)
- **Pages 4–5** How do astronauts prepare for space travel? (They practice in simulators.)
- **Pages 6–7** What can you learn from going inside a replica of the space shuttle? (You see the flight deck, where astronauts control the spacecraft, and the mid deck, where other work is done.)
- **Pages 8–12** What do the different teams on a space mission do? (One works in the control center, outside the shuttle; one works inside the shuttle.) Who observed space from Earth long ago? (Galileo and Newton)

Reread Have students reread the book with a partner, in small groups, or independently. Have them complete the Study Guide on page 271.

RESPOND

Answers to the Reader's Inside Back Cover:

Talk About It

1. It shows and labels the different parts. (Graphic Sources)

2. It lets them pretend to be astronauts in simulated training and missions.

Write About It

3. Possible responses: *Fact:* At space camp you may eat freeze-dried food. *Opinion:* Freeze-dried food isn't as good as fresh food. (Fact and Opinion)

Support writers at various English proficiency levels.

Beginning Write facts from the text on the board. Ask students to work in pairs to devise related opinions.

Intermediate Ask students to page through the book to find facts about space camp, then write related opinions.

Advanced Have students write at least three facts and three opinions in their charts.

Extend Language without weight

Answers to page 271:

1. Neil Armstrong, Buzz Aldrin
2. a piece of equipment that lets astronauts practice being in space
3. There is no gravity, so doing those things is very different in space.
4. getting the shuttle safely back to Earth
5. scientists who observed space hundreds of years ago

Family Link Read aloud the Family Link activity on page 271 before sending copies of the Study Guide home with students. Later, have students share what family members say about space travel.

Name ______________________________

Welcome to Space Camp

- **Read** *Welcome to Space Camp* again.
- Use the information in the book to **answer** the questions.

pages 2–5

1. Who were the first men to walk on the Moon?

____

2. What is a simulator?

____

____

page 6

3. Why do astronauts need to learn how to walk, work, sleep, and eat in space?

____

____

pages 8–9

4. What is one of the jobs of the team at the control center?

____

page 10

5. Who were Sir Isaac Newton and Galileo Galilei?

____

Family Link

Would anyone in your family like to travel into space? Where would they like to go? What would they like to see? What would they like to do in space? How would they feel about you becoming an astronaut?

Multilingual Lesson Vocabulary
Unit 1

English	Spanish	Chinese	Vietnamese	Korean	Hmong
Week 1: Because of Winn-Dixie					
grand	estupendo	盛大	to lớn	장려한, 웅대한	loj heev
memorial	conmemorativa	紀念	đài kỷ niệm, lễ kỷ niệm	기념물	nco txog cov dhau los
peculiar	peculiar	奇怪	lạ kỳ	기묘한	txawv txawv
positive	segura	正面	tích cực	긍정적인	yam zoo ntxiv
prideful	orgullosa	傲慢	kiêu căng	자존심이 강한	khib oom
recalls	recuerda	回憶	nhớ lại	생각해내다	nco qab, hu rov qab
selecting	seleccionando	選擇	chọn ra	선택	xaiv
Week 2: Lewis and Clark and Me					
docks	puerto	船塢	bến tàu	부두	ntug dej uas nkoj los nres
migrating	emigrando	移居	di cư	이동하는	tsiv teb tsaws chaw
scan	escudriñar	搜索	nhìn lướt qua	자세히 조사하다	luam
scent	aroma	氣味	mùi hương	냄새	ntxhiab
wharf	embarcadero	碼頭	bến cảng	선창	ntug dej ua neeg taug ua si
yearned	anhelaba	想念	khao khát	~하고 싶어하다, 동경하다	siab nco
Week 3: Grandfather's Journey					
amazed	maravillaban	驚奇	bị kinh ngạc	놀라다	ceeb
bewildered	desconcertaban	迷惑	bị hoang mang	당황한	yuam kev, tsis paub qab hau dab tsi lawm
homeland	tierra natal	家鄉	quê hương	모국	yus teb chaws
longed	deseaba	渴望	khao khát	열망하다	khuam siab, siab nco
sculptures	esculturas	雕塑	các tượng điêu khắc	조각	mlom pob zeb

English	Spanish	Chinese	Vietnamese	Korean	Hmong
still	calmar	靜止	yên tĩnh	움직이지 않는, 조용한	tseem, tab si
towering	imponentes	聳立	cao chót vót	우뚝 솟은, 아주 훌륭한	loj siab
Week 4: The Horned Toad Prince					
bargain	pacto	交易	mặc cả	거래	hais nqi
favors	favores	厚待	ân huệ	친절	yam (dab tsi) thov ua
lassoed	enlazó	用套索捕捉	bắt bằng dây thòng lọng	~을 올가미 밧줄로 잡다	txoj hlua ua muaj ib voj
offended	ofendida	冒犯	bị xúc phạm	감정을 해치다, ~을 위반하다	ntxuam
prairie	pradera	大草原	đồng cỏ rộng lớn ở Mỹ	대초원	plag tiaj nyom
riverbed	lecho	河床	lòng sông	강바닥	paj dej uas tus dej ntws los rau
shrieked	chilló	尖叫	kêu thét	비명을 지르다	quaj txias siab
Week 5: Letters Home from Yosemite					
glacier	glaciar	冰川	dãy băng hà	빙하	(thooj) dej khov
impressive	impresionante	印象深刻	gây ấn tượng sâu sắc	인상적인	ua tau ntxim nyiam
naturalist	naturalista	博物學家	nhà vạn vật học	동물(식물)학자	neeg tshuaj xyuas yam nyob hauv ntiaj teb
preserve	preservar	保存	bảo quản	보존하다	tseg cia
slopes	laderas	斜坡	những dốc	경사지다	toj
species	especies	種類	các loài	종	tsiaj
wilderness	zona silvestre	荒野	miền hoang dã	자연 보호 구역, 다수	hav zoo

Unit 2

English	Spanish	Chinese	Vietnamese	Korean	Hmong
Week 1: What Jo Did					
fouled	hizo una falta	弄髒	phạm luật	반칙하다	thawb
hoop	aro	箍	rổ	(농구의) 링	tawb pov basketball
jersey	camiseta	緊身運動套衫	một loại vải, đồng phục bóng rổ bằng loại vải này	(운동선수가 입는) 셔츠	cev khawb ncaws yas nyias nyias
marveled	se maravillaban	驚奇	thán phục	놀라다	xav txog
rim	canasta	外緣	vòng rổ	(농구의 골망을 달아 매는) 테	sab ntug
speechless	boquiabierto	無言	không nói nên lời	말로 표현할 수 없는, 말을 못 하는	hais tsis tau lus, tsis muaj lus hais
swatted	le dio	猛擊	đập mạnh	세게 치다	npuaj
unbelievable	increíble	難以相信	không thể tin được, lạ kỳ	믿을 수 없는	ntseeg tsis tau
Week 2: Coyote School News					
bawling	berreando	大喊	la hét	크게 외치다	quaj, qw
coyote	coyote	凱奧特	sói nhỏ ở sa mạc	코요테	coyote
dudes	dandis	花花公子	(từ lóng) mấy thằng bạn	멋쟁이	ib tug txiv neej
roundup	rodeo	召集	gom lại, lùa về	총괄, 요약	sau, suaj kaum, khi cia
spurs	espuelas	踢馬刺	bộ đinh thúc ngựa	격려하다	khau ncaws thos neeg
Week 3: Grace and the Time Machine					
aboard	a bordo	登上	lên tàu	~을[에] 타고	nce rau
atlas	atlas	地圖集	tập bản đồ	지도책	pees theeb teb chaws
awkward	incómodo	笨拙	lúng túng, ngượng nghịu	서투른	txawv txav
capable	capaces	可勝任	có thể	유능한	ua tau

English	Spanish	Chinese	Vietnamese	Korean	Hmong
chant	cantan	歌頌	hát hoặc đọc theo nhịp nhiều lần	노래	hu, hais
mechanical	mecánicas	機械	thuộc về cơ khí	기계의	raws li tshuab
miracle	milagro	奇迹	phép mầu	기적	muaj hmoo
reseats	vuelve a sentarse	使復位	ngồi lại	새 좌석을 마련하다	rov zaum dua (tshiab)
vehicle	vehículo	車輛	xe cộ	탈것	tsheb
Week 4: Marven of the Great North Woods					
cord	pila de leña	繩子	sợi dây	끈	hlua faim fab
dismay	consternación	沮喪	sững sờ, thất thần	당황하게 하다	tu siab
grizzly	pardo	灰色的	màu hoa râm; gấu nâu	회색의	dub
immense	enormes	巨大	to lớn mênh mông	거대한	loj loj, dav fo
payroll	nómina	工資單	danh sách trả lương	급료 지불 명부, ~에 자금을 지급하다	them nyaij ua hauj lwm
Week 5: So You Want to Be President?					
Constitution	Constitución	憲法	Hiến Pháp	헌법	Mis kas txoj cai
howling	rotundo	嚎叫	hú lên	쓸쓸한	quaj qw
humble	humildes	謙卑	khiêm nhường	겸손한	tus paub siab paub qis, hwm niam hwm txiv
politics	política	政治	chính trị	정치	kev ua nom
responsibility	responsabilidad	責任	trách nhiệm	책임감	saib xyus txoj dej num
solemnly	solemnemente	莊嚴地	nghiêm trang	엄숙하게	tus coj tiag tiag tsis dag
vain	vano	自負	vô vọng	우쭐대는, 공허한	muaj phlus

Unit 3

English	Spanish	Chinese	Vietnamese	Korean	Hmong
Week 1: The Stranger					
draft	corriente de aire	草稿	bản nháp	외풍, 통풍	kos thawj lwm
etched	grabadas	銘刻	đã khắc vào	선명하게 그리다, 마음에 새기다	rias kos
fascinated	fascinaba	迷住	bị thu hút	매혹하다, 마음이 끌리다	ntxim siab
frost	escarcha	結霜	sương tuyết	서리	dej khov
parlor	salón	客廳	phòng khách	응접실	chav tsev tos qhua
terror	terror	恐佈	nỗi kinh hoàng	공포, 겁	ntshai
timid	tímido	怯懦	rụt rè	겁많은	txaj muag
Week 2: Adelina's Whales					
biologist	bióloga	生物學家	nhà sinh vật học	생물학자	tus kawm txog txua yaj muaj sia
bluff	despeñadero	懸崖	lừa phỉnh	(해안, 곶 따위가) 깎아세운 듯한, 절벽	tso ya, tso hem
lagoon	laguna	礁湖	hồ nước biển	초호 (환초로 둘러싸인 얕은 바다)	av suav puam uas kem tus dej me thiab tus dej loj
massive	inmensas	巨大	khổng lồ	육중한	ntau ntau
rumbling	retumbante	隆隆響	kêu ầm ầm	우르르 하는 소리	suab ua zog
tropical	tropical	熱帶	về vùng nhiệt đới	열대의	chaw sov
Week 3: How Night Came from the Sea: A Story from Brazil					
brilliant	brillante	明亮	ngời sáng	훌륭한	tsw yim zoo heev
chorus	coro	合唱	dàn hợp xướng, dàn đồng ca	합창	nqi xab
coward	cobarde	懦夫	người hèn nhát	겁쟁이	tais caus

English	Spanish	Chinese	Vietnamese	Korean	Hmong
gleamed	relucía	閃爍	lấp lánh	빛나는	duab ci
shimmering	centelleante	閃閃發光	lung linh	아른아른 빛나는	ci nplas
Week 4: Eye of the Storm					
destruction	destrucción	破壞	sự phá hủy	파괴	tsoo pov tseg
expected	esperaba	期望	được mong đợi	예상하다	vam tias
forecasts	pronósticos	預報	tiên đoán	일기예보	huab cua
inland	tierra adentro	內陸	trong đất liền	내륙의	saum qhuab
shatter	hace añicos	震裂	làm vỡ tan	산산이 부서지다	ntsoog
surge	oleada	浪湧	sự dấy lên	큰 파도	txav ze
Week 5: The Great Kapok Tree					
canopy	copas (de los árboles)	樹冠層	vòm cây	그늘	ntaub dai ntawm taub hau txaj
dangle	colgar	搖晃	treo lơ lửng	매달리다	dai
dappled	salpicada	花斑	có điểm lốm đốm	얼룩덜룩한	teev cim
fragrant	fragante	芬芳	thơm	향기로운, 유쾌한	ntxhiab tsw qab
pollen	polen	花粉	phấn hoa	꽃가루	hmoov paj
pollinate	polimizar	授粉	thụ phấn	수분하다	kev ua hmoov paj
slithered	se deslizó	滑行	trườn	미끄러지다	swb
wondrous	maravilloso	奇妙	lạ lùng	놀랄 만한	zoo heev

Unit 4

English	Spanish	Chinese	Vietnamese	Korean	Hmong
Week 1: The Houdini Box					
appeared	apareció	出現	đã xuất hiện	나타나다	tshwm ntawm
bustling	bulliciosa	奔忙	nhộn nhịp	바쁜 듯한, 떠들썩한	ua hauj lwm
crumbled	se desintegró	粉碎	đã sụp đổ, vỡ vụn	산산조각이 되다, 맥없이 무너지다	ntsoog
escape	escapar	逃跑	tẩu thoát	탈출하다, 사라지다	khiav dim
magician	mago	魔術師	nhà ảo thuật	마술사	tus ua yees siv
monument	monumento	紀念碑	tượng đài	기념비	tej yam tsim los nco txog yav tag los
vanished	desapareció	消失	đã biến mất	사라지다	ploj ntsis, ploj ntais
Week 2: Encantado: Pink Dolphin of the Amazon					
aquarium	acuario	水族館	bồn hoặc tòa nhà nuôi cá	수족관	tsev rau tsiaj deg
dolphins	delfines	海豚	cá heo	돌고래	dolphins
enchanted	encantado	迷惑	bị mê hoặc	매혹되다, 황홀해지다	zoo nkauj
flexible	flexibles	靈活	uyển chuyển	유연한, 다루기 쉬운	yooj yim
glimpses	vistazos fugaces	瞥見	nhìn thoáng	힐끗 보기	pom ib muag
pulses	impulsos	脈衝	nhịp tim	맥박	plawv nrhia
surface	superficie	表面	bề mặt, hiện lên bề mặt	표면	saum daim tawv

English	Spanish	Chinese	Vietnamese	Korean	Hmong
Week 3: The King in the Kitchen					
duke	duque	公爵	công tước	공작	tus neeg qib siab nyob rau lub As Kiv teb chaws (England)
dungeon	mazmorra	土牢	ngục tối	지하 감옥	chav kaw neeg
furiously	furiosamente	憤怒地	giận dữ	맹렬히	npau ntaws
genius	genio	天才	thiên tài	천부의 재능, 능력	tus neeg ntse thiab muaj txuj ci tshaj
majesty	majestad	雄偉	tráng lệ	위엄	vaj ntxwv
noble	noble	高尚	quý phái	고귀한	muaj meej mom
peasant	campesino	農夫	nông dân	소작인	pej xeem ua teb
porridge	gachas de avena	粥	cháo	포리지 (오트밀 따위의 죽)	mov kua dis
Week 4: Seeker of Knowledge					
ancient	antiguo	古老	cổ xưa	고대의	qub qub
link	conexión	連接	nối	연결 고리	kev mus rau lwm qhov
scholars	eruditos	學者	các học giả	학자	tub kawm ntawv
seeker	buscador	尋找者	người tìm tòi	탐구자	tus nrhiav
temple	templo	寺廟	đền thờ	사찰	tsev teev hawm
translate	traducir	翻譯	phiên dịch	번역하다	txhais (lus)
triumph	triunfo	勝利	đắc thắng	승리	yeej
uncover	descubrir	揭露	phát hiện	노출하다	qhib tau, nrhiav tau

English	Spanish	Chinese	Vietnamese	Korean	Hmong
Week 5: Encyclopedia Brown and the Case of the Slippery Salamander					
amphibians	anfibios	兩棲類動物	động vật lưỡng cư	양서 동물	cov tsiaj muaj peev xwm nyob hauv dej thiab ntawm av
baffled	perplejo	使人困惑	bối rối, hoang mang	난처한, 당황한	xav tsis thoob li
crime	crimen	罪行	tội	범죄	ib qhov kev phem yuam cai
exhibit	exposición	展覽	trưng bày, biểu lộ	전시하다	qhib saib, nthuav ntawm
lizard	lagarto	蜥蜴	thằn lằn	도마뱀	nab qa
reference	referencia	參考	việc tham khảo	참조	txheeb ze
reptiles	reptiles	爬行動物	loài bò sát	파충류	tsiaj muaj nplai thiab yug qe
salamander	salamandra	火蜥蜴	kỳ nhông	도롱뇽	nab qa salamander
stumped	perplejo	連根挖去	bị bí lối	난처하게 하다	pob ntoos

Unit 5

English	Spanish	Chinese	Vietnamese	Korean	Hmong
Week 1: Sailing Home: A Story of a Childhood at Sea					
bow	proa	鞠躬	mũi tàu	절하다	tais
cargo	carga	貨物	hàng hóa	화물	cov khoom xav uas nkoj thiab dav hlau thauj
celestial	celestial	神聖	thuộc về bầu trời	천상의	qaum ntuj
conducted	condujo	舉辦	đã thực hiện	행동하다	ua
dignified	digno	授以榮譽	có hoặc biểu thị phẩm giá	위엄 있는	zoo tshaj tsis muaj dab tsi pauv ntau
navigation	navegación	航海	việc lái tàu, ngành hàng hải	항해	nrhiav hau kev
quivered	estremeció	顫抖	run nhẹ	흔들리다	tshee
stern	popa	船尾	đuôi tàu	선미	hais tiag tiag, nyaum nyaum
Week 2: Lost City: The Discovery of Machu Picchu					
curiosity	curiosidad	好奇心	trí tò mò	호기심	xav paub
glorious	gloriosa	光榮的	vinh quang	영예로운	zoo nkauj
granite	granito	花崗岩	đá hoa cương	화강암	pob zeb granite
ruins	ruinas	殘留的廢墟	các tàn tích	폐허	yam khoom puas ntsoog tag
terraced	en terrazas	臺階形的	làm thành bậc thang	계단식 땅을 만들다	qab tsib taug, chaw ua si
thickets	matorrales	叢林	các bụi cây	덤불	tsob nyom
torrent	torrente	洪流	dòng nước chảy mạnh	급류	ntws
Week 3: Amelia and Eleanor Go for a Ride					
aviator	aviadora	飛行員	phi công	비행사	tus tsav dav hlau
brisk	fresco	輕快	nhanh nhẹn	활발한, 상쾌한	nrawm nrawm, maj maj

English	Spanish	Chinese	Vietnamese	Korean	Hmong
cockpit	cabina	駕駛艙	chỗ phi công ngồi lái máy bay	조종실	chav tswj hwm cav tshuaj
daring	valiente	大膽	liều lĩnh	대담한	tsis ntshai dab tsi
elegant	elegante	典雅	thanh nhã	고상한	zoo nkauj
outspoken	franca	坦率	bặt thiệp	거리낌 없는, 솔직한	hais taus
solo	sola	單獨飛行	một mình	혼자서	ib leeg
Week 4: Antarctic Journal: Four Months at the Bottom of the World					
anticipation	anticipación	預期	sự trông đợi	예상	tos tos, cia siab
continent	continente	大陸	lục địa	대륙	teb chaws
convergence	convergencia	匯合	sự hội tụ	집합점	sib sau
depart	salir	分離	khởi hành	떠나다	sib ncaim
forbidding	inhóspita	禁止	cấm đoán	금지하다	txwv tsis pub
heaves	sube	隆起	ráng sức nâng lên	들어올리다, 물결치다	tsaws
icebergs	icebergs	冰山	các tảng băng	빙하	thooj dej pob zeb khov tshwm sau dej
Week 5: Moonwalk					
loomed	surgía	隱約地出現	đã hiện ra lờ mờ	어렴풋이 나타나다	ua ntos
rille	valle lunar	溝	đường rãnh trên mặt trăng	골짜기	ib lub hav nyob rau saum hli
runt	pequeño	矮子	nhóc tì	작은 동물(식물)	tus tsiaj me me
staggered	se tambaleó	搖擺	đi loạng choạng	비틀거리다	nyob tsis ntseg
summoning	armándose	召喚	kêu gọi	호출하는, 요구하는	hu tuaj ua kev
taunted	burló	嘲笑	đã khiêu khích	비웃다	thuam
trench	zanja	溝槽	mương, hào	깊은 도랑	tsev qhov av
trudged	caminaron fatigosamente	費勁地走	đã lê bước	터덜터덜 걷다	mus kev li pob tw nyav nyav

Unit 6

English	Spanish	Chinese	Vietnamese	Korean	Hmong
Week 1: My Brother Martin					
ancestors	ancestros	祖先	tổ tiên	조상	poj koob yawg koob
avoided	evitaba	避免	đã tránh	피하다	ua txuj tsis pom, nkaum
generations	generaciones	世代	các thế hệ	세대	tiam
minister	ministro	部長	mục sư	목사	xib hwb
numerous	numerosos	眾多	rất nhiều	매우 많은	ntau ntau (leej, tus)
pulpit	púlpito	講壇	bục giảng	설교	qhov chaw sawv (qhia lus ntseeg)
shielding	protegiéndonos	防護	che chở	보호하는	thaiv
Week 2: Jim Thorpe's Bright Path					
boarding school	internado	寄宿學校	trường nội trú	기숙 학교	tsev nkawm ntawv them nyiaj
dormitory	dormitorio	宿舍	ký túc xá	기숙사	tsev pw rau cov tub ntxhais nkawm ntawv
endurance	resistencia	忍耐	sức bền bỉ	참을성, 시련	nyiaj, uv
manual	manual	手工的	bằng tay	수동의, 육체를 쓰는	yam ua los ntawm tes
reservation	reserva	保護區	sự dè dặt	보류, 조건, 제한	chaw tseg cia
society	sociedad	社會	xã hội	사회	zej zog
Week 3: How Tía Lola Came to Stay					
affords	ofrece	負擔得起	có tiền để mua	할 수 있다, 여유가 있다	yuav tau, khwv tau
colonel	coronel	上校	đại tá	대령	thawj coj
glint	destello	閃閃發光	sáng lấp lánh	반짝 빛나다	ci
lurking	acechando	潛伏	ẩn núp chờ đợi	숨은	nkag los, nyiag los
palettes	paletas	調色板	tấm nâng hàng; giường hẹp và cứng	팔레트	daim rau xim uas tus neeg thas xim, tuav rau ntawm tes

English	Spanish	Chinese	Vietnamese	Korean	Hmong
quaint	pintoresco	古雅	kỳ lạ	진기한, 별난	txawv
resemblance	semejanza	相似	sự giống nhau	닮음	zoo li
Week 4: To Fly: The Story of the Wright Brothers					
cradle	soporte	托架	chiếc nôi	요람	me nyuam txaj
drag	arrastrar	阻力	kéo	끌다	rub
flex	doblar	電線	co giãn	구부리다	ntsuas (zog)
glider	planeador	滑翔機	máy lượn	글라이더	dav hlau rau ib tug neeg
hangars	hangars	飛機庫	nơi để máy bay	격납고	chaw rau thiab kho dav hlau
rudder	timón	舵	bánh lái	방향타	dav hlaus tus khov tw
stalled	entró en pérdida	失去作用	bị chết máy	(비행기를) 실속 시키다	khuam kev
Week 5: The Man Who Went to the Far Side of the Moon: The Story of Apollo 11 Astronaut Michael Collins					
astronauts	astronautas	太空人	phi hành gia	우주 비행사	tus neeg mus saum qaum ntuj
capsule	cápsula	密封艙	khoang có thể tách ra trên tàu vũ trụ	캡슐	lub nkoj mus saum qaum ntuj
hatch	escotilla	艙口蓋	cửa ra vào trên tàu vũ trụ	(항공기, 우주선의) 출입문	kab pleb nyob rau hauv lub dav hlau
horizon	horizonte	地平線	chân trời	수평선	npoo ntuj
lunar	lunar	登月	về mặt trăng	달의	lub hli
module	módulo	小艇	khoang có thể tách ra trên tàu vũ trụ	착륙선	xws li lub tsheb
quarantine	cuarentena	檢疫	cô lập	격리하다, 검역하다	lub sij hawm raug kaw cia (vim tej zaum yus muaj kab mob kis tau)